South Carolina's Turkish People

South Carolina's Turkish People

A History and Ethnology

Terri Ann Ognibene
and
Glen Browder

The University of South Carolina Press

© 2018 University of South Carolina

Published by the University of South Carolina Press
Columbia, South Carolina 29208

www.sc.edu/uscpress

Manufactured in the United States of America

27 26 25 24 23 22 21 20 19 18
10 9 8 7 6 5 4 3 2 1

Library of Congress Cataloging-in-Publication Data
can be found at http://catalog.loc.gov/.

ISBN: 978-1-61117-858-6 (cloth)
ISBN: 978-1-61117-859-3 (ebook)

This book was printed on a recycled paper
with 30 percent post consumer waste content.

To those from whom I come and of whom I am one, the Martin Frazier Ray and Lani Hood Ray family. Your life experiences have moved me, perplexed me, inspired me, strengthened me, encouraged me, and molded me into the person that I am today. May this feeble attempt lend to your voices: Martin Sr. (Papa) 1910–1996; Lani (Granny) 1911–1996; Melissa (Aunt Sis) 1932–2006; Josephine (Aunt Jo) 1934–2010; Martin Jr. (Uncle Bubba) 1936–1992; Bufort (Uncle Bufort) 1938–1963; Loretta (Aunt Ret) b. 1940; Pearl (Mom, the most intelligent woman I know) b. 1942; Della Mae (Aunt Della) 1945–2008; and Floyd (Uncle Floyd) 1948–2000.

Terri Ann Ognibene

To my daughter, Jenny, and wife, Becky. This project has made me more appreciative of our family than ever before.

Glen Browder

Contents

List of Illustrations

ix

Preface

xi

Acknowledgments

xvii

Introduction: A New People and Voice in Regional Life

1

~ *Part One* ~

Who Are the Turkish People of Sumter County?

~ *Chapter One* ~

A Community Like No Other

15

~ *Chapter Two* ~

The Traditional Story of Oral History

30

~ *Chapter Three* ~

Probing the Legend of Origins

41

~ *Chapter Four* ~

Documenting the Patriarch and His People

63

~ *Chapter Five* ~

The Turkish Traditional Narrative Is Confirmed

101

Table of Contents

~ Part Two ~
We Are the Turkish People of Sumter County

~ Chapter Six ~
Our Voice: A Family Discussion
109

~ Chapter Seven ~
Our Journey: From Isolation to Assimilation
127

~ Chapter Eight ~
Reflections on Our Ancestry, Ethnicity,
Community, Race Relations, and Systemic Oppression
145

~ Chapter Nine ~
Life at the Dalzell School for
Turks and Integrating the White Schools
169

~ Chapter Ten ~
The Turkish Community Today
184

~ Chapter Eleven ~
Our Story Has Now Been Told
208

Conclusion: What Have We Learned?
212

Bibliography
219

Index
227

Illustrations

Charts

Map of South Carolina and Sumter County, showing the Dalzell community   4

Excerpt of a survey plat dated 1815   74

Figures

General Thomas Sumter (1734–1832)   3

Joseph Benenhaley (ca. 1753–1823)   5

Eleazer Benenhaley   35

Matilda Ellison Benenhaley (1842–1936)   75

Lawrence "Curly" Benenhaley (1848–1923)   76

Noah Benenhaley (1860–1939)   79

Rosa Benenhaley (1857–1937)   80

Isaac Benenhaley (1927–2011)   81

Family and relatives of Noah Benenhaley (1860–1939)   86

Martha Ann Benenhaley Hood (1855–1919) and her niece Martha Jane Oxendine Benenhaley (1866–1951)   86

John Benenhaley (1853–1923)   87

Family of William Joseph Benenhaley (1858–1920)   87

Jesse Noah/Noah Jr. (1896–1960) and Maybelle (1898–1972)   88

Isaac Benenhaley (1927–2011) and his sisters Leah and Lillie   88

The cemetery behind Long Branch Baptist Church   90

Springbank cemetery   91

List of Illustrations

Some gravesites in the cemetery behind High Hills of Santee Church   92

High Hills of Santee Church   129

James Ray (1878–1929)   130

Nellie Benenhaley Ray (1879–1952)   131

The first minister and deacons of Long Branch Baptist Church   132

Long Branch minister and leadership burning the mortgage   133

The congregation celebrating paying off the debt of their church   134

Long Branch Baptist Church in Dalzell   135

Springbank Baptist Church   135

The Dalzell School for Turks   136

Students and their teacher at the Dalzell School   136

More Dalzell students and their teacher   137

Greg Thompson   190

Ognibene interviewing Turkish descendent Chip Chase   195

Schoolteacher Adrienne Love   200

Reilly Ray   206

Preface

Every so often, a pearl of poignant beauty comes our way. Something happens—something that is simultaneously painful and inspiring—enriching our lives and helping us better understand the world around us. Such is the beauty of the Turkish people of Sumter County, South Carolina. Their full history and true story—presented here for the first time—reveal a beleaguered society that struggled as a rural southern enclave through isolation, segregation, discrimination, and oppression for almost two centuries. They had to fight and win their full rights as citizens; and only in the last few decades have they begun assimilating into mainstream American society. In this book, the authors investigate and reveal the Turkish community's origins; and the Turkish people, shedding their traditional reluctance to talk about themselves, share the heretofore untold, inside account of their extraordinary community in Dalzell, South Carolina.

Actually, this book is two books. There are two authors, with two different objectives, pursuing two separate investigations; but the efforts come together to resolve a mystery that has confounded everyone for two centuries. First, Browder, a Sumter native, will present academic research documenting the ancestral background of the fabled Turkish patriarch and the chronological history of the Turkish community. Second, Ognibene, a Turkish descendant herself, will get the Turkish people to tell their own story about what life was like in this rural settlement; and she will share her personal feelings about the enigmatic heritage of this unique group. Overall, this work is a breakthrough analysis of South Carolina's Turkish community. You will find the Turkish people a revelational pleasure, and the following pages should prove both provocative and enlightening.

Notes on Authors, Objectives, and Analytic Model

The Ognibene-Browder partnership is recent and happenstance—but their backgrounds bonded them together for presenting this poignant pearl of Turkish life and history. They are revealed more personally in the following pages; however, as the following biographic entries reveal, they both have special reasons for trying to tell the true story of the Turkish people.

The captions include information derived from documents of varying nature over the past two centuries. Errors and inconsistencies are inevitable; however, the authors have exercised due diligence to minimize those problems.

~ Objectives ~

The authors hope to make several contributions through this project. The first objective is to try to solve the mystery that has plagued the Turkish people and outsiders from the beginning: Exactly who was Joseph Benenhaley? What was his role in the origin of the Turkish community? Is the Turkish traditional narrative true?

The second objective is to help the Turkish people tell their own story about who they are and what life was like within their community. Their voice has been a critically missing element of this part of South Carolina and southern history.

A third objective is to present the Turkish experience during segregation and integration in the middle of the past century. The participants interviewed here lived through their own struggle in this area at the same time that our nation was focused on the national civil rights movement.

A final purpose of this project—reflecting the authors' responsibilities as teachers—is to inspire today's educators to embrace all students in the classroom. South Carolina, the South, and the United States of America have changed considerably over the past half century and continue to diversify in the twenty-first century. The story and voice of Turkish citizens who lived through those experiences should be very instructive in dealing positively with marginalized groups in contemporary society.

~ Analytic Model ~

The authors have designed a very clear, credible, and successful model, that is, a conceptual framework of propositions and strategies for discovering and telling the true story of the Turkish people. Presenting it here will help readers navigate the twists and turns of the rest of this book.

Seven Propositions

The authors started this project with many questions, premises, and hunches; and, as the work moved forward, the most constructive notions were refined into a concise list of propositions hypothesized as the main currents and nature of Turkish life over the past two centuries. Actually, readers can consider these propositions not only as the basis of the evolving project but also as the enduring principles in a conclusive conception of Turkish history.

Here are the seven propositions of the analytic model:

First and most significantly, the authors asserted that the Sumter County Turkish family began, ancestrally, with Joseph Benenhaley, the original Ottoman Turk, during the early years of the American nation. This was a central truism, based in logic and simplicity.

Propositions two and three were judicious elaborations of connectedness in the evolving community. They posited that Turkish lineage extended, mainly, to and through Benenhaley's descendants. Outsiders who married descendants thereby gained entry to the Turkish group; and being born to Turkish parents carried birthright inclusion.

Proposition four related to the ethnic makeup of the Turkish settlement in its formative years—and this historically involved racial connotations and practices. As already acknowledged, the original Ottoman Turk sat atop the family tree. White Europeans (the wives of Benenhaley and Scott) were part of the group from the beginning and others married in later; and some persons of partial American Indian descent married in during the first few generations. The Turkish people thus comprised a mainly dark-skinned gathering; however, Sub-Sahara Africans—whether runaway slaves or free black individuals—were not received in this community. Of course, the group became more diverse over time, especially during the twentieth century.

The fifth proposition was the reality of isolation in rural Sumter County for these people. Trapped by the social dynamics of southern history, most of them settled among relatives in the Dalzell area, and they were estranged from the rest of the county for almost two centuries. Furthermore, it seemed to be a case of mutual estrangement. The Turkish people were generally leery of outsiders, and they may have preferred living among themselves almost as much as they were spurned by the outside world.

The sixth proposition was the ordeal of discrimination. Many years of isolation and segregation engendered personal and systemic mistreatment of the Turkish people, and this abuse had deep, lasting, and oppressive impact on the Turkish community. This adversity kept them from realizing their potential, and many lived their entire lives as second-class citizens.

The seventh and final proposition was that Turkish people consciously identified with the Turkish community as an outcast society throughout their history. Whatever the reason—their self-perceptions, physical isolation, or treatment by the broader population—they mentally bonded and banded together.

Summarily and fundamentally, this analytic model held that "the Turkish people" have comprised a powerful cultural experience—with definitive subcultural character—rather than a simple geographical, genealogical, or friendship network. Just living in this area, or associating with Turkish individuals, or even being loosely related to the Turkish people did not make one a member of the Turkish community; that stature was determined by a cultural combination of patriarchy, blood, marriage, color, isolation, discrimination, and identity. Apparently, there was something in the ancestral genes, or cumulative background, or evolved psyche of "true Turks" (as one recently called herself online) that encouraged strong allegiance to family and homeland for many generations.

Of course, there has never been an official code of qualifications and conduct for Turkish membership; and compliance with all seven criteria—particularly Joseph Benenhaley's bloodline—was not a rigid requirement for Turkish identification. Over the years, some have considered themselves Turkish people and have been considered among the group, even without traceable lineage to the patriarch; and this has been especially true for individuals in the twentieth century. So the authors would not presume to deny their cultural identification with the community. But, as we began to investigate the traditional narrative, we realized that it was necessary to focus on the communal beginnings of these people; and that required us to operationalize the definitive, distinguishing character of the original group in the formative period of the nineteenth century. Therefore, our research plan was devised in accord with the essential elements—as described in the propositional criteria—of the historical community.

Two Strategies

The authors then employed two different but connected research strategies in examining—and confirming or denying—these propositions. First, we analyzed countless documents relating to Turkish history, with the discussion organized around their thematic question: "Who are the Turkish people of Sumter County?" Second, we asked the Turkish people themselves to talk with us personally about Turkish history, with the comments reflecting their thematic answer: "We are the Turkish people of Sumter County."

Here is a review of specific efforts in the two research strategies—some routine but others innovative—that helped us evaluate the propositions. In the documentary approach, we started by scouting the Internet and talking with many people—insiders and outsiders, scholars and everyday citizens—in the search for records and information about this community. We researched the usual public sources—such as the US Census, vital records, and genealogical reports. We attempted to round up everything that had been written possibly relating to Joseph Benenhaley and his life. We dug up arcane and unusual material—such as old property surveys, long-hoarded letters from discreet relationships, and genetic tests—to shed light on hidden aspects of his life and the nature of his people. We compiled our own data—such as a "master list" of individuals who lived back then and a full inventory of headstones in local church cemeteries—to chart the historical Turkish family. We compiled academic, news, and journalistic accounts of the Turkish community's adversities as a subcultural society; and we scoured legal papers relating to the integration of the public schools. In short, we have thoroughly documented the history of the Turkish people.

Just as important, we interviewed living Turkish persons in depth about their lives and their versions of these issues. We questioned the Turkish respondents about their ethnic identity and the traditional narrative. We got the Turkish respondents to talk about what it meant to be a "Turk" during difficult days of the past. How did they deal with discrimination and adversity? What were their relationships with whites and blacks in Sumter? Were they really Indians? How was life at the Dalzell School for Turks? What were their memories and feelings about the struggle for educational opportunity at Hillcrest High School and Edmunds High School? And how are things different for Turkish people in today's world? For the first time ever, the respondents told their own story in their own words. These interviews not only provided substantive information about Turkish history but also revealed the enduring strength of Turkish spirit.

Glancing ahead, it is clear that the propositions in the analytic model were substantiated by these research strategies. Newly discovered historical documents revealed the history of the patriarch and community; and the informants corroborated and elaborated that research with the human story of this group's past and present.

Acknowledgments

As stated in the preface, this publication is two books in one—written by two different authors with different objectives and methodologies—but with a common mission. There are many people to whom Terri Anne Ognibene is indebted for their help and support on this project. First, she would like to thank the Georgia State University faculty members who guided her in college. Joyce E. Many served as mentor, advisor, and chair, offering encouragement and peace. Other faculty members who deserve to be recognized include Mary Ariail, whose expertise in identity theory helped this author to discover her own; Dana Fox, who taught her how to organize and conduct a study effectively; Carol Semonsky, who has worked with and supported her since undergraduate school; and Randy Fair, who challenged her to discover the voices of the segregated, and to provide the means through which their voices could be heard. She followed his advice and has become a new person. Thank you goes to all of them. In addition to the professors mentioned, she would also like to thank the entire MSIT Department at Georgia State University, as well as her professors from Kennesaw State University. She learned a great deal from all of them, and she wants them to know that this project is for them too. Her thanks go to Peggy Albers, Lori Elliott, Amy Flint, Gertrude Tinker-Sachs, Lynn Fideli, Judy Holzman, Elaine McAllister, and Lucia Ribera. She would also like to thank the four participants of this study: Boaz, Tonie, Helen, and Jean. Their stories have touched her heart. She thanks them for enduring difficult times and for taking action against oppression and for trusting her enough to tell her about their educational experiences. Their courage has brought educational freedom to the younger generation of Turkish people, and she is eternally grateful to them for fighting the good fight. Without their struggle, she would not be free. God bless them. Thanks also go to Pearl Corcoran (Mom), Daniel Ognibene (Dad), Denise Ognibene, Michael Ognibene, Rebecca Brown, Jasper Kohlby Brown, Susan Crooks, Eleazer Benenhaley, Helen Team, Bertie Jean Noordhoek, Sue New, and Blanche Ray for their support and wise counsel. Finally, and most important, thanks to her Heavenly Father, for guiding her to his purpose. May his will be done, and may he be glorified.

Acknowledgments

Glen Browder is most grateful to the Turkish people of Sumter County. This has been a worthwhile but sometimes sensitive experience for this community, and many of them have graciously shared their homes and stories with him. Without their courage, cooperation, and treasured family histories, his research would never have gotten off the ground, and the authors would never have solved the mystery of the Turkish narrative.

Also vital for both authors were Eleazer Benenhaley and Greg Thompson, as stout champions and historical sources in this project. Benenhaley is the most respected Turkish person alive today, and his participation was necessary for gaining support in the community. Thompson was similarly critical with his friendships in the community, and his collection of historical material has proven to be the single most useful documentary source in the project. Each could have written this book on his own. In fact, Benenhaley has already authored two publications about life among the Turkish people; and Thompson is working on his own manuscript dealing with interactions among the early Turkish people, with detailed research on the Graham, Miller, Benenhaley, and related families. The authors feel privileged that they worked with them, and it has been a pleasure working with them.

The authors are indebted, too, to the non-Turkish people in Sumter County and throughout the state and country who helped them to deal with difficult issues of southern history. Furthermore, a word of gratitude is in order for many people of various callings—whom the authors have pestered over the years to help them find, validate, and document the material presented in this publication. Their service has been invaluable (and the authors apologize for any inadvertent errors or misrepresentations in the final product).

Various institutions and individuals have assisted the authors throughout this process. Georgia State University and Jacksonville State University have been supportive in various ways; in particular, their library personnel proved responsive and reliable as the authors requested and worked through countless research documents. Likewise, the South Caroliniana Library (particularly Brian Cuthrell) at the University of South Carolina provided valuable historical materials for scrutiny. Also, numerous academic colleagues—too many to begin to mention here—were helpful with their reviews and suggestions regarding the text. David Peagler and several other individuals and churches in the community shared precious photographs of Turkish history. The Sumter County Museum allowed the authors to include their portrait of General Thomas Sumter among the book's images; and Summerton artist Charles Marsh contributed his sketch of Scout Joseph Benenhaley. Graphic artist David M. Smith and photographer Mark du Pont of Jacksonville, Alabama, professionally designed and enhanced charts and photographs.

The authors specifically acknowledge the following individuals for permissions to quote them in this book: Limame Barbouchi, Brian Benenhaley, Eleazer

Acknowledgments

Benenhaley, Harold Benenhaley, James Bindon, Jonathan Bradshaw, Chip Chase, Charles Cobb, Pearl Ray Corcoran, Randy Fair, Michael Gomez, Sara Jernigan, Adrienne Love, W. A. McElveen Jr., Steve Miller, Roosevelt Miott, Sue New, Richard Ray, Reilly Ray, Carl Steen, Wesley Taukchiray, Helen Team, Greg Thompson, Thomas Sumter Tisdale Jr., and Donald Yates.

The authors especially appreciate their experience with the University of South Carolina Press—specifically acquisitions editor Alexander Moore and Linda Fogle, assistant director for operations. This has been a truly collaborative effort.

Finally, and this may sound unusual—the authors acknowledge each other. Both brought different backgrounds and research agendas to this project, and it has been a mutually rewarding and educational process.

Introduction
A New People and Voice in Regional Life

For too long, those engaged as professional scholars in the study of southern history and culture have focused on the monotonous, insensitive notion of "black and white, and sometimes red," in regional affairs. As Celeste Ray generalized in The New Encyclopedia of Southern Culture, such scholars conventionally and simplistically structured their discussions of the region within the perspective of the three continents from which most southerners originated (2007, 1).

Moreover, too often scholars have analyzed the dynamics of slavery, segregation, and the civil rights movement as though white southerners and black southerners represented the totality of important regional society and experience. Bioethicist Carl Elliott noted this inclination in the *Wilson Quarterly*: "Most Americans, and even many Southerners, believe that Southerners come in two varieties, white and black. Yet groups that don't quite fit either mold have been living in the South for centuries, often in isolated communities" ("Adventures" 2003, 13–14). Such fixation has limited understanding of the region, particularly the character and consequence of its cultural diversity. Again, as Ray observed: "The diverse ancestral origins of early southerners have only recently become a subject for recovery among scholars and in popular culture" (*New Encyclopedia* 2007, 1).

Fortunately, attention is now shifting to other aspects of the South, and scholars are discovering the richness of culture interwoven into southern history while probing more sophisticated societal concepts related to gender, religion, ethnicity, and other considerations of human history.

This new sense of discovery extends far beyond local and regional folks. The Southern Studies Forum (an international group that operates within the European Association for American Studies) regularly convenes outside the United States to talk about southern topics—such as race, religion, immigration, the

Confederate flag—and persistent themes of southernness in the literature of writers such as William Faulkner, Flannery O'Connor, and Harper Lee. Their 2003 annual conference in Greece showcased southern ethnicities because of renewed fascination with the South's multicultured history. According to Youli Theodosiadou, an associate professor in the Department of American Literature and Culture at host Aristotle University in Greece, "The heterogeneous multi-ethnic character of the American South can easily be identified from its beginning" and "in recent decades so much interest has been generated in issues connected to ethnicity in the American South" (*Southern Ethnicities* 2008, 7).

Sociologist John Shelton Reed, for example, has drawn our attention to the "odd . . . enclaves" of the southern ethnological landscape. The South has always been more diverse than many have thought, he notes in a brief essay; besides the British whites, West African blacks, and American Indians are numerous "odd enclaves" such as the Creoles, Cajuns, Hungarians, and Canary Islanders of Louisiana; the German, Czech, and Polish settlements in Texas; Greeks in Florida; the Chinese and Lebanese in Mississippi; and the Italians in Louisiana, Arkansas, and North Carolina ("Mixing" 1997, 25).

Especially mysterious, Reed has asserted, are the "little races": "Few of these exotic groups have been as little known or poorly understood as the South's so-called 'little races.' Every southern state except Arkansas and Oklahoma has at least one group like the Red Bones of Louisiana and Texas, the Turks and Brass Ankles of South Carolina, the Issues of Virginia, the Lumbee and Haliwa and so-called Cubans of North Carolina, or the Cajans of Alabama. The 1950 census identified over twenty of these populations in the South, numbering from a few hundred to a few thousand, often isolated in swamps or mountain coves" (25).

South Carolina presents a golden opportunity for probing the richness of southern culture. As claims Walter Edgar, the Palmetto Sate's premier historian, this state is "different" and "special" in its history (*South Carolina Encyclopedia* 2006). Before the Europeans there were as many as forty different Indian nations; and by the end of the eighteenth century there were at least twenty-five West African ethnicities and nine European ethnic groups. "Thus South Carolina's population is a rich mosaic, a variety of people from three continents. Over the centuries the interaction of these peoples produced a culture that made South Carolina a special place" (xvi).

Of particular pertinence to this project, historian James W. Hagy pinpoints South Carolina's rich diversity prior to the Civil War ("Muslim Slaves" 1993). Hagy writes that one can find non-Europeans and non-Christians with exotic ethnic backgrounds, including Muslim slaves, abducted Moors, African Jews, and even "misnamed Turks," who contributed to the state's early experience. And with a reference to the famed culinary dish of the Palmetto State, he said that "while pilau has rice as its base, the other ingredients give it taste" (12).

Most recently, according to historian Arlin Migliazzo, academics have begun probing and documenting—with sophisticated scholarship—the ethnic diversity of South Carolina communities "shrouded in relative obscurity" (*To Make This Land* 2007). "During the past fifteen years," he writes, "social historians of the American South have combined sophisticated social science methodology with increased historical narrative to illuminate the variegated textures of life for a number of the region's peoples and communities." As he also notes, "Colonial and antebellum South Carolina has been the focus of many of the finest of these studies" (2).

~ The Turkish People of Sumter County ~

Among those "odd enclaves" and "little races" are the Turkish people of Sumter County, South Carolina. For most of our country's history, they endured as a quiet, reclusive settlement near Dalzell, in the midlands of the Palmetto state.

General Thomas Sumter (1734–1832). According to oral history, the "Gamecock" recruited Joseph Benenhaley for his military unit in South Carolina during the American Revolution. This is a copy of a portrait originally painted by Rembrandt Peale around 1795 and now located in the Sumter County Museum. Courtesy of Sumter County Museum.

According to oral history, the founding father of this community was Joseph Benenhaley (also called Yusef ben Ali by some), a "Caucasian of Arab descent." The story goes that he was chosen by General Thomas Sumter himself to be a scout for his regiment fighting the British in the Revolutionary War, and he proved to be such a valiant scout that, at the end of the war, Sumter gave him some land from his own plantation for farming and raising his family. Joseph Benenhaley thereafter was hailed as patriarch of this settlement, and his name and ancestry have been imprinted upon all generations of its members, known from early times as the "Benenhaleys" or "Turks."

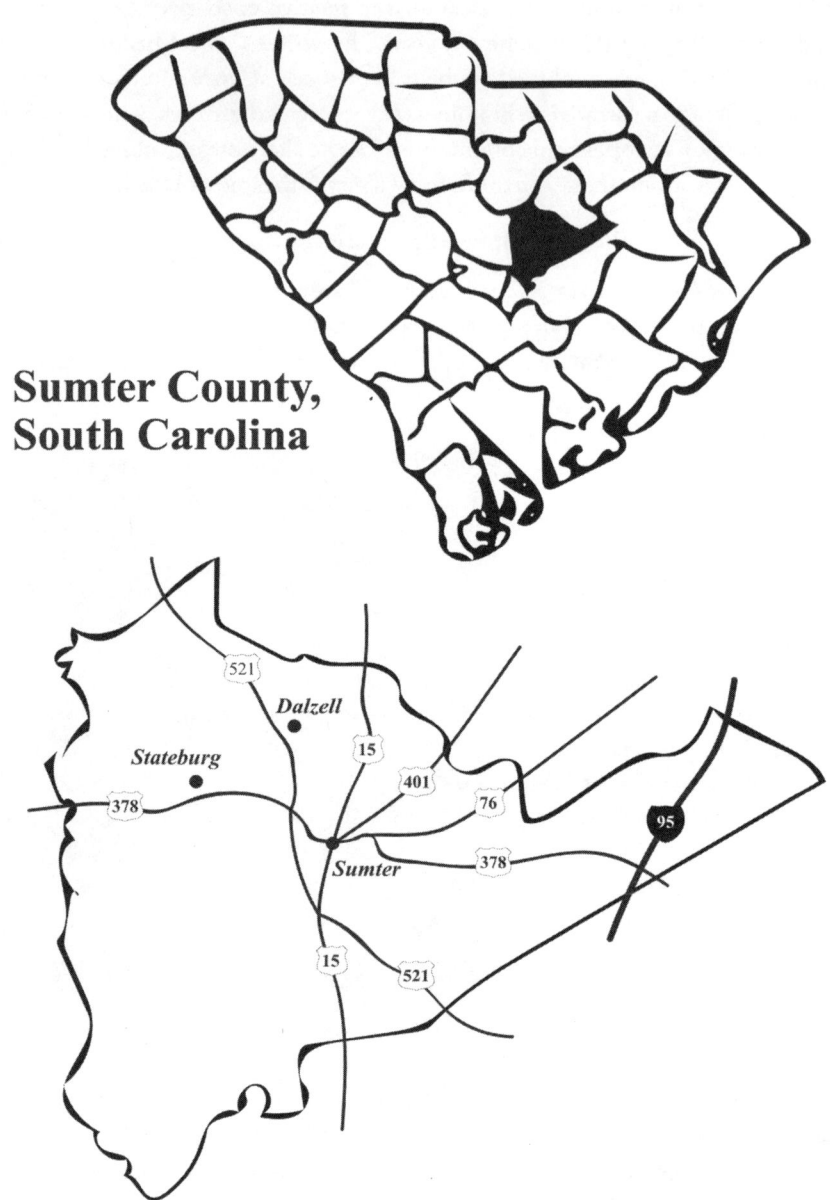

Map of South Carolina and Sumter County, showing the Dalzell community where the Turkish people lived for two centuries.

Introduction

Joseph Benenhaley (ca. 1753–1823) was the patriarch of the Turkish people of Sumter County. He reputedly was from the Ottoman Empire and helped General Sumter as a scout in the American Revolution. Original sketch by artist Charles Marsh of Summerton, S.C.

There have been questions about the designation of this community as the "Benenhaleys" and the "Turks"; however, an exhaustive search of records found that these terms have been used throughout two centuries to refer to the Turkish people of Sumter County. Among countless documents using these very same terms, no historical source could be found that might raise serious doubts about Joseph Benenhaley and his Turkish ancestry as the reason for these designations.

If this discussion thus far were the extent of the tradition, then the drama would have ended long ago; however, the saga of Joseph Benenhaley and his beleaguered descendants has now extended into its tenth generation, and it merits more than a footnote in regional histories and social science journals.

The rest of that narrative held that Thomas Sumter vouched for Benenhaley as a white man in the racially structured South and helped his family throughout the general's lifetime. But the Benenhaleys and their kin never assimilated into the mainstream populace of that area. Instead, these tightknit folk suffered isolation and segregation; and they kept mainly to themselves in rural Sumter County for the next two centuries. Amazingly, they persevered as an enclosed society— numbering about five hundred persons at mid-twentieth century—separate from both white and black South Carolinians. They fought back and won their full rights as citizens in the 1950s and are assimilating into mainstream American society.

For the Turkish people, this history has always been an important tale of both pride and pain.

The problem is that the traditional narrative of Joseph Benenhaley and the Turkish community has often been considered no more than myth, a fable concocted to sustain them through unpleasant realities of hard history. There have always been doubts and questions about these people and their interesting experience. Critics scoffed at the idea of an Arab warrior helping win the American Revolution; they dismissed the notion of a community of dark-skinned Ottomans surviving so long in rural South Carolina; and they disparaged the identity and culture of the "so-called Turks." Many believed that this settlement originated as an indistinct haven for societal remnants—poor white settlers, disassociated American Indians, and runaway or freed African slaves—and that the Turkish narrative is either a racist artifact of oral history or a fairy tale for comforting a scorned community.

The obvious question is: "Why is their true story unknown?" Or, more precisely, "Why has their history never been told completely and accurately?" The Turkish people have been referenced and reported many times, as will be noted in the rest of this project. Nevertheless, little is known about them for sure beyond the basics of their draggled existence in Dalzell. The pertinent question, "Why is their true story unknown?" can be answered simply and with certainty. Thus far, no one has been able to produce any authoritative evidence or contemporaneous testimony—only vague oral history—relating to their epic tale. Generations of scholars, journalists, and activists have referred to the community's traditional narrative and attempted to tell the story of the Turkish people of Sumter County. But they have been stymied by a lack of documentary records; and they have been unable to overcome the reluctance of these people to share whatever information they had or to talk about life in their enclave.

An inquiring visitor learned a half century ago that the Turkish community has always resisted being asked anything by outsiders. University of South Carolina graduate student Mike Boliver tried to interview them for a study in the 1970s and he got nowhere (White, *A History of the Turks*, 1975). In an unpublished report based on that experience, he said: "The mood of the community strictly opposes any sort of historical investigation. The people will tell any would-be historian that they don't know anything, don't think that anyone else does either, don't see any point in it, and think that he should go talk to some other member of the community." One Turkish old-timer told the visitor that some sort of historical study should be done—but he "found himself old and with a bad heart and unable on that account to stand up against the rest of the community." In short, these reclusive people have refused to talk about themselves, and outsiders have not and cannot tell "their story" (n.p.).

In addition to a scarcity of historical documentation, laypersons and scholars encounter inconsistency in names, places, dates, grammar, spelling, and word usage in references to this community. For example, the Turkish people's historical home is usually identified as Dalzell, a small community in Sumter County; however, others have noted their residence as Stateburg and one will find early references to Providence. Most of the inconsistencies occur because of dealing with many documents over a wide span of sources and history; thus informed choices must be made in some cases and estimates in other cases. However, such instances have been kept to a minimum and are irrelevant to the substantive essence of this manuscript.

For generations, this shadowy drama has haunted the Turkish people and defied study by professional scholars. Now, many people—including both blood descendants and outside observers—are asking questions and demanding answers. They want to know the truth about Joseph Benenhaley and the Turkish people of Sumter County.

It was not until a century after their origin that anyone compiled a written, credible account of their narrative. General Sumter's great-grandson, Thomas Sebastian Sumter, was the first to record the special status and character of this community (*Stateburg and Its People* 1920): "In my narrative of the people of Stateburg, I have heretofore made mention only of the Bennanhaly and Scott families. These people deserve more than a mere mention as they know no other country than this, and claim no other home than the ones they now live in, among the old hills of Stateburg, enjoying the respect of every one, with a flurishing school, and a church where they and their children assemble each Sunday to worship their Creator" (43).

Others subsequently have recorded different views of the Turkish community. For example, almost a century ago an unidentified writer for the *State* newspaper painted a dreary, fatalistic picture of this community in a front-page story entitled "Sumter County Colony Locally Called Turks" (Mar. 18, 1928): "Most conspicuously characteristic of all, however, is their utter lack of spontaneous joy. They wear, one and all, the air of patient and unquestioning acceptance of life as they find it. But what does the future have to promise them? Bits of flotsam from life's ebb-tide, left stranded between two layers of a civilization which provides no place for a third element. Prevented by racial instinct from amalgamation with the Negro; seeing in the future nothing but a continued marriage and intermarriage with those of their own clan, and a repetition of the age-old struggle for existence; they are faced by a problem the solution of which only the future can tell"(1).

Additionally, here is the cryptic, concluding paragraph of a provocative report ("Pockets in America," late 1930s) written by another unidentified author for the Federal Writers' Project: "Unobtrusively they go their lonely way. In spite of their Baptist affiliation, their Mohammedan ancestry has stamped them with an utter lack of spontaneous joy. With tragic patience they apparently accept as unalterable their struggle to exist in abject poverty. Fired with no zeal to unite in common endeavor, beset with no adventurous spirit to roam beyond the limited radius in which they have remained since the settling of their earliest progenitors, they remain a submerged and isolated group. It is kismet" (3).

Normally such characterizations would be considered unacceptable because of their uncertain authorship, disparaging nature, and lack of supportive documentation. There were no identified authors for the assessments of the *State* or the Federal Writers' Project. That latter report was an especially curious statement consisting of four pages and only two sources (Thomas Sebastian Sumter's *Stateburg and Its People* and "Personal observation and interviews with the Turks by Lucy G. Platt"). It reflected the tone and style of a local person of some education and was written assumedly to convey the origin, history, and ways of an outcast society. While there is no way to be sure, Lucy G. Platt is believed to have written "Pockets in America." Information about Platt was not found, other than US Census records showing that she was a widowed teacher in her late forties who lived in the same rural area as the Turkish people during the time when that report was written. These assessments appear in this introduction because they apparently were the sources, thereafter, of many published characterizations—positive and negative—about the Turkish community. Some of these sentiments have found their way into accepted historical accounts; they also were repeated in court testimony during the fight for educational equality in the 1950s, and they persist today in some circles. Such stereotypical references—repeated often by outsiders—command the Turkish people to discover their voice and tell their story today.

~ Why Should Anyone Care? ~

Why should anyone care about the Turkish people and their history? The big picture reason is that they represent a hidden history that needs to be revealed. Their story will be a valuable new contribution to our knowledge about the diversity of southern history and culture; and it will serve as an analogy for the classic American experience, demonstrating a difficult but successful journey through adversity to triumph and redemption as part of the American family. Their particular story of Americanization is both similar to and different from other regional or national subcultures, and that story should be told. In a sense, for all—and particularly for the mainstream citizens of this little corner of the world—"their story" is everyone's story. More immediately, it is important to pay attention to their story because of their fading presence as an ethnic identity.

~ Urgency of Fading Ethnicity ~

This distinctive community of South Carolinians has long endured adversity, from their struggle for basic rights during the formative years of this country through their fight for educational opportunities in the twentieth century. Now the Turkish people of Sumter County seem to be drifting away from a shared conception of who they are, losing their way as a distinct culture. Older members are dying, younger members are assimilating into the broader society, and census statistics indicate that their numbers are shrinking.

The need for quick and sound research on this community is clear. As Calvin E. Beale noted long ago, in reference to other southern subcultures, increasing outmarriage and abolition of legal segregation threaten the continued existence of such societies ("An Overview" 1972). Furthermore, as time marches on, it may be impossible to capture their history as an interesting ethnic culture.

Just as ominously, a growing debate among local cultural activists threatens their historical identity. Some argue that the Turkish people of Sumter County are really American Indians (Hill, *Strangers in Their Own Land*, 2010); and others want to subsume them among the Melungeons, a diverse group reflecting "a mixed ethnic, cultural, and religious heritage" (Kennedy and Kennedy, *The Melungeons*, 1997). Many, of course, continue to consider them tri-racial isolates, the notion that they are all just an ill-defined hodgepodge of European, African, and Native American origins (Gilbert, "Memorandum," 1946; Price, "Geographic Analysis," 1953; Beale, "American Tri-Racial Isolates," 1957).

Through historical research and social science techniques, it can be verified that the Turkish people have a proud and distinct heritage, based as much on culture—two centuries of an isolated, enclosed way of life—as ancestral origins and genealogical lineage. Through this unveiling process, the Turkish people are allowed to define their own identity and history. And it is critical that they tell their story soon, because their time may be running out.

~ Compelling and Valuable Testimony ~

Our historical research and findings are original and significant as well as timely. But the real strength of this project is the compelling voice and valuable story of the Turkish people themselves. Their voice and story are important, not only as historical clarification but also because they bring recognition and dignity to the Turkish people of Sumter County; and, they represent a worthwhile addition to our conception of South Carolina, the South, and America. They demonstrate that our historic regional culture is much richer than thought in earlier times; also, they tell something about the changing dynamic of contemporary society.

The Turkish people profiled and interviewed in this project add substantively and substantially to our understanding of the changing world around us. They symbolically represent and passionately articulate the evolving, diverse, and sometimes troubled nature of the South and southern culture; and their story speaks similarly to our broader definition of America and the American experience.

~ Candid Conversations and Painful Declarations ~

From the outset, the Turkish people in this project engage in candid discussions of their hazy origins and shout out painful declarations about their history. For example, they have never been able to articulate or celebrate their own heritage; and while they proudly claim their identity as "the Turkish people of Sumter County, South Carolina," they sometimes bristle at the term "Turks" as a slur that has been used over the years to disparage and separate them from the mainstream society of this area. Ironically, too, the Turkish people acknowledge that they helped create their historic isolation from both white and black people and, for most of their existence, accepted segregation in their churches, schools, and social lives. They also try to explain their folkways, such as pronounced intermarriage among the few family lines in their community. Throughout, there are personal accounts of being insulted and harassed, both verbally and physically.

This project clearly portrays a long, murky, difficult ordeal about who the Turkish people are and from whence they came; it also details their many struggles in the rural South because of their blurred history and the tones of their skin. Consequently, some of the upcoming analysis deals with troubling aspects of ancestry, ethnicity, and especially race. Many professional scholars contend that race is an artificial and meaningless construct; and some of our colleagues have warned that discussing such issues as is done in this project risks condemnation. However, it will be impossible to tell this story effectively in accord with the sentiments of our academic friends.

This is not a study of race; but the mystery of the Turkish people cannot be solved without frank discussion about the problem of missing information, misconception, and misinterpretation regarding the racial history of this community. Thus the authors wade—cautiously and sensitively but candidly—into the mire of race and racism to unravel almost two centuries of isolation, segregation, discrimination, and oppression. For example, the authors talk about faulty racial ideas and unwarranted racial presumptions regarding this community. Scholars and journalists have long cited the typology of triple-mixed origins—white European settlers, Native American Indians, and runaway or freed African slaves—to dismiss the Turkish traditional narrative; and they have made it hard for the Turkish people to understand their history or to celebrate their heritage. It will be necessary for us to assert contradictory ideas and present new evidence, for legitimate purposes, about these topics.

Also, throughout this book—in both the academic discussions and conversations with Turkish individuals—terms commonly used as self-descriptors are employed by the authors and populations of interest in this community. References to the "Turkish people" and "Turkish people of Sumter County" frequently appear throughout the text. As will be apparent in these pages, such references are not literally and solely about people from Turkey; nor do such references designate an aggregation of Turkish individuals only. This phrase is used to refer to a distinct ethnic enclave of people in Sumter County, South Carolina, many of whom claim to be of Turkish descent or who have been accepted into the Turkish communal family, and who are viewed by themselves and outsiders as the Turkish people of this area. The phrase "Turkish people" is also used because the word "Turk" or "Turks" has always and still conveys pain to these individuals; it has been used commonly in the past as a derisive term, declaring them different and unworthy citizens. That connotation has moderated now; but it is still hurtful to some of them. In the interviews for this book, most of the Turkish people expressed preference for the "Turkish people" designation.

Additionally, throughout this text various terms are used by the authors and Turkish respondents—for analytic purposes and in line with common discourse in this area—to refer to the other three ethnic populations discussed in this book. These groups have indicated to us that they prefer these terms—"white," "black," and "Indian"—and readers should consider them as neutral designations, with absolutely no negative connotations; they are simply practical and useful terms for analyzing historical interactions among those groups in this county.

The term "white" is used to refer to people who are non-Turkish and who claim to be white. They are also referred to as white Europeans or as Euro-Americans. This ethnic group has been the privileged group throughout the history of Sumter County, South Carolina, and the United States. The Turkish people claimed to be white but the white people did not accept them as being white. Thus, the differentiation of the term Turk was used by white people to justify their exclusion from schools for white individuals and mainstream society.

The term "black" is used to refer to people who are not white or Turkish and who identify as and claim to be black. They are sometimes called Africans or Sub-Sahara Africans when referencing the slave era. They were commonly described as Negroes back then and throughout most of American history, and the term African American did not become a functional designation until more recent times. This ethnic group has never been a privileged group locally. Generally, black and Turkish people steered different courses from the beginning; but their skin tones placed them beneath white individuals socially in this county. Turkish people did not claim to be black, and black people did not claim that the Turkish people were black.

The term "Indian" is used to refer to the indigenous peoples of the southeast and to their descendants, including many of the latter who are of mixed ancestry and who identify and prefer to be called Indians. These individuals are also sometimes called Native Americans or American Indians. Knowledgeable authorities advise that proper usage depends upon the nature of the discussion; and associates in that group note that the simple "Indian" designation is used among themselves and is appropriate in academic and analytical context. The Indians have lived a history different from white, black, and Turkish people. They have never been a privileged group in American society; in fact, they have been somewhat hidden and invisible for most of the history of this county and in this region. As various tribes have asserted themselves in recent times, their designation as Indians has shifted from a tone of disrespect to one of pride; and the term is now used as common, accepted parlance. As this section will show, the uncertain relationship between the Indians and Turkish people has been a topic of discussion for many decades.

Finally, readers should note in this manuscript—especially in the review of the slave-trade era—a variety of terms referring to the subjects of the Ottoman Empire. As will be covered at a later point, the historical literature has lacked precise ethnic and cultural distinctions; and several related terms could have varied meanings—but they most often and generally refer to the people of this dynasty that reigned far and wide for six centuries. Therefore, the designations "Turk," "Arab," "Moor," and "Muslim" are used interchangeably as historical descriptors of Ottomans; and sometimes they are referenced geographically, as Mediterraneans, Middle Easterners, and North Africans. This is not a matter of personal whim or ignorance; it simply represents necessary reliance on the terminology of available documents in the search for the conjectured homeland of Joseph Benenhaley. Rest assured, however, that in all aspects of this investigation, reputable experts and local citizens have been consulted along the way to avoid egregious violations of academic theory, mutual respect, and common sense.

The task taken on in the rest of this book is both educational and exciting. First, Browder compiles historical documents and other analytical material to identify Joseph Benenhaley and appraise the traditional narrative. Then, Ognibene tackles the awesome mission of helping the Turkish people discover their voice and tell their story about Turkish life as they lived it. Readers should pay particular attention to the individualized assignments and styles of these two authors. Browder has written as an academic investigator hot on the trail of a baffling historical mystery; and Ognibene has engaged her relatives in a personalized, passionate drama that has never been shared outside this reclusive community. Their coordinated effort has proved both unusual and productive.

~ *Part One* ~

Who Are the Turkish People of Sumter County?

~ *Chapter One* ~
# A Community Like No Other

There are many different renditions of fact and legend regarding the Turkish people of Sumter County, South Carolina. One historian, Marina Wikramanayake, exercised unusual bluntness for an academician by putting it this way in A World in the Shadow, a publication celebrating the Palmetto State's tricentennial anniversary (1973): "A stranger visiting Sumter County today may come across a baffling breed called 'Turks.' In recent years these Turks, known also as 'Free Moors,' have claimed and received recognition as white citizens. Their status in ante-bellum South Carolina was less clear, and their origin has been the subject of much speculation. So meager are the facts relating to them that the wildest conjectures, based on what must surely be flight of fancy and geographical ignorance, have been advanced to support their origin" (20).

Among those wild conjectures was the fantasized account of Charlestonian Herbert Ravenel Sass in *South Carolina Lowcountry* (1956). According to Sass, these people may have been descendants of "golden women of the East." He speculated that the Turkish people originated from "slender, raven-haired, golden-skinned creatures," stolen by pirates known as the Red Sea Men from nobles of the Great Mogul's Delhi court, who were on a pilgrimage to Mecca and brought to South Carolina three centuries ago (82). Almost as curiously and somewhat ironically, *Ebony Magazine* called the Dalzell group a "raceless" people who distrusted whites and disliked blacks ("South Carolina's Raceless People" 1957, 53–56).

Are the Turkish people of Sumter County a "baffling breed" whose origins are cloaked in fanciful ignorance? Are they descendants of "golden-skinned creatures" kidnapped and brought here by pirates? Is their enclave a "raceless" yet racist clan? These are strong and strange proclamations; and, indeed, there is solid documentation that the Turkish people have lived a peculiar history. To generalize, these and numerous other reports support the notion that this is a unique people in the American experience.

Actually, there is another community—the Moors of Delaware—whose traditional narrative bears some resemblance to that of the "Sumter Turks," at least until the Delaware legend was discredited in the 1940s. The Delaware Moors had been considered for many generations as, possibly, the dark-skinned descendants of exotic ancestry, specifically the union of an Irish princess and a Moorish slave. But C. A. Weslager long ago explored their mythical heritage and concluded that the group's background was a racial mixture of unknown calculation, likely Native Americans, white Europeans, and some of black African origin (*Delaware's Forgotten Folk, 1943*). Our work documents important differences between the Sumter Turkish people's history and that of the Moors in Delaware and confirms the fascinating narrative of the South Carolina community.

Many of the strange proclamations about the Turkish people relate, of course, to their ancestry and ethnicity. However, from a broader perspective, it is clear that a driving factor in the formation and evolution and reputation of this subculture was their precarious situation in southern history. These people developed their secluded existence and tightknit folkways in an especially difficult regional environment. Negotiating uncertain paths among white and black individuals, they have lived separately and suspiciously within the raucous racial realities of their time and place.

Consequently, scholars and journalists have never been able to tell the full and true story of the "Sumter Turks." Previous analysts have presented only partial, disjointed snapshots of the Turkish people, and many have expressed fuzzy observations and serious misrepresentations. The chief reason for these varied depictions arises from ignorance and skepticism regarding their history; and complicating the situation is the fact that a certain awkwardness has always permeated discussion of this community.

~ Awkward Questions ~

Outside observers—no matter their backgrounds—are usually puzzled as they attempt to make sense of the Turkish people and their history. They raise awkward, insensitive questions and receive awkward, blunt answers in return, because many members of this community find discussions of such matters uncomfortable and offensive. Accordingly, an attempt to field the most common questions and provide answers has been made—with a balance of candor and sensitivity—based on personal experience and with help from some academic colleagues and Turkish friends.

For outsiders, two questions are automatic wonderings about this community: (1) "Are the Turkish people of Sumter County really Turks from Turkey?" (2) "Are the Turkish people white or black people, or something else?" These questions reveal normal curiosity about the history of southern society but they also reflect a gawking fixation on race.

This is not the place for an anthropological treatise on ancestry, ethnicity, and race. However, these terms need to be examined. For the purposes of this work, ancestry is defined as one's origins as a lineage of human beings, or "whatever I am as determined by my biological ancestors." Ethnicity is the cultural essence of one's self-identifying group, based on ancestry, history, religion, language, experience, and other aspects of that society. Race is the common designation of one's group, based on perceived physical differences, like skin color. Unfortunately, discussions of ancestry and ethnicity are too often grounded upon "race," the least reliable method of establishing identity.

Differentiation of groups by such factors as skin tone is a practice based on dubious science and steeped in the bias of Western civilization. Its most simple form is a binary distinction between Caucasians (usually called "whites" or "light-skinned people" originating from places such as Europe, North Africa, and the Middle East) and everyone else (usually known as "persons of color" or "dark-skinned people"); it sometimes consists of a five-color chart of white, black, yellow, red, and brown but can range to dozens of complex categorizations. Finally, most modern analysts consider race, as commonly depicted, an invalid concept; and they argue that there are gradations of characteristics among and between different groups of people rather than precise and distinct races.

Unfortunately, Americans seem to have always been driven to divide and define society by sometimes real and sometimes imagined differences in ancestry, ethnicity, and race; and they have usually resorted to the aforementioned metaphorical classifications as shorthand tools for sorting out various cultural groups. Academicians, particularly anthropologists, are divided on this practice, with most of them rejecting such typologies as value-laden discrimination; they prefer other approaches for understanding peoples and groups. Governments have also struggled with this concept; but the practice persists because, despite its faults, it is familiar and functional for most users of government publications. Laypersons seem to like it because it is simple and easy reading. Consequently, the practice of defining and categorizing human beings is often used for a variety of questionable endeavors.

Since the current discussion deals with such a complex and controversial topic, the authors asked a reputable anthropologist, via email, to render an opinion on our commentary about race as a topic of analysis in this project. James Bindon, former chair of the anthropology department at the University of Alabama (whom the authors did not know prior to this project), is a longtime teacher and expert on such matters. Bindon wrote back thus in an October 10, 2014, message: "I heartily concur with your portrayal of modern notions on the use of race—that's what I spend my classes trying to get across to the undergrads." (Readers looking for more extensive and comprehensive discussion of such issues relating to small southern enclaves such as the Turkish people may want to consult the introduction to *The New Encyclopedia of Southern Culture: Ethnicity*, edited by Celeste Ray, 2007.)

Who Are the Turkish People of Sumter County?

Particularly in this region of the country, many have considered it a matter of primary concern whether a person was of European or African origins—that is, a white or black person or some mixture of presumed consequence. Various designations have been contrived and implemented to convey different status for certain social groups—such as "free person of color," "colored," and "mulatto"—all of which reflect the black or white dichotomy.

Especially illustrative and instructive for our project is the strange and changing approach to officially identifying the Turkish people of Sumter County in selected censuses. An examination of US Census designations of the Benenhaley family in several decennial counts reflects the shifting tenor of the times, and the patterns of usage reveal the arbitrary and racist results of these practices. In 1810, the Joseph Benenhaley household of seven individuals was identified as "other free persons" (i.e., not white, not Indian, not slave); and in 1820, the Benenhaley family of twelve was listed as three "free white males" and nine "free white females." But sixty years later in 1880, all twenty-two Benenhaleys were labeled as "mulattoes." In the 1940s, the hundred-plus Benenhaleys were designated as "Negro" (69 percent), "Turk" or "Turkish" (21 percent), and "White" (10 percent). In perhaps the clearest specific example of the suspect and capricious nature of official record-keeping, one Benenhaley individual was recorded as a "White" person in the 1930 census and as a "Negro" in the 1940 census.

Similarly, analysts of all callings—scholars, journalists, activists, and genealogists—have tried, for whatever their reasons, to pigeonhole the Turkish people into their favored typology of white European/Native American/Sub-Sahara African background. Without any record or basis for judgment, academic analysts decreed long ago, and many contemporary observers still presume, that the Turkish community originated as "tri-racial isolates." The definition of that term is tangled in uncertainty; but these groups were usually described as an enclosed, remnant mixture of poor white settlers, disassociated American Indians, and runaway or freed African slaves. Also, those analysts were quick to stereotype the isolate communities with references to backwardness, drunkenness, violence, and crime.

For example, William Harlen Gilbert Jr. wrote the following comment in the 1940s: "The characteristics of illiteracy, poverty, and large families mark them as members of the more backward section of the American nation" ("Memorandum" 1946, 439). Calvin L. Beale compiled a litany of common stereotypes about them in the 1970s, including "a reputation for violence, drunkenness, and crimes of passion within the group and for petty thievery against outsiders" ("Overview" 1972, 705). Like many others who knew little about the Sumter County group, both writers included the "Turks" among these marginalized enclaves.

The Turkish people have always resented such unfounded presumptions and crass characterizations of their community; and there should be little wonder about their reactions to continuous interrogations of cultural and racial nature.

The first question usually posed by outsiders about the Turkish community deals with their ancestry and, by extension, their ethnic heritage: "Are the Turkish people really Turks from Turkey?" The answer to this simple question is not so simple. The key merit of this book is that it demonstrates without ambiguity the Turkish origins of Joseph Benenhaley; but, just as clearly and interestingly, the authors have found no evidence of Ottoman culture among the people of this rural enclave in Sumter County.

What we have here is a qualified version of ancestry and ethnicity. None of the Turkish people, except their alleged patriarch, was born in Turkey or anywhere in the Ottoman Empire. But most of them have believed that Joseph Benenhaley was truthful in declaring his ancestry; and they have considered and still consider themselves of similar descent, with certain stipulations. Thus, while they have claimed allegiance to their Turkish forefather and experienced ethnic distinction for two centuries, they do not adhere to Old World culture as part of their heritage. Their lives hark not to the days and ways of ancient Turkey or the Middle East. Instead, as will be demonstrated in the rest of this book, their heritage mainly reflects their long experience as common folk harried by isolation and discrimination in rural South Carolina.

The second automatic question is a clumsy and simplistic inquiry about race. Outsiders eventually embrace the binary vernacular of southern life when they ask, "Are the Turkish people white or black, or something else?" Some suspect that they may be American Indians, and a few speculate about other racial mixtures. Most Turkish people of Sumter County have adhered historically to an ancestral understanding that they are "white people" descended from Joseph Benenhaley, a "Caucasian of Arab descent"; and, today, they are considered white by most citizens in the area. Their skin color has been described over the years as dark brown, light brown, olive, and tanned; but it is not uncommon for them to be light skinned with blond hair and blue eyes. Our DNA investigation among Benenhaley descendants mainly found Mediterranean/Middle Eastern/North African, white European, and Native American backgrounds, with no significant markers for Sub-Sahara Africa. It appears certain that a full genetic accounting of all Turkish people over the past two centuries would provide more complex and diverse configurations; but the authors also are convinced that their reported results, viewed collectively and combined with our other historical research, accurately depict the origins and early history of this community.

It is undeniable that whispers of "dark blood" in the lineage have been problematic over the years, revealing the same attitudes and practices as have existed throughout regional and national society. Many local white people have looked down on the Turkish people on this count; and some in the Turkish community continue to be skittish about the question of African ancestry. The historical record is one of prejudice and discrimination over the past two centuries; and sworn testimony during the school Integration Movement of the 1950s reflected poorly on all sides of the issue. Interestingly, skin tone has been a topic of gossip—and sometimes amusement—among the Turkish people themselves. Some Turkish informants in our project commented about the variety among their relatives—from dark hair, dark eyes, and olive skin to light-skinned, blue-eyed blondes. But a few also told us that their parents instructed them not to date or marry certain other Turkish youngsters because "they're too dark."

On a more humorous note, a Turkish minister who used to serve a church in Dalzell recounted an incident that reveals changing times in this community. "I had some girls at church who had gotten good tans; they used to come up and put their arm up against mine and say, 'I'm as dark as you are now.' I said, 'Yes, but how long will it last?' And we'd just have a big laugh over it. But I'm glad that things have changed to a large extent with the younger people coming along."

Sometimes, inquiring types are also very curious about a third issue, that is, "Do the Turkish people only marry among themselves?" Being isolated, regardless of the cause, meant that from the start the Turkish people were cautious about outside society. Thus few outsiders were accepted in the community, and Turkish people mainly married within their own crowd for generations. This was a common pattern for other ethnic groups as well. The difference is that the Turkish population was geographically isolated and smaller than other ethnic populations, hence the repetition of family surnames throughout the generations. While it seems unlikely that society absolutely forced the Turkish people to marry within their ethnic group, it is very likely that there were unwritten societal customs in each group regarding the acceptable parameters of marriage.

This marital practice produced a growing community with a handful of common surnames. In addition to the Benenhaleys, the most prominent families were the Oxendines, Rays, Hoods, Buckners, and Lowreys. The practice of intermarriage among these families produced inevitable complications within the community and impacted their reputation among outsiders. Fortunately, assimilation into the broader society has relieved such issues, since almost all Turkish descendants now marry outside the traditional community.

In light of this nuanced version of historical origins, skin color, and marital practices, two essential follow-up questions are posed: "Did the Ottoman Turk sufficiently forefather these people for us to pronounce them a community of Turkish descent?" and "How has that heritage impacted them in Sumter County?" The summary answer is that historical, legal, census, genetic, genealogical, and vital records (to be presented in following pages) clearly support the veracity of the traditional story that Joseph Benenhaley—a "Caucasian of Arab descent"—was the patriarch and forefather of this group; and, from the beginning, most members of this enclave (including those who "married in") considered him their leader and identified themselves, generally, as people of Turkish descent.

Certainly, the Turkish people have never claimed singular bloodline; and it would be ridiculous to say that this community subscribed to strict notions of heritage. Just as certainly, however, their distinctive ways brought upon them two centuries of isolation and adversity—as the "Sumter Turks"—in the Carolina backcountry. Indicative of their special sense of historical discrimination and group affinity was the comment of a contemporary descendant, who told us about the indignities inflicted upon her late father: "He suffered for being a Turk—and that had great impact on my proud identification as a Turk."

Today, most of the individuals traditionally included among "the Turkish people" still identify with their community's ancestry and ethnic heritage. However, some members have determined that they are descendants of American Indians. Others, particularly younger people, never think about their lineage and simply consider themselves part of the white mainstream.

The questions raised here have proven to be difficult issues in Sumter County. The inability to prove Joseph Benenhaley's Turkish background bedeviled their identity, and uncertainties of racial nature strained their relationships with other groups in southern society. Additionally, intermarriage, while no longer practiced, is still a sensitive matter.

The "asking and answering" process regarding such matters in the prior paragraphs has been an uncomfortable experience for many people among the four population groups in this area. As historian Malinda Maynor Lowery has written so insightfully regarding her work among the Lumbee Indians of North Carolina, identity is a conversation among insiders and outsiders (*Lumbee Indians* 2010). It is always evolving, sometimes uncomfortably. "Identity often involves conflicts, threats, selfishness, and silences as much as trust, loyalty, sacrifice, and freedom" (xii).

This probing is particularly difficult for today's Turkish people. While most of them appreciate the fact that this project may vindicate their tribulations and triumphs, it also brings pain to some of them. They are a proud but shy people who dislike the attention that this project focuses on them. Also, although never the intention, hurtful memories and divisive arguments have been stirred up during the course of this investigation. In some ways, the development of this book has subjected the Turkish people to a renewed unpleasantness of the bad old days.

~ Unique Cultural Situation ~

The cultural peculiarity of this little patch of America derives from several unusual circumstances that early shaped these people and their ways. Most important is the fact that the Turkish community commenced from Joseph Benenhaley, a subject of the Ottoman Empire.

Greg Thompson, a native Iowan who married into the Turkish community and lives in the Stateburg area, compiled a feature story about the original family for a special progress edition of *The Item* (April 2000). He wrote: "The children of Joseph Benenhaley and John Scott intermarried and formed the nucleus of the 'Turk' descendants. Until the late 1880s, this core family rarely married outside its own except for the Oxendines, Rays, Hoods and Buckners and a few others who joined the community. These related families also became known as 'Turks' by association with the Benenhaleys, even though they all had their own origins and history." But there is more to this story than bloodlines and folklore.

Historian Michael Gomez, who has compiled an encyclopedic account of African Muslims in the Americas, pointed to the Benenhaley community as a singular cultural experiment in New World history (*Black Crescent* 2005). He focused generally on the significant presence, in eighteenth- and nineteenth-century North America, of North Africans who functioned in their various locales as "Founding Mothers and Fathers of a different sort." Some of these immigrant communities helped shape the development and history of regional localities in the South, particularly along the South Carolina and Georgia coasts. Furthermore, he identified other Moors who merged and mingled extensively with their neighbors "to create transracial, polycultural formations in the hinterlands (185)."

Gomez said that Joseph Benenhaley may be the "lone clear example" of an individual North African Muslim who took a third course, deviating from both regional prominence and multiracial blending (186). Benenhaley and his followers went their own, separate way, with limited intermingling, into cultural isolation and struggle in Sumter County.

Eventually, Benenhaley and his descendants established a unique and concentrated presence. US Census records show that the Turkish community expanded slowly but steadily throughout our country's existence. The "Benenhaleys" began as a single family of seven persons in 1810; a century later, in the early 1900s, there were approximately three hundred Turkish people. At midpoint of the twentieth century, the Turkish population consisted of about five hundred persons, most of them congregated in a ten-square-mile radius in the area originally settled by Benenhaley (based on estimates from various local sources and genealogical sites, such as Kaye 1963; White 1975; New 2002–2005).

Census data further documented the special nature of this cultural group in the latter half of the twentieth century. The authors of a reputable atlas of America's diversity calculated, based on self-ascribed designations in the 1980 US Census, that Sumter County had the highest percentage of Turkish-identifying persons among all counties in the United States (Allen and Turner 1988, 139). Additionally, in 1990, more people claimed Turkish ancestry in Sumter County than in all forty-five other counties in the state combined. As a local official once declared to a *New Yorker* reporter: "Right here, all within ten miles of where you're sitting, is the only Turkish community on the continent of North America. Oh, there may be a Turk who has come over and lives in New York, or something, but this is the only Turkish community" (Trillin 1969, 104).

The local speaker may have stretched his declaration for dramatic impact; but there was indeed a remarkable aggregation of people in this area of Sumter County. Defined originally by ethnic distinction and pressed thereafter by racial realities of southern history, they have survived for generations as a reclusive society.

~ Eclectic Academic Depiction ~

Among academic chroniclers, the Turkish community has been depicted eclectically, reflecting what was available from local lore, limited evidence, and reasoned interpretation.

South Carolina historian Anne King Gregorie crafted this account for the *History of Sumter County* (1954):

> Up in the High Hills between Stateburg and Dalzell, is a community of dark-skinned farming people known as the Turks, whose obscure and undocumented origin has long been a subject of speculation.... For many generations the land was held in common, and yielded a more or less meager living for all the Turks, who intermarried through the years and gradually increased. Holding themselves aloof from Negroes, and segregated by long custom from the whites, the Turks occasionally married outside of their community.... Always a law-abiding people, the Turks of Sumter County are said to be singularly lacking in "spontaneous joy. They wear, one and all, the air of patient and unquestioning acceptance of life as they find it. (467)

Respected local educator Cassie Nicholes offered the following assessment in *Historical Sketches of Sumter County* (1975):

> No history of Sumter County would be complete without mention of a group of people who are among the oldest inhabitants of the county and compose the only such community in North America.... The Turks until recent years eked out a meager living from the lands on which they have lived for almost 200 years. Most of them are poor and someone has said that they "seem to accept their lot with truly Eastern fatalism." ... The Turks are not of an exuberant nature; rather their mien is one of patient endurance of the lot that is theirs. Their favorite recreational sports are hunting and fishing, also portraying their quiet nature. They have always been law abiding and peaceful, deserving and receiving the respect of those who know them well. (136–38)

There was also interesting depiction of the Turkish community in the pre–Civil War era biography of a black slave-owner in this part of the state. Historians

Michael P. Johnson and James E. Roark wrote that William Ellison, a prosperous free person of color, enjoyed a special relationship with the Turkish inhabitants of the Sumter District (*Black Masters* 1984):

> The one local group with whom the Ellisons could safely enjoy social relations was the Turks, whose racial status was ambiguous. The Turks professed to be Caucasians and for generations the white Sumter family steadfastly defended the claim. Most other whites in Sumter District perceived the swarthy Turks as people of color. Elsewhere in the state, other groups—variously called Brass Ankles, Red Bones, Red Legs, and Buckheads—shared the Turks' indeterminate race. Most of these individuals descended from remnants of Indian tribes who intermarried with poor white and freed or escaped slaves. Whites discriminated against them as if they were Negroes, but they tried to give themselves a separate status, aloof from blacks. (145–46)

Other scholars have noted the peculiar standing of the Turkish people in this area. Historian Margaret Burr DesChamps, a native of Sumter County, discussed them briefly in her research on the "free agricultural population in Sumter District" preceding the Civil War. She identified small groups of "poor whites," and a considerable number of "free Negroes" in the 1950s; and, among the latter, she said, "were people of uncertain origin and race who were commonly called 'Turks' by Sumter citizens" (1955, 87–89).

Historian David W. Dangerfield similarly described the Turkish people as marginalized "free people of color" during the antebellum period (2014). In his research on free black farmers of that era, he wrote about an extraordinary community of people who enjoyed association with whites in Sumter County because of their service in the Revolution: "Even though they were not considered quite the same way as freed slaves or otherwise freed people of black descent, they were still marginalized as people of color and dependent on the Sumter family's paternalism for their degrees of freedom" (69–71).

Sociologist Brewton Berry provided dour commentary on the Turkish people of Sumter County in a 1945 article ("Mestizos"). He characterized them and other outcast groups as mixed-blooded people who did not fit into the biracial system of South Carolina: "These outcastes insist that they are white, and they claim the privileges and courtesies of white people. Some of them, if pressed, will not deny a strain of Indian, though they take no pride in the fact; and most of them are offended even at that suggestion. The dominant whites, on the other hand, are convinced that there is a trace of Negro blood in them and, on the theory that 'one drop of Negro blood makes one a Negro,' are reluctant to accept them and regard their claim to white status with various and mixed emotions, ranging from amusement to horror" (34).

In his later book (*Almost White* 1963), Berry criticized the mythology of the "so-called 'Turks'" as cover for their antiblack racism; and he depicted them as continuously struggling to assert their whiteness against intransigence and discrimination by the local establishment (186–90).

~ Mixed Media Coverage ~

The news media and journalists have paid sporadic attention to this unusual community. Their coverage ranged widely, from straight news to compassionate analysis to candid commentary about the Turkish people's lot in life, often with superficial, insensitive references to both their folkways and the people of Sumter County.

One of the earliest and most pertinent newspaper stories was the aforementioned 1928 feature story in the *State*. The unknown author wrote this about the Turkish people: "In that part of the High Hills of the Santee lying in Sumter County and mostly in Stateburg township lives a group of people known locally as 'the Turks.' Within a radius of less than ten miles there are about three hundred of them—a people who since Revolutionary times have lived in this limited area, and made a third element in the race problem of the community. They have their own church, their own schools, and socially, they have preserved their own distinct identity through five generations"(1).

A few reporters visited the area for serious, in-depth interviews with the Turkish people. For example, William D. Workman penned several sympathetic articles at mid-century for the *Charleston News and Courier*. Among his observations were the following: "Their story begins, so far as South Carolina is concerned, back in the early days of the American Revolution. And that story is vouched for by the descendants of General Thomas Sumter, the "Gamecock" of the Revolution and the man for whom Sumter county is named"(Dec. 16, 1950). As the years passed, the 'Turks' (as they came to be known in the community), grew into a numerous clan. They lived mostly unto themselves, keeping apart from whites and Negroes"(Sept. 10, 1953). That clannishness, manifested also by a patriarchal type of leadership only now fading away set the Turks up as a group separate and distinct from their neighbors" (Dec. 17, 1950).

Most scholars and journalists gathered their information from afar or in brief, hit-and-miss visits; and their professional assessments usually focused on their own particular views of this unusual settlement. This was especially true as the Turkish people began pushing for the right to attend white schools.

For example, *Ebony Magazine* profiled the Turk "colony" and "clan" as a "raceless" people who distrusted whites and disliked blacks ("South Carolina's Raceless People" 1957). The magazine article included a picture of a Benenhaley descendant as a "Typical Turk" with "tawny complexion and coarse, black hair" (53–56).

Harry Golden—a Charlotte civil rights partisan and publisher of the *Carolina Israelite*—wrote a jumbled version of the Turkish community as a sidelight in *Mr. Kennedy and the Negroes* (1964). He considered the Turkish people one of "the small segregated enclaves of people of 'questionable' origin, neither white, Negro, or Indian," and his account reflected the usual mix of fact and fiction. "In South Carolina are 'the Turks' who recently won their fight for freedom in the courts. The Turks of Sumter County live between the towns of Stateburg and Dalzell, some three hundred of them within a ten-mile radius. There has never been a recorded case of a Turk committing a crime. The story is that they were brought over by General Thomas Sumter to fight in the American Revolution. After the war General Sumter settled the Turks upon his lands but neither he nor his descendants ever gave them a deed. When they married, they married outside their community, usually with Indians" (63–64).

The New Yorker's Calvin Trillin journeyed southward to write about the area's racial and ethnic bickering ("Sumter County" 1969). He belittled the claim of Arab origins and trivialized the Turkish community's cultural heritage. "The Turks still tend to stick together," he quipped; but "they have no special traditions to carry on except a love of hunting and an obsession about being white" (109).

~ Glimpses of Everyday Life ~

For a variety of obvious reasons, these analysts rarely attempted a full picture of the Turkish community. Accurately portraying the Turkish people has been difficult because there are few firsthand, authoritative, detailed accounts of public life in this community. However, some documents of the past century provide interesting glimpses into their daily activities and folkways. For the most part, these snippets seem rather trivial and routine, depicting a small village of struggling families in the rural South; however, in important ways, they convey the stark isolation and adversities of Turkish existence in Dalzell.

One of the earliest references to the Turkish community was in a church newsletter in 1887. The annual report of the High Hills Baptist Church to the Baptist association of that area reported thus: "The Sunday school at the Hills is in two sections for the convenience of the children who live at a distance from the church. The branch presided over by Mr. Noah Benenhaley contributed $5.50 to State Missions. It is composed mainly of the Turks who have long resided in that section" (Thompson Collection and Interviews).

Another early mention of "the Turks" was a well-meaning citizen's letter-to-the-editor of a nearby newspaper, the *Manning Times*, (Mar. 31, 1909). J. D. Huggins wrote: "I have recently had the pleasure of a week's trip over on your side of the Santee. . . . For three successive years I have been helping in a meeting, in March, with the Turks, a colony of people well known in the High Hills of Santee, living nearly entirely to themselves in a community near Stateburg.... They are earnest christians and good citizens"(2).

Another local newspaper reporter, J. C. Dunbar, observed in the *Watchman and Southron* (May 20, 1916): "They are a quiet and inoffensive people, who attend to their own business; they are industrious and have an ambition to build themselves up in a moral and intellectual way and should have the sympathy and encouragement of all right-thinking people"(3).

A few years later, in 1928, the previously cited and unidentified writer for the *State* included the following observations: "The men are mostly of the small farmer or tenant class and most of them are poor. They are not aggressive and seem to accept their lot with truly Eastern fatalism. They are capable of learning and their teachers say the children are bright and eager to take advantage of the opportunities afforded them.... The theory of the "Turkish" origin of these people is supported very substantially by the physical characteristics of the present generation.... There are no Indian characteristics to be found in these people, except perhaps a similarity of complexion.... There is no Negro ingredient in the makeup.... One of the most outstanding characteristics of these people is their inherent respect for law and order. They are a law-abiding people"(1).

The unidentified author of the Federal Writers' Project paper was equally eager to share personal observations, many of which closely parallel the previous article ("Pockets in America," late 1930s): "Their homes straggle along over a territory known on old maps as the High Hills of the Santee.... No characteristic marks their homes from those of Negroes living along-side, except a greater cleanliness.... Politically these people rank as Democrats and vote as white people.... Mostly small tenant farmers, day laborers and farm hands, they are hired by the white farmers of the district indiscriminately along with Negroes.... When a white man or woman marries into the group, he or she and the offspring of the union become accepted as Turks.... This is a people whose hand is raised against no man. On the contrary, the Turks are self-respecting and law abiding, with high moral standards"(1-4).

Another unattributed account produced by the Federal Writers' Project ("South Carolina" 1941) similarly characterized their lives as an ambiguous, reclusive existence: "In and around DALZELL, 85 m. (80 pop.), live a colony of several hundred 'Turks,' all said to be descendants of two pirates, a Turk and a Frenchman, who joined the Revolution as scouts under General Sumter. Their dark complexion and wary habits have left them an ambiguous group, farming their land in isolation. They refuse to associate with Negroes, and, despite prevailingly Caucasian features, are ignored by the whites"(312).

These are interesting depictions. Mostly, they reflect "outsider" perspectives; they offer gratuitous judgments; and they repeat stereotypes. Fortunately, other individuals with extensive personal experience have written useful, first-hand reports about the community.

F. Kinloch Bull grew up in Stateburg and spent considerable time with the Turkish people during the early 1900s. In *Random Recollections of a Long Life, 1896–1986* (1986), he recalled them as farmers and laborers who liked to fish, hunt, and play poker. "In all they were a cheerful people," he wrote, "and with some a drooping mustache and fierce look belied a pleasant disposition. The girls were pretty at an early age, but what with working in the fields and bearing many children, they looked older than they were" (106).

Bull's memoir also provided interesting insight into the structured nature of authority in their community. "The acknowledged head of the clan was an old veteran called 'Tom Turk,' but I do not remember ever hearing his real name. It was said that old Tom exerted almost supreme authority, so that when disturbances of any kind, including domestic, he would step in and settle things with firmness and dispatch. With so much influence he even dictated how they voted. . . . Politicians running for office made it a practice of standing in with the old man and getting a good bloc of votes" (107).

The brief autobiography of Eleazer Benenhaley (*Moulded Clay,* 1983) represents the only narrative written by a Turkish person about life in the Turkish community of the twentieth century. Benenhaley, a lineal descendant of Joseph Benenhaley, was born in 1934 and has been deeply embedded in the community for most of his life. In plain language, he talked about his life as a product of that culture." Those early years were lonesome, but good years for me. . . . We did not have the abundance of food or clothes that people so take for granted today, but we did appreciate what we had. Although she had a limited education, my mother worked at odd jobs to keep us going. Because we did live on a farm, we had our own hogs and chickens. As a result of this, we had meat and eggs which made the eating pretty good" (11–12). His childhood games were similar to those of many young boys of that time: "When I was alone at home, I became Superman, the Lone Ranger and all of the comic and radio heroes" (12).

Eleazer Benenhaley's teenage dreams likewise extended to sports (although those dreams could not be realized because of the social constraints of that era): "Back during the late forties and early fifties, I listened excitedly to the Sumter American Legion baseball games over the radio. I never saw a game, but I dreamed of what it would be like to have a uniform and step out on the diamond. Young boys of Turkish descent could not take part because they were not wanted and no one had ever shown them the essential rules of baseball. Think of it now, eleven years of school and not one coach to show a boy how to hold a bat or how to throw a curve ball. You can only wonder how many major league prospects were never found" (17).

Eleazer Benenhaley's remarks also reflect some sadness about the old days, particularly the impact of discrimination on life in the Turkish community. "The Dalzell School had been provided for the people living in Sumter County whose ancestral background was Turkish. I was too young to understand the hatred and prejudice which had developed against the people of my ancestral background by some living in the area. It is so tragic that people let their feelings color their intelligence. This feeling of superiority by some deprived many Turkish children of a good education" (14).

These accounts demonstrate that, in many ways, the everyday lives of the Turkish people were similar to those of other southerners in rural areas. Their existence revolved around the family, their school, their church, their farms, and whatever jobs they could find in the local area. But the underlying reality was that they were shunned outside Dalzell. So they kept to themselves. Thus it was probably impossible for anyone in the past to convey the full nature and extent of what made Turkish community life different from that of their Sumter County neighbors. Various accounts—both professional and personal—described the trivialities, exaggerated the peculiarities, and referred to some of the afflictions of life in Dalzell; but no "snapshot" could sufficiently communicate the compelling drama that pervaded the group's everyday existence.

To summarize this discussion, the Turkish people of Sumter County indeed appear to have lived an unusual history. But no one has been able to tell the full and accurate story of this settlement, because there were no clear historical records and the Turkish people did not respond well to outsider interrogation. Nor could anyone adequately address the traditional narrative that sustained their existence in Dalzell. So, perhaps, it would be worthwhile to begin our investigation by examining that narrative—from the perspectives of both supporters and critics of Turkish oral history.

~ *Chapter Two* ~
# The Traditional Story of Oral History

The Turkish people of Sumter County have always had to deal with cultural ambiguity. They often have been depicted as a mysterious community, and they have had to endure distortions of their heritage. Therefore, most of them have clung generally and loyally to their traditional narrative.

There is certainly no shortage of material—some of it credible but much of it questionable—about these reclusive people. (Readers can consult the following key sources, listed chronologically, for the evolving literature: High Hills Baptist Church Annual Report 1887; Huggins 1909; Dunbar 1916; Sumter 1917, 1920; "Sumter County Colony" 1928; Gregorie 1931, 1954; Federal Writers' Project late 1930s, 1941; Mitchell 1943; Berry 1945, 1963; Workman 1950, 1950, 1951, 1953, 1953; "Timmerman Refuses" 1955; DesChamps 1955; Sass 1956; "Turks Lose" 1956; "South Carolina's Raceless People" 1957; Bass 1961; "'Turk' Case" 1961; Kaye 1963; Golden 1964; Trillin 1969; Nicholes 1970, 1975; Griessman 1972; Wikramanayake 1973; White 1975;Macron 1979; Benenhaley 1983, 2008; Bull 1986; Myers 1989; Hagy 1993; Bullard 1995; McElveen 1996; Thompson 2000; New 2002–2010, 2005; Baker 2004, 2006; Gomez 2005; Woody and Thigpen 2005; Dolan 2007; "Yesteryear" 2009; Failinger 2012; Considine 2013; Dangerfield 2014; Hilton 2014.)

What is the true story of the Turkish people of Sumter County? What has it meant to be a Turkish person in the past? What does it mean to be a Turkish person now? What can be learned from the Turkish experience in this part of the world? First, in seeking answers to these questions—pro and con—the traditional narrative of Sumter's Turkish people needs to be reviewed.

~ The Traditional Narrative ~

It had been impossible to verify Turkish oral history with documents available thus far. However, we were able to piece together a rough collage based on the words and works of Turkish friends, academic scholars, and amateur genealogists.

The main elements of the story revolve around the fabled patriarch, Joseph Benenhaley, a "Caucasian of Arab descent" and subject of the Ottoman Empire, who somehow ended up in South Carolina. He served as a scout for General Thomas Sumter, the "Fighting Gamecock," during the Revolutionary War. After the war, Sumter gave him some land from his estate to grow food and raise his family. Sometime early in the 1800s, the general dramatically pronounced Benenhaley a white man. Joseph Benenhaley founded a familial settlement, and the Turkish people lived as an enclosed community for two centuries in rural Sumter County.

~ Supporting the Narrative ~

Various analysts and historical sources have provided both support for and opposition to the traditional narrative. The central and most interesting written testimony in support of the traditional narrative of Joseph Benenhaley and his people came from General Sumter's great-grandson, Thomas Sebastian Sumter (1852–1934).

Thomas Sebastian Sumter spent his life in the Stateburg area. Some question his story; but he claimed that he got most of his information from his father, who had spent a lot of time talking about these matters with the general. The great-grandson knew some of the Turkish people by name, including the elderly widows of both Benenhaley and Scott, who lived near where the great-grandson was born and grew up.

Great-grandson Sumter authored a newspaper article, "An Interesting People," for the *Watchman and Southron* (1917) and his book, *Stateburg and Its People* (1920), in part so that the young Turkish men from this community might take their proud history with them as they went off to fight in World War I. Since Thomas Sebastian Sumter is witness number one for the traditional narrative, he is quoted extensively here, beginning with the initial encounter between the General and Benenhaley.

As reported in *Stateburg and Its People*, Benenhaley was one of the men who joined General Sumter and fought with him during the Revolutionary War. The great-grandson provided the following anecdote detailing how the "Gamecock" got his nickname and recruited Benenhaley in Goose Creek Parish, near Charleston. (The blue game hen mentioned in the following paragraph was a prized specimen whose offspring were famous in those parts for courage and winning bloody battles.)

It was during this period the war of "American Independence" broke out. It was not long before he had a following of friendly Indians and whites to join him in the fight for freedom. It was on one of his recruiting trips he came upon a crowd of men fighting some chickens at a cross road, and upon his remonstrating with them many agreed to follow him and fight for their country. One in the crowd called out "Boys that's the blue hen's chicken, let's follow him, he is the game cock."

Hence he got the soubriquet "Game Cock." It was from this crowd he enlisted Joseph Bennanhaly, and a man who gave his name as Scott. He made Joseph Bennanhaly his scout, in which capacity he continued during the war. He was a Caucasian of "Arab" descent. (43)

There is no solid historical documentation for this particular account of Thomas Sumter's nickname. Some have credited a British general for supposedly saying that the general fought like a gamecock; however, historians Rufus Griswold et all had recounted a more authoritative story that was roughly similar to the tale of great-grandson Sebastian (*Washington and the Generals* 1847, 297–98). Furthermore, there are discrepancies regarding how and where and when Benenhaley may have been recruited by the general. Whatever the circumstance of that encounter in the wilderness, history might have accommodated the true essence of such an event on any number of occasions. Thomas Sumter served in various military capacities throughout South Carolina, especially in the lowcountry and Charleston area, in North Carolina, and as far south as Savannah, Georgia. He constantly recruited followers whenever and wherever he was fighting, including Goose Creek near the South Carolina coast, down toward Georgia, and across the border in North Carolina. (For detailed accounts of Sumter's military career, see Buchanan 1997; Griswold 1847; McCrady 1902; Sumter 1920, Gregorie 1931; Bass 1961; Flood 1976; Heitzler 2005; and Southern Campaigns of the American Revolution 2007). After the war, reported his great-grandson, "General Sumter . . . gave the two old soldiers a piece of land near his home at Stateburg, S.C., where they lived and he cared for them during his lifetime" (1920, 44).

Early in the 1800s, General Sumter rendered another service to Benenhaley and Scott and their descendants. The two men were involved in a court case in Sumter County and their race was a factor of consideration. Some citizens at the time objected to the right of these two men to vote and to sit on a jury. Because General Sumter was a well-respected man, he was called to testify on behalf of these two individuals. Thomas Sebastian Sumter related this incident thus: "On one occasion the fact of their dark complexion brought up the question of their having a right to sit on a jury and when General Sumter was sent for—the writer was told this by the late Col. Jas. D. Blanding, who was about 18 years old, who said he saw General Sumter walk in, place his pistol on a desk and deliberately shake hands with both men and turning, asked if that was sufficient" (1920 44). The great-grandson further added that "Joseph Benenhaley and the man Scott were either pirates or had escaped from pirates—the writer has forgotten which, but they were, 'white men'" (1920 44–45).

General Sumter was one of South Carolina's most distinguished citizens and founders of the Republic, and his word was respected. The case was quickly dismissed because, at that time in history, white men and black men did not shake hands with each other. The fact that he recognized and defended their status carried a great amount of weight in the community and established the Turkish people of Sumter County as being white citizens.

Thomas Sebastian Sumter's nephew, F. Kinloch Bull, related similar memories of growing up in Stateburg (*Random Recollections* 1986). Bull (1896-1986), previously referenced as an eyewitness to Turkish life in the early 1900s, supported the legendary origin of that community; and he observed that "with their straight black hair and copper colored complexion, they looked like Turks" (105).

There are some differences in the words and stories of Thomas Sebastian Sumter and F. Kinloch Bull, both of whom were relatives of General Sumter and who spent most of their lives in that part of the county. However, their written accounts provided significant support for the traditional narrative. Subsequently, as the following entries attest, their belated reports have been incorporated into most accounts of Joseph Benenhaley and Sumter County's Turkish community.

Noted historian Anne King Gregorie authored the standard academic version of the story in her *History of Sumter County* (1954). "Numbering more than three hundred persons, living within a radius of ten miles, they are among the oldest inhabitants of Sumter County, their arrival having coincided with the coming of General Thomas Sumter to the Hills soon after the Revolution" (467). She also wrote that "Benenhaley is said to have been the General's scout, and as his name is evidently Moorish in origin, he is probably the reason for the local name of Turk" (467).

Local educator Cassie Nicholes similarly conveyed the same essential tale of the Turkish community, along with other miscellaneous material, in *Historical Sketches of Sumter County* (1975). "The origin of this colony in the area dates back to the Revolutionary War. Tradition says that once when General Thomas Sumter was recruiting men to fight for American independence, he came upon a group of men in the low country engaged in the doubtful sport of cock fighting. After the group had been chided by the general for such activity, many of them, impressed by this spirit, decided to follow him into the fight against Britain" (136).

Revolutionary War scholar Robert D. Bass rendered his lengthier and more colorful version of the relationship between General Sumter and his foreign recruits in *Gamecock: The Life and Campaigns of General Thomas Sumter* (1961). Bass noted that Benenhaley and Scott were among the early enlistees in the General's militia: "And from the Barbary coast came Yusef ben Ali and one who called himself John Scott. The Gamecock welcomed the corsairs, making a scout of Ben Ali and a bugler of Scott" (78). Bass also wrote: "After the Revolution, John Scott and Yusef ben Ali squatted on his land near Home House. . . . But the dark complexion of the two North Africans brought up the question of their right to sit on a jury. His neighbors sent for the old Gamecock to say whether or not they were white. He strode into the meeting, laid his pistol on the table, and shook hands cordially with Scott and ben Ali. Then turning to the gathering, he asked, "Gentlemen, are there any other questions?" (237).

Mary Haddad Macron, author of a history of Arab Americans for the ethnic heritage program at Cleveland State University, subscribed even more enthusiastically to the traditional legend ("Arab Americans" 1979). Citing Yusef Ben Ali and his friend among those who were inspired by the ideals of the American Revolution, she wrote: "They served with General Thomas Sumter, who like Francis Marion and Andrew Pickens, had formed a guerilla band to fight an unorthodox kind of warfare in the forests and swamps of the South against Cornwallis. Coming from North Africa where this type of warfare was common, Yusef Ben Ali acquitted himself well. Indeed, in later years it was General Sumter's support that won him the right to serve on a jury although he was 'dark of skin'" (98). This rendering of Benenhaley's service has also been repeated in numerous Muslim accounts of New World history.

Even the US government has incorporated the traditional version of Turkish history into the public record. During the Great Depression, an anonymous writer with the Federal Writers' Project provided a detailed account of their story, including the following statements: "The most commonly accredited theory as to the origin of the colony is that General Thomas Sumter, recruiting near Charleston during the Revolutionary War, enlisted two men who had recently disembarked from a pirate ship. Whether they were pirates or escaped ship's prisoners is uncertain. One of the two was a Turk, Ben Ali. The other, said variously to have been of French or English descent, called himself Scott, admitting that such was not his true name. Ben Ali and Scott served through the Revolution with General Sumter, the first as his scout, the second as his bugler." After the Revolution, according to this source, "the General rewarded both faithful recruits with small farms near his estate in the Stateburg community. During his lifetime he looked after their welfare and championed their standing as Caucasians. Due to their swarthy appearance, insinuations concerning their race were common and came to a head when their right to serve on a Sumter County jury was questioned. To settle the dispute, General Sumter was summoned. Walking into the room, the doughty and aristocratic Gamecock laid his pistol on the desk, and then very cordially shook hands with both his proteges, after which he inquired of those present if there were still any doubt as to the men's being white." Also, it was commonly believed that the two men married white women; and one of Ben Ali's daughters married an

Oxendine man thought to be a Redbone. "The descendants of these three families intermarried among themselves in truly Biblical fashion and the names still predominating among them are Benenhaly and Oxendine" (Federal Writers' Project, late 1930s, 1-4).

At about the same time, another report on the Turkish people appeared as part of the Federal Works Progress Administration survey of state and local historical records. Local worker Anna L. Sinkler answered a question about the origin and history of Long Branch Baptist Church thus: "This is a congregation of Turks. Gen Sumter brought some Turks to his plantation and these are the descendants. They have their own school and church as neighborhood objected to their attending theirs" (Works Progress Administration 1936).

Eleazer Benenhaley, ca. 1970s. Author of two books about life among the Turkish people, Eleazer is probably the most famous and respected member of the community. Courtesy of Eleazer Benenhaley.

Most recently, in a 2006 archaeological resources review for Shaw Air Force Base, the Air Combat Command mentioned Joseph Benenhaley and his descendants as "some of the most interesting residents of the Stateburg area," with references to North Africa, pirates, General Sumter, the Revolutionary War, dark complexions, and separate schools and churches (United States Air Force 2006, 66–67).

Finally, there is personal testimony from Eleazer Benenhaley. Benenhaley was born in 1934, is a lineal descendant of Joseph Benenhaley, attended the segregated Dalzell School for Turks, helped integrate a local white high school, and preached for ten years at the Long Branch Baptist Church. He now lives in North Augusta,

South Carolina, with a doctor of ministry degree and a long string of pastored churches on his resume.

Eleazer Benenhaley has authored two brief but moving publications, his biography *Moulded Clay* (1983) and *An Analysis of Neophytes and Would Be Historians* (2008). When it comes to Joseph Benenhaley and the origin of the Turkish community, Benenhaley expressed complete confidence in the traditional narrative: "But as for me, I trust the oral tradition of my grandmother and those before her" (2008, 36). "Oral Tradition and family biblical records can have more creditability than records kept by those whose views are colored by bigotry" (2008, 22). Certainly, Eleazer Benenhaley had no doubts about who he is: "God knew what He was doing when He created me.... I have lived 73 years as being of Turkish descent. I have no desire to be anything else" (2008, 37). He also spoke with pride when writing about the role of Joseph Benenhaley and the Turkish people in the history of this area: "What other family group in Sumter can trace their ancestry further? Parks and schools are named after General Thomas Sumter, but what other group can claim closer association with the General than the people of Turkish descent?" (1983, 17–18). What seemed to most irritate Eleazer Benenhaley on this matter was "neophytes and would be historians." He said: "What really bothers me is the obscure research that is presented and assumptions that are printed as facts." (2008, 29).

~ Skeptics and Naysayers ~

Of course, many skeptics have been less impressed with the exotic tale of Joseph Benenhaley, and some naysayers have been brutally dismissive of the traditional narrative.

Included among the harshest critics have been noted South Carolinians. For example, Chapman J. Milling—medical doctor, historian, and poet born in Darlington County—described the Turkish people and other such communities as remnants of "doubtful stock" who "endured a rather miserable existence and gradually merged with the surrounding population" (*Red Carolinians*, 1940, 3). Sociologist James Brewton Berry, originally from Orangeburg, characterized them as "so-called Turks" ("Mestizos" 1945, 34–41); and historian James W. Hagy of Charleston labeled them "misnamed Turks" ("Muslim Slaves" 1993, 12–27).

Many scholars have discounted the Turkish people's traditional narrative based on the logic and reality of early American history. To these critics, the story of Joseph Benenhaley rang hollow; and the tribulations of Native Americans, as recounted in the following paragraphs, seemed a more likely explanation for the strange history of the Dalzell community.

At the end of the eighteenth century and the beginning of the nineteenth century, white settlers began flooding the southern backcountry and laying claim to lands occupied by Native Americans. Armed conflict and various treaties pushed the original inhabitants westward; and the Indian Removal Act of 1830 relocated most of them west of the Mississippi River. By 1840, the major southern tribes had been relocated; however, others remained in their homelands, some in defiance of the law and others because they were independent groups not covered by the Removal Act. Those who stayed behind often were forced to submerge themselves into out-of-the-way settlements that served as common refuge for whites, Indians, and Africans who had nowhere else to go. Hence the origin and nature of the Dalzell group according to these analysts. (For the history and politics of the Indian Removal Act, see Howe, *What God Hath Wroght*, 2009, 342–67; for its impact on Indians who remained in their ancestral home, see Hobson et al, *The People Who Stayed* 2010, 4–9.)

Later on, these Native Americans faced struggles of a different sort because of speculation that they were African descendants; and some mixed-race and lighter-toned Indians attempted to avoid recrimination by redefining themselves as variations of acceptable ancestry for white authorities and white society (Berry, *Almost White*, 1963; Bird, *Light, Bright, and Damned Near White*, 2009). Historical archaeologist Carl Steen, president of Diachronic Research Foundation, has done extensive research on Native Americans in this area ("An Archaeology" 2012), and he personalized their desperation in an October 25, 2014, e-mail: "Native Americans in SC during the historic period have been faced with the threat of enslavement and discrimination based on the suspicion that they might have African heritage, so many denied being anything but white, and hid their heritage—even from their children." Unsurprisingly, the Dalzell group was similarly suspected of convenient transformation through a contrived oral history.

Numerous other analysts based their doubts about the Turkish narrative, more systematically, on field observations, biological data, and historical records in the southeast. They concluded that the many small communities in this part of the country originated as enclosed mixtures of white European, Native American, and African ancestry.

Cultural anthropologist William Harlen Gilbert Jr. first identified and labeled groups of this nature as "mixed-blood racial islands" ("Memorandum" 1946). Gilbert introduced them, generically, as people with no known history who lived separately from both the white and black castes of America. He described them as "complex mixtures in varying degrees of white, Indian, and Negro blood"; and he said that early whites considered them as "mere squatters" rather than legitimate settlers (438).

Gilbert said that the South Carolina groups were called different names locally but generally resembled each other. He listed the "Turks in Sumter" along with other stereotypically disparaged groups, such as the "Brass Ankles," "Croatans," "Red Bones," "Red Legs," "Buckheads," "Marlboro Blues," "Greeks," "Portuguese," "Clay-eaters," "Yellow-hammers," "Summerville Indians," and "those Yellow People." Regarding their history, he simply noted that there were "many theories regarding their origin," and they had "only attracted attention of writers recently" (439–40).

A few years later, geographer Edward T. Price produced further research on the "mixed-bloods" of the Eastern United States ("Geographic Analysis" 1953). Price cited the "Turks" among the smaller mixed-blood groups, who "may have formed around the small lowland Indian tribes as nuclei, picking up both white and Negro blood" (146). He also wrote, "They live somewhat apart from other groups in rural settings with their own clusters of shacks" (146).

Shortly thereafter, demographer Calvin L. Beale attempted a more thorough inventory; and he formally labeled most of these groups as tri-racial isolate communities ("American Tri-Racial Isolates" 1957). According to Beale, the tri-racial isolates numbered not less than seventy-seven thousand persons in more than one hundred counties in seventeen and perhaps a couple more Eastern States, with settlements ranging from less than fifty to more than twenty thousand people. Like Gilbert and Price, he included "the Turks of South Carolina" among their ranks. He said that "the precise origin of these groups is unknown in most instances," but "they seem to have formed through miscegenation between Indians, whites, and Negroes—slave or free—in the Colonial and early Federal periods" (187–88). In a later publication ("Overview" 1972), Beale characterized them as marginal people who were "wary until recently of being Black, aspiring where possible to be White, and subject to rejection and scorn on either hand" (705).

Anthropologist William S. Pollitzer provided more objective insight into these populations in his study of "Caucasian-Negro-Amerindian Isolates" of the Southeast ("Physical Anthropology" 1972). He took previous analysis a step forward by accumulating biological data from studies of eight such groups, and he was able to reconstruct the approximate ancestral contributions of parental populations to these hybrid communities. Pollitzer's research amended the literature in important ways. Most important, his research of estimated genetic admixture demonstrated variations among the isolate communities; and he reported major differences in the contributions of specific parental populations—"English," "Negro," and "Indian"—from one group to another (725-33). Like his predecessors, Pollitzer cited the "Turks of South Carolina" among the ranks of tri-racial isolates, although none of his data were obtained from this small population (722).

More recently, Paul Heinegg continued this line of inquiry with a series of controversial publications about the origins of tri-racial isolates in the Southeast ("Free African Americans" 2001). Heinegg, an engineer, conducted extensive research of family names in old court records, census reports, and other documents. He concluded that there was only limited Indian ancestry in many of the isolate communities (5); and he claimed that most groups originated from the union of white servant women and slaves or free African Americans (1). Heinegg also ridiculed the "fantastic theories" fabricated about the origins of such communities (21); and, of course, he, too, included the Turkish population of South Carolina in his listing of tri-racial isolates, without any special discussion or data for this group.

As a result of the aforementioned research, the term "tri-racial isolates" became the standard categorization for such groups; and early analysts presumed that the small enclave of Turkish people shared commonalities of origin with those settlements. Their presumptions soundly trumped oral history, apparently without any reliable evidence from the Dalzell area to support those presumptions. Perhaps as a consequence, numerous other observers—as recounted in the next few paragraphs—have pronounced the story of Joseph Benenhaley doubtful history and the notion of Turkish ancestry as functional legend.

Historian Rosser H. Taylor put it curtly in the 1940s: "One of the groups, the Turks, settled near Stateburg. Their origin is obscure. The belief commonly held that General Thomas Sumter had a Turkish or Arab bugler in his command during the Revolution, who settled at Stateburg and sired the group, is not susceptible of proof" (*Ante-Bellum South Carolina* 1942, 88).

Sociologist Brewton Berry ("Meztizos" 1945) was also one of the early skeptics: "The so-called 'Turks,' of Sumter County, are said to be descendants of laborers imported from Turkey by General Thomas Sumter, or of Turkish pirates stranded on the Carolina coast, or of refugees who escaped from their pirate captors. The legends are numerous and never convincing" (35).

Mike Nassau, a librarian-geneticist who has written widely about mixed-race people, commented on his website that General Sumter resolved the early racial predicament with a suspect and self-serving explanation: "Fearful of losing them as they were unhappy with their treatment by neighboring whites, he took action to have their status as whites recognized. He presented an affidavit to the authorities that they were indeed Turks which he had personally imported from the Ottoman Empire as contract labor. Never mind that Turks were the ruling people of that Empire and not likely to contract out as hired hands, or that the Turks of South Carolina knew no Turkish and were not Muslim" ("Melungeons and Other Mestee Groups" 1994).

Independent scholar Mary Ricketson Bullard (*Roger Stafford*, 1995) termed the traditional narrative a "psychological and legal" defense for a vulnerable subculture: "The so-called Sumter Turks of the 1840s, allegedly Moors who had entered South Carolina in the late eighteenth century, probably shared with the Delaware Moors and the Carolina Yellowhammers a psychological and legal need to whitify their racial origins in order to satisfy the curiosities of state authorities" (88).

Sylviane Diouf (*Servants of Allah* 1998), an award-winning historian of the African Diaspora, was less charitable: "Such confusions could reach ridiculous proportions: the members of a Muslim family who had lived in Sumter County, South Carolina, since the Revolutionary War were reputed to be alternatively 'Turks,' 'Free Moors,' 'nobles of the Delhi Court,' and 'subjects of the Emperor of Morocco.' Then in a complete turnabout, they were labeled 'free blacks' in 1830;

but another shift in perception allowed them to serve in white regiments during the Civil War" (99).

Most recently critical has been Native American activist Steven Pony Hill (*Strangers* 2010). Hill, who claimed family links to the South Carolina group, dismissed "the fantastical origin theory" and insisted that they are descended from American Indians. He attacked the term "Turks" as an outdated slur, asserting that "these copper-skinned, high cheek-boned people whose grandparents learned that they could gain equality under the identity of 'Turks' that they were denied as 'Indians,' have in the most recent generations begun to reclaim their rightful birthright as persons of Indian descent" (41).

We attempted to visit and interview the current chief, former chief, and chairperson of the Sumter Tribe of Cheraw Indians for their comments about the Turkish traditional narrative; but those efforts were unsuccessful. There seemed to be pressing tribal matters and health issues on their end of the scheduling issue. Also, as is clear in the text, relations between these two ethnic groups have been pretty sensitive for several years; and it appeared there was little interest among these Native American leaders in meeting with authors whose avowed purpose was giving voice to the story of the Turkish people.

~ True Story Yet To Be Told ~

The traditional story of Turkish oral history has engendered sharp division among supporters and opponents of that narrative for most of the past century; and the critics have held sway. Despite the impassioned drama sometimes articulated by supporters and believers, other analysts have persuasively invoked early American history and supposedly similar communities in rejecting the legend of Joseph Benenhaley. The standard approach among these latter analysts—without any real research or evidence of the situation in Dalzell—was to list the Turkish people among the muddled ranks of "tri-racial isolates," generally defined as enclosed, complex mixtures of white European, American Indian, and African origin.

Many subsequent commentators have assumed the validity of the tri-racial paradigm or considered the Turkish people a group with uncertain, indefinable ancestry and/or ethnicity. Also, published accounts have been replete with damning doubts and outrageous opinions about these folks. Some expressed derogatory stereotypes; some charged them with racist mythmaking; and some claimed that they were really Native American Indians.

Our contention is that these assessments and criticisms have been unwarranted, and it was premature to dismiss the traditional narrative of oral history. Two full centuries into their existence, the true story of South Carolina's Turkish people had yet to be told.

~ *Chapter Three* ~

Probing the Legend of Origins

Through the years, there has been much discussion about the "Sumter Turks"; and most of that discussion consisted of oral history and recollections. The problem was that Turkish oral history as articulated by insiders lacked evidentiary authority, and almost all recollections by outsiders postdated, by a century, the pertinent persons and events of interest in this case.

Consequently, as covered in the previous chapter, considerable dispute has occurred in historical and genealogical circles. The general conversation has consisted of rehashed versions of folklore and hearsay, supported by skimpy records and faulty research; and much of it was argumentative, contradictory, and simply inaccurate.

This problem was especially pronounced as previous analysts tried, unsuccessfully, to address the background of the presumed patriarch. Readers may recall the review of supporters and critics in the previous chapter on the traditional story; those accounts were rife with supposition and opinion rather than factual discussion of the Ottoman Turk and his Old World origins. Therefore, the authors conducted their own assessment of this mysterious wanderer, based on reasonable interpretation of available sources. It was hoped through this exercise, to figure out who he really was and whether and how he made his way from the Ottoman Empire and established a Turkish community in South Carolina.

Here is the essence of the origins legend as passed down from generation to generation among the Turkish people. According to this version, they were descendants of Joseph Benenhaley—or Yusef ben Ali, his perhaps Arabic name. He was thought to have been born in Morocco or somewhere else in the Ottoman Empire during the latter half of the 1700s and somehow made his way to South Carolina. Apparently, he self-proclaimed as a "Caucasian of Arab descent," was known locally as a "Turk," and served as a valiant scout for General Thomas Sumter in the Revolutionary War. Afterward, he founded a settlement of Turkish descendants who endured for two centuries in rural Sumter County.

There will always be assumptions, uncertainties, and inconsistencies among sources from so many years ago, particularly when that research involves oral tradition; and such has been the case with the Turkish people for many generations. Therefore this probing inquiry is designed to help clarify what we knew, thought we knew, and did not know from previous research and analysis of Joseph Benenhaley and the Turkish community. In this chapter, we discuss (1) the assumptive identity of the Turkish patriarch, as revealed or suggested in available sources; (2) the hypothetical trail whereby he may have journeyed from the Ottoman Empire to the New World; and (3) the plausibility of Joseph Benenhaley's legendary origins. First, we will review some of the assumptions, uncertainties, and inconsistencies—along with the authors' own speculations— will be reviewed regarding the legendary patriarch's background and journey.

~ Joseph Benenhaley/Yusef ben Ali ~

There are many interesting accounts, alternative theories, and wild ideas about the man at the center of the Turkish traditional narrative. Some have called him a Barbary pirate; others have pronounced him a hero of the American Revolution; and, most recently, it has been suggested that he was a distant relative of Elvis Presley.

Even the best scholars have been unable to decode, with any degree of satisfaction, the background of Joseph Benenhaley and the early history of the Turkish community. For example, Anne King Gregorie—a history professor, president of the South Carolina Historical Society, editor of the *South Carolina Historical Magazine,* and author of *Thomas Sumter* (1931) and *The History of Sumter County* (1954)—was thoroughly stumped to explain the origins of Joseph Benenhaley and the Turkish people. In her biography of the general, she abstrusely referenced Sumter's tenant this way: "and there was one Benenhaly, a mysterious Ben Ali possibly"; and she described Benenhaley's descendants as dark-skinned people who "are as much a mystery to their neighbors as the mound builders" (1931, 264–65).

In her later work on the history of Sumter County, Gregorie noted the Turkish group's "obscure and undocumented origin" and couched her assessment in terminology like "a confused tradition," "it is possible," and "believed to be descended" (1954, 467–68). She further admitted in personal correspondence that she had "never seen any documentary evidence'" and never solved the "mystery" of Joseph Benenhaley and his people. (See brief discussions of this matter in Johnson and Roark, *Black Masters,* 1984, and *No Chariot Let Down,* 2001; Gregorie's letters regarding the topic can be accessed in the Anne King Gregorie Papers, South Carolina Historical Society, Charleston, South Carolina.)

For the purpose of this analysis, there are several elements in the traditional story of Joseph Benenhaley that reflect our previous discussion about "assumptions, uncertainties, and inconsistencies"; and they therefore bear elaboration. (See traditional accounts of his story in the following sources, listed chronologically: Sumter, *Stateburg and Its People*, 1920; Gregorie, *History of Sumter County*, 1954; Nicholes, *Historical Sketches*, 1975; and Bull, *Random Recollections*, 1986.)

The first issue of debate is the presumed patriarch's name—sometimes he was called "Joseph Benenhaley" and at other times he was identified as "Yusef ben Ali." Neither name can be nailed down with authoritative and absolute certainty; so he is normally referred to in this book as "Joseph Benenhaley," because that is how he was referenced in most situations and sources; and he is addressed as "Yusef ben Ali" when that name seems appropriate within the context of the particular circumstance or quotation.

Expectedly, the spelling of our central character's colloquial name has been recorded variously over the years—including Benenhaley, Benenhaly, Benanhaly, Bennahaly, Benenhale, Benenhali, Benenhala, Benenhaile, Benengeli, and others—creating confusion at times. These varied spellings may explain some of the problems experienced as scholars and genealogists tried to sort out the information of historical documents. For example, historian James Hagy ("Muslim Slaves" 1993) reported that Benenhaley was in the first US Census in 1790, but never thereafter; while Sue New, a descendant of Benenhaley lineage, said that he can be found in the censuses of 1810 and 1820 ("Census Data for the Turks" 2002–2005).

"Yusef ben Ali"—the Arabic name—was less grounded in written sources; it appeared much later, after the passing of Joseph Benenhaley. "Ben-En-Ali" was mentioned in an 1889 letter from Sebastian D'Amblimont Sumter ("Furman Papers"); and he can be found, as "Ben Ali," in Thomas Sebastian Sumter's writings in 1917 and 1920 and in the Federal Writers' Project documents of the late 1930s and 1941. He has been incorporated simultaneously and synonymously with "Joseph Benenhaley" in many other accounts since then.

Another issue is Benenhaley's imprecise point of origin in the Ottoman Empire. His most commonly suggested homeland was Morocco or the North African coast, due likely to the fact that historical accounts of Ottomans in the New World have overwhelmingly referenced seafarers, scouts, and slaves from that area (al-Ahart El, "Early American Settlers"; Lowery, *Spanish Settlements*, 1959; Wheat, "Mediterranean Slavery," 2010). Accordingly, Morocco and North Africa have often been cited as Benenhaley's native region in local conversations and genealogical discussions; and this geographical inference has made its way into various published reports (Considine, "George Washington," 2013; and White, *A History of the Turks*, 1975). Benenhaley may well have come from Morocco or North Africa; however, thus far, no hard evidence substantiating the claim has been found.

Also puzzling is the phrase "Caucasian of 'Arab' descent," which was how General Sumter's great-grandson precisely described Benenhaley (Sumter, *Stateburg*, 1920, 43–44). It is not shocking that Joseph Benenhaley might have tried to set the record straight at the outset in South Carolina by declaring himself in such manner. Race, ethnicity, and ancestry were of great consequence in that time and place; and his declaration apparently was acceptable to his newfound associates, most particularly the general. This phrasing also was reasonable considering complexities of such nature in his Ottoman homeland. The Ottoman Empire was situated at the intersection of Europe, Asia, and Africa; and patterns of ancestry, ethnicity, and race have always been multifaceted and mingled among the variously hued peoples of the Mediterranean world. Over time, that Empire stretched from Southeast Europe to Asia Minor and the Middle East and across North Africa; and it was populated by groups of diverse backgrounds, such as Turks, Arabs, Berbers, Kurds, Moors, Persians, and others. The spoken language likely would have been hybrid versions or dialects reflecting the many ethnicities of that region; and the prevailing religion would have been Islam. The people of the Empire would have differed in important ways from those of Christianized Europe and Asia; however, many of them would have been considered within the broad classifications of white and Caucasian. Immigrants to the New World from that part of the Old World might have legitimately claimed to be a "white person," a "Caucasian," and an "Arab" or any number of identities.

It also is understandable that South Carolinians called the dark-skinned Benenhaley a "Turk" in everyday parlance. "Turkey" and "Ottoman Empire" were synonymous back then; and the term "Turk" was a common appellation, sometime with derogatory connotation, for people from that region of the world. Furthermore, Westerners have always generalized about "Turks," "Arabs," "Moors," and "Muslims" without clarifying distinctions. Both terms—"Caucasian of Arab descent" and "Turks"—therefore have to be accepted as suggestive elements of the traditional narrative; however, too much significance cannot be attached to their usage as historical evidence. Historian Michael Gomez, an expert on Islam and the Middle East, suggested a possible explanation, in an e-mail message, for these generalizations. He said that outsider comprehension of the Muslim world was very limited in past times: "We have to remember that Europe had a difficult time distinguishing between various Muslim polities in the 18th and 19th centuries" (May 24, 2015). Also, as DNA investigator Donald N. Yates wrote, again in an e-mail: "In the colonial period the word Turk could have been used of Moroccans, Tunisians, Egyptians and Sephardic Jews as well as any people coming from the Ottoman Empire, which once spread from Hungary to Persia and across North Africa" (February 13, 2014).

Another aspect of Benenhaley's story that merits mention in this discussion is his participation in the American Revolution. Numerous analysts over the past century have cited his service in General Sumter's regiment (al-Ahart El, "Early American Settlers"; Considine, "Honoring Muslim Americans," 2013). However, his name could not be found in any listings of military personnel; and he did not file for a veteran's pension. Nor was there anything in written correspondence back then that referenced his contribution to the war.

Also, although many sources have ascribed "scout" status to Benenhaley, there is an argument to be made that he worked in some capacity keeping Sumter's wagons rolling. In an old letter to be presented in the next chapter, his service to the general was described "as his wheelwright"; and census reports from the 1850s listed "wheelwright" as the occupation of his son Francis. While this account is different from the traditional narrative of Joseph Benenhaley being a "scout" for the general, it makes some sense as he probably did not know much about South Carolina or its geography.

Finally, there has been no solid documentation of Benenhaley's role as founder and progenitor of the Turkish community. Despite countless reports as already noted in this manuscript, the only substantive evidence of his existence consisted of US Census records showing him as head of a family in the area. Subsequently, we have had to rely on flimsy foundations for Joseph Benenhaley's evolving story.

These ambiguities—relating to the presumed patriarch's name, ethnicity, homeland, war record, and family history—make for interesting discussion. But they leave us with no resolution of serious questions about his story. It is possible to posit a fit between what we have heard and read about Benenhaley and the traditional narrative among the Turkish people; and nothing of historical evidence contradicts the legend. On the other hand, there is little official documentation of that story. The 1810 and 1820 census enumerations were the beginning and ending notations of his life as recorded in public records commonly available and known prior to our investigation. The story seemed reasonable; but various aspects were open to conjecture and debate.

Thus, numerous questions loomed large while researching the true history of the Turkish people; and the biggest challenge was resolving Joseph Benenhaley's origins: How did a "Caucasian of Arab descent" wind up founding a Turkish settlement in rural South Carolina? This has been the most divisive topic from the very beginning as major doubts existed about this part of oral tradition. Therefore, we devote considerable attention to the question about how he may have journeyed from the Ottoman Empire to his destiny in Sumter County.

~ Meandering Saga of the Turkish Patriarch ~

The notion that an Ottoman warrior ended up in the Carolina backwoods and started a Turkish settlement is indeed a fascinating story. So fascinating, in fact, that an early minister of Long Branch Baptist Church studied the matter for many years and concluded that the idea of Turkish origins likely was true. Joseph H.

Mitchell, who pastored that church from 1904–1908, wrote in an article for the *Baptist Courier* ("Long Branch Church" 1943) that Joseph Benenhaley might indeed have been an Ottoman subject. He reasoned that "since a large segment of Turkey is Arabic and migrated freely into North Africa, there is some real ground for the Benenhaleys to be called Turks."

Mitchell also tried to explain how an Ottoman named "Yusef ben Ali" might have been renamed "Joseph Benenhaley" in the Dalzell community. He referred to the literary character Cide Hamete Benengeli, an Arabian historiographer in Cervantes's *Don Quixote*, in order to support his position. Mitchell said that Benengeli was described as being of Arab origins, "a Moor, a Mohammedan, an Arabian," and that the pronunciation of this character's name, Benengeli, sounded somewhat like both Benenhaley and ben Ali. Mitchell's literary musings provided interesting context while charting Benenhaley's journey from the Old World to the New World.

From the beginning of this project, a simple idea seemed worth considering. Why not examine old photographs from Sumter's Turkish community to see how their physical features matched up with those of residents in lands that once comprised the Ottoman Empire? The news media and interested partisans on both sides of this debate have always made references and inferred conclusions about the physical appearance of the Turkish people. For example, William D. Workman, a newspaperman with Charleston's *News and Courier*, cited their "distinctive" appearance as a reason for their social isolation (Dec, 17, 1950); *Ebony Magazine* printed a picture of the "typical Turk" with "tawny complexion and coarse, black hair" (1957, 53–56); F. Kinloch Bull said they "looked like Turks" with "their straight black hair and copper colored complexion" (*Random Recollections* 1986, 106); contrarily, S. Pony Hill described them as "copper-skinned and high cheekboned people" to buttress his claim that they were Native Americans (*Strangers* 2010, 41).

This seemed like a reasonable effort—but it led nowhere. Charles R. Cobb, then chair of the anthropology department at the University of South Carolina and now professor of historical archaeology at the Florida Museum of Natural History, told me that "one cannot tell ancestry just by general characteristics. There's so much variation and overlap between groups that, short of DNA testing, most anthropologists are highly cautious about any broad attributes related to body type" (e-mail message, January 13, 2014). Another anthropologist, Emeritus Professor James Bindon at the University of Alabama, stressed "how difficult it is to judge ancestry from photos." Furthermore, he added, "I'd be very leery of anyone who claims to be able to do what you're asking" (e-mail message, January 14, 2014).

The next effort was trying to track Joseph Benenhaley's route backward to Turkey, or Morocco, or North Africa—using his Anglicized and Arabic names along with his approximate birth year—in whatever records might exist in that part of the world. Other regional scholars had failed to resolve questions about his status (as a pirate, slave, refugee, or contract laborer) and his geographical route to the New World; but we hoped that perhaps there might exist some mention of him in news reports, travel logs, commercial books, or population counts tucked away somewhere in the Old World.

Contact with Limame Barbouchi, an academic colleague from Western Sahara/Morocco, was made, and he enlisted "search" help from his associates in Turkey and elsewhere in the region. Considering the intervention of hundreds of years, it was not surprising that this wild-shot inquiry came up dry for "Joseph Benenhaley," and "Yusef ben Ali" was "unrecognizable in the region" except possibly in reference to a long-ago religious leader and a district in Marrakesh (e-mail exchange, November 2013–January 2014).

It quickly became apparent that there would be a lot more to this task than comparing old photographs or e-mailing a few colleagues. It would involve a huge research effort; but it was important to figure out, at least theoretically, if the speculative patriarch could have sailed out of the Mediterranean, crossed the Atlantic, and settled in backwoods South Carolina.

~ Hypothetical Trail from the Ottoman Empire to Dalzell, South Carolina ~

The next stage of this inquiry included camping out at libraries (physically and electronically) and scouring diverse historical documents for clues about the possible journey of the Ottoman Turk. The immediate task was getting a handle on Ottomans in early America. Was there a historical Turkish presence here, and might that history suggest how Joseph Benenhaley made his way from the Old World to the New World?

It was clear that the Ottoman Empire's involvement in the New World was limited during the Age of Discovery, which encompassed the fifteenth through the seventeenth centuries; and the Empire never participated as a colonial power in this area during the eighteenth century. However, some elites were knowledgeable about and attentive to the Americas. (See Goodrich 1990, 9; McIntosh 2000 (5-6); Faroqhi 2006, 194–99; Kupperman 2007, 39–41; and Emiralioglu 2014, 117–43.)

For example, in 1513 an Ottoman admiral and geographer—Piri Reis, a native of current-day Turkey—created a map for Sultan Suleiman the Magnificent that reportedly incorporated lost documents used by Columbus and roughly displayed much of the world, including parts of the Americas (McIntosh 2000). Also, an extensive compilation of information and maps regarding this area of the globe was compiled for the Ottoman court by an anonymous author in 1580, although it was not formally published until 1730 (5-6). Historian Karen Ordahl Kupperman (2007) noted the curious nature of the original compilation thus: "At the same time a manuscript account of the Americas, mostly from Italian translations of Spanish sources, was compiled for the use of Ottoman rulers. For centuries this remained the only Turkish book about America. The manuscript was called 'Hadis-i nev,' which means 'fresh new,' but when it was published in 1730 it was given the title *Tarih-i Hind-i Garbi*, 'A History of the India of the West.' Twice in the manuscript the author expressed the hope that someday the Dar ul-Islam would extend even to the New World" (39–49).

It is hard to identify Ottomans who came to this area centuries ago with precision or exactness, because available documents are scarce and of indefinite sourcing; and historians and other observers have tended to reference most Islamic persons in the New World simply as "Muslims" or "Moors." This practice commonly and confusingly lumped together interesting historical figures from diverse ethnicities and regions of the Old World; furthermore, some analysts asserted differing versions of the backgrounds of these individuals.

Nevertheless, historical accounts have sufficiently documented the presence of Muslims and Moors—including Ottomans—in the New World; and it is clear that individuals of mixed background were among the earliest explorers of the Americas.

Amir Nashid Ali Muhammad, a former Baptist and converted Muslim, has claimed that West African Muslims came to this hemisphere almost two centuries before Columbus, including a journey through interior North America, via the Mississippi River, in 1312 (*Muslims in* America, 2001, 3). Muhammad, now president of the Islamic Heritage Museum and Cultural Center in Washington, DC, also wrote: "History shows that Muslims came to the Americas in four different waves, the first as explorers, then those fleeing the Spanish Inquisition, during the Barbary Coast Wars and the enslavement of Africans, and by immigration starting in the mid- to late 1870s" (7).

Detailed reports of Muslim contributions to exploration of the Americas can be found; but the effort requires keen sleuthing and tedious attention to arcane documents. According to Jerald Dirks—a former Methodist minister who now embraces Islam—Muslims played critical roles in the feats of Christopher Columbus and later Spanish explorers: "However, contemporary histories seldom bother to report that many of these early 'Spanish' explorers were Muslims of Arab and Berber descent" (*Muslims in American History* 2006).

No less an authority than Admiral Columbus confirmed the role of Moorish participants in his New World exploits. Reputable compilations of his writings and related material have shown their critical and substantial involvement in his original and later voyages (Irving, *A History of the Life*, 1828; Markham, *The Journal* 1893). Columbus had hoisted his flag on the Santa Maria; and two Muslim brothers—Martin Alonzo Pinzon and Vicente Yanez Pinzon, reputed relatives of a Moroccan Sultan—commanded, respectively, the Pinta and Niña in the 1492 adventure. Also, a Muslim navigator—Pedro Alonso Niño, a Spaniard of African descent—helped Columbus make charts and plot his route during that excursion (Irving 1828, 110–15; Markham 1893, 17, 69, 173; Muhammad 2001, 4–5).

More spectacular, a Moroccan guide—Mostafa al-Azemmouri, a "black Arab" sometimes known as "Estevanico the Moor"—was an almost mythical character in early travels through what is now the United States. He played an important role as scout and interpreter for Spanish conquistadors in Florida in the 1520s and in the American Southwest during the 1530s (Lowery, *Spanish Settlements*, 194–293).

Also, some have reported that Muslims of Berber origin were among the settlers of Santa Elena Island, a Spanish colony in present day South Carolina, in the mid-1500s (Kennedy and Kennedy 1997, 113–14); and others have contended that perhaps a couple hundred Turkish and Moorish slaves were loosed upon the North Carolina coast in the late 1500s (Abd-Allah, "Turks, Moors, Moriscos," 2010; and Quinn, "Turks, Moors, Blacks, and Others," 1982, 97–104).

Early relations between the American nation and the Barbary States were checkered and difficult, and conversation about positive interaction seems to get lost in debates over historical piracy and current jihadism. Significantly, however, Muslims contributed sporadically to the aspiring colonies and the United States. For example, it is reported that Islamic individuals served in the Continental Army during the Revolutionary War and several distinguished themselves in historic engagements, such as the Battle of Bunker Hill (Considine, "George Washington," 2013; al-Ahart El, "Early American Settlers," n.d.). Additionally, Mohammed III, the Sultan of Morocco, proved to be a special friend at times during and after that revolution. In 1777, he intervened on behalf of American merchant ships against attack from Barbary raiders, declaring that those ships sailed under the protection of his sultanate; and the Moroccan-American Treaty of Friendship, signed in 1786 and still in force today, is the longest unbroken treaty in United States history. In fact, President George Washington himself penned a 1789 letter of gratitude to Sultan Mohammed for his "friendship and magnanimity" toward the United States. (For these and other details on this historic relationship, see the following websites as referenced in the bibliography: "Embassy of the Kingdom of Morocco," "Morocco's Contribution to American Independence," and "United States Department of State, Historian.")

Available reports also demonstrated that a few Muslims lived in South Carolina, and an occasional Moorish visitor appeared in the area in the eighteenth and nineteenth centuries. For example, according to historian James Hagy, certain "exotic ethnics" showed up in South Carolina and created quite a stir in 1786 ("Muslim Slaves" 1993). "Two men appeared in Charleston 'dressed in the Moorish habit' and aroused a great deal of suspicion by their strange ways." They were taken to the home of an Arabic-speaking woman who was born in the Barbary States and resided in Charleston. They explained to her that they had sailed from Algeria to Virginia, where they were arrested as suspected Algerines, and they somehow made their way overland to South Carolina (26). To summarize these sources, Muslims and Moors—undoubtedly including Turkish individuals—helped explore and settle North America; some sided with the American struggle for independence, and a few lived in or visited South Carolina during its early history.

It also was evident in the literature that many of these individuals were slaves or had been victims of forced servitude. As religion professor Kambiz GhaneaBassiri (*A History of Islam* 2010) has remarked, "From the time Christopher Columbus crossed the Atlantic, West and North Africans served as involuntary servants to Europeans arriving in the Americas" (10). Readers also should keep in mind that many African slaves from regions of Islamic influence in the Old World—including some who were literate in the Arabic language and knowledgeable of the Koran and Bible—were imported and distributed throughout the southeastern colonies and states; and remnants of Islamic culture can still be detected in communities along the Carolina coast.(See, for example, Austin 1997; Diouf 1998; Gomez 1998; and Hagy 1993.) Clearly, dark-skinned people from non-European backgrounds have been a conflicted and neglected part of the American story from the beginning.

That generalization about forced servitude provides critical context when paired with obscure but relevant material in the South Carolina Department of Archives and History. Those records indicate in detail how some Ottomans had arrived in this colony and state—mysteriously and involuntarily—around the time that our person of interest showed up in this area. According to the archived files (*Journals of the House of Representatives* 1790; *South Carolina Royal Council Journal* 1753), several Moorish individuals found themselves in difficult situations during the eighteenth century, and they submitted formal petitions to the colonial council and state government of South Carolina in which the petitioners explained their forced journey from North Africa to North America and asked for help.

The first petition, filed with the Royal Council of South Carolina in 1753 on behalf of two individuals with Arabic names—Hamed and Guylance—claimed that they were Moroccans born on the Coast of Barbary, were soldiers by trade, and had been captured by the Portuguese. According to their petition, a Captain Henry Daubrig arranged for them to work for him in South Carolina for five years, after which they would be set free. Unfortunately, they came to Carolina and were required to work for a Daniel LaRoche, alongside his black African slaves, for fifteen years. Desperate, they appealed to the Royal Council: "We have often humbly demanded our liberty but cannot obtain it. And instead of any prospect of liberty, we understand that we are very shortly to be sold at Public Sale with Mr. Laroche's negroes. We most submissively fall down and prostrate ourselves before your Excellency, pray for your most gracious protection, and with the utmost humility submit ourselves and our most miserable circumstances to your Excellency's most sublime goodness. And may the Almighty God guide your Excellency in the fervent prayer of your lowest servants." The North Africans eventually secured their freedom after twenty years of labor in America. According to scholars at the Moroccan Cultural Studies Centre, documents filed in that country show that South Carolina officials investigated the situation and issued papers certifying their freedom; and they returned to Morocco that very same year (Beyond Borders "Moroccans in Britain and America").

Another petition was filed in 1790 on behalf of eight "sundry Free Moors"—four men and their wives, all with Arabic names—who claimed to be subjects of the Emperor of Morocco and residents of the state of South Carolina. Their story was that they were captured as prisoners of war and brought to this area as slaves but they had been able to buy their freedom. In this petition to the South Carolina General Assembly, they asked, as free-born citizens of an American ally, to be treated under the same laws as other citizens of the state, instead of under "the negro law":

> That your Petitioners some years past had the misfortune while fighting in the defense of their Country, to be captured with their wives and made prisoners of War by one of the Kings of Africa. That a certain Captain Clark had them delivered to him on a promise that they should be redeemed by the Emperor of Morocco's Ambassador then residing in England, in order to have them returned to their own Country: Instead of which he brought them to this State, and sold them for slaves. Since that period they have by the greatest industry been enabled to purchase their freedom from their respective Masters; And now prayeth your Honorable House, That as free born subjects of a Prince now in Alliance with these United States; that they may not be considered as subject to Law of the State (now in force) called the negro law; but if they should unfortunately be guilty of any crime or misdemeanor against the Laws of the Land, that they may have a just trial by a Lawful Jury.

Their petition was sent to a committee, from which it was reported to the floor of the House and agreed to, thusly: "Report That they have considered the same and are of opinion that no Law of this State can in its Construction or Operation apply to them, and that persons who were Subjects of the Emperor of Morocco being Free in this State are not triable by the Law for the better Ordering and Governing of Negroes and other slaves." Thus these eight Moroccans achieved their desired status as free people.

The archived accounts of these Ottoman refugees were an intriguing development. But what happened next was like a bolt out of the blue. A "secret witness" was discovered from long ago in the Turkish community who had proclaimed, in writing, a similar account of Joseph Benenhaley's adventure in bondage and emancipation. An old letter from this source will be presented later in this section;

but the essence of her testimony was that Benenhaley was indeed "an Ottoman," had been "bonded by the Spanish at sea," "kept from freedom in the Indies," but "persevered" and was "made free," and served with "General Sumter in the War" (Thompson Collection and Interviews).

This letter from inside the Turkish community was a breakthrough development, and it squared with a collection of research and ongoing revisions by Wesley White Jr., an ethnological historian who investigated the Turkish community decades ago (1975, n.p.). White originally concluded in a Smithsonian manuscript that "Benengeli seems to have been a native of Turkey, and of Arabic descent"; and there is a scribbled footnote in his handwriting on the bottom of the pertinent page of his updated papers insinuating slavery as a circuitous route for Benenhaley's journey to South Carolina. The note mentioned the 1753 case of enslaved Moors and added: "I think now that Joseph Benengeli was born in S.C. and that his father/grandfather came from Morocco." In a lengthy telephone conversation in January, 2015, he also offered an interesting comment: "I don't think anybody can say for sure how Joseph Benenhaley got to South Carolina. In any coastal area, many people are going to show up from somewhere else. Some people were on the lam and just landed there."

These possibilities might also help explain the mystery of the man who called himself Scott and "was always thought to be of partly French descent and had an assumed name" (Sumter, *Stateburg*, 1820, 43). Historians Bass and Flood apparently doubted his French background. Bass, in his 1961 biography of the Gamecock, wrote of both Benenhaley and Scott as "corsairs" from the Barbary Coast (78) and as "the two North Africans" with "dark complexion" (237); he also mentioned them as "Turkish tenants" (274) on Sumter's land; and Flood referred to them as "the Arabs" and "Sumter's North Africans" (*Rise and Fight Again* 1976, 312). Many historical documents have demonstrated the strong slave trade to the French West Indies in the eighteenth century; and it also has been reported that some of those slaves made their way to the southeastern coast of North America, as either slave chattel or as runaways. So it seems logical that the individual called Scott might have come to South Carolina in some manner akin to what is surmised for Benenhaley. The darkly hued man could have been from the Mediterranean area, picked up his "French" credentials in the Caribbean basin, and introduced himself thereby as "Scott" and "of French descent" in Carolina.

The discovery of a dramatic old letter from within the Turkish community and suggestive documents at the South Carolina Archives altered and expanded this investigation significantly. This line of inquiry would involve a lengthy and challenging study of slavery in world history; but we knew it was necessary to determine if the slave trade might have brought Joseph Benenhaley from the Mediterranean Sea to South Carolina.

~ Slave Trade Connection ~

The idea that human trafficking might be the connective key to our transatlantic mystery is not as strange as it seems; and investigating this theory would prove to be a critical and rewarding part of our pursuit of the Turkish patriarch, as explained in the next few pages.

To begin, there was widespread slavery and a thriving slave trade in the Western Hemisphere during the sixteenth through the nineteenth centuries, most famously involving Sub-Sahara Africans and indigenous Americans but also others of different races, religions, ethnicities, and nationalities. This was particularly true in the Mediterranean area, where powerful entities preyed on adversaries and innocent victims. (See, for example, Adams and Adams 2006; Baepler 1999; Davis, 2004; Davis, 2009; Games 2009.)

"All who traveled by sea in that region, whether statesmen, tourists, mariners, or traders, were vulnerable" to captivity, conversion, and enslavement, according to historian Alison Frazier Games in her analysis of the British Empire (Games, *The Jamestown Project*, 2009, 64). In fact, she claimed, "The extent of Mediterranean captivity was considerable, equaling the Atlantic slave trade until the middle of the seventeenth century" (68). Another historian, Robert C. Davis, focused on white slavery among Muslims of the Barbary Coast, and his calculations indicated the extent of that trade over several centuries. His rough estimation was that the number of European Christian enslavements approximated "a total that easily exceeds 1 million, probably 1.25 million, all told, between 1500 and 1800" (*Christian Slaves* 2004, 60).

More interesting and pertinent to this project, there is solid research showing that Muslim subjects also were enslaved by the Europeans. According to the Lowcountry Digital History Initiative at the College of Charleston, these enslavements grew out of papal efforts to counter Islamic transgressions during the fifteenth century: "In response to these conflicts, a series of fifteenth century popes argued for the enslavement of non-Christians as 'an instrument for Christian conversion.' According to church law, Christians were protected from slavery, but Muslim 'infidels' and non-Christian 'pagans' were acceptable to enslave" ("European Christianity and Slavery"). This theological doctrine was articulated in France a century later by a Sorbonne judge, who declared that Christians could not enslave other "believers" seized in combat, but "in a just war, however, Christians have every right to deprive [unbelievers] of their liberty and make them slaves" (Weiss, *Captives*, 2013, 91). Also, a French official explained that it was permissible for Ottomans and Moroccans who had violated no laws to be imprisoned because "this kind of commerce is established" in foreign countries (91).

Consequently, many Muslims ended up as captives and slaves of the Christians. As reported by Lhoussain Simour, an English teacher who specializes in

Moroccan Cultural Studies: "Captivity and enslavement were not exceptionally a Barbary activity; they were a concentrated Western preoccupation as well. The archives of history are replete with Barbary names who endured western bondage in many ways" (Simour, *Recollections,* 2014, 26). Simour claimed that these slaves contributed to early history of the Americas; but, he said, they have been slighted in the official record. With specific reference to enslaved people from his home country, he wrote: "A number of Moroccan captives were held in America and were an integral part in the great Atlantic passage, but they were occluded in historiographical practice and almost nothing is left of their traces in the annals of history. . . . The presence and contributions of Moroccan captives in the New World have largely been unrecognized in historical writings, and their physical routes have also been less tracked in academic undertakings" (26).

There are isolated reports of such presence and contributions of Ottoman slaves, in addition to those cited above. For example, historian Jeremy Black wrote that, early on, prior to the massive transatlantic slave trade, Moorish captives from Mediterranean conflicts were sent to work in Spanish/Portuguese colonies in the Americas (*The Atlantic Slave Trade,* 2015, 24); historian Herbert Klein mentioned that Moorish captives preceded and coexisted with African slaves in the Caribbean (*African Slavery* 1986, 16); and English professor Nabil Matar noted that Britons encountered Moorish and Turkish captives of the Spanish in the Caribbean during the Age of Discovery (*Turks Moors,* 1999, 101).

Umar Faruq Abd-Allah, scholar in residence at the Nawawi Foundation, has covered these prisoners more thoroughly in an online article, "Turks, Moors, and Moriscos in Early America" (2010). He concluded that there were significant numbers of Muslims in this region: "Recent historical studies have brought to light the fact that there were significant numbers of Muslims in the New World during the colonial period, who lived a generally clandestine existence as slaves and occasionally free laborers" (3).

Abd-Allah noted that most of those Muslims were Africans from West Africa; however, he said that there were other Muslims of different backgrounds among them, such as the Moors from the Mediterranean. He provided elaboration regarding these "other Muslims" and their specialized role as galley slaves in the Caribbean; and he cited a 1586 expedition of Sir Francis Drake, in which the Englishman liberated or stole several hundred Turkish and Moorish oarsmen. According to Abd-Allah, Drake's Turks and North African Moors likely had ended up in the Caribbean as captives from the Old World (4).

Historian David Wheat has provided additional research on galley slaves, who constituted a major Spanish contingent in the Caribbean during the sixteenth and seventeenth centuries ("Mediterranean Slavery" 2010). "In the Caribbean," he wrote, "this specialised labour was carried out by Mediterranean Muslims" (330). He continued with the following observations in his report:

From 1578 until the early 1630s, galley squadrons based in Cartagena, Santo Domingo, and Havana relied on the labour of several hundred Mediterranean Muslims (and a handful of moriscos). Viewed as skilled and experienced oarsmen, these 'Moors' and 'Turks' rowed alongside enslaved sub-Sahara Africans, and convicts drawn from various corners of the Iberian empires (328)....

Like many North Africans, these men were most probably captured from Ottoman vessels in the course of Mediterranean naval warfare, and forced into galley slavery (332)....

Most had probably been captured in amphibious raids conducted by Spanish naval forces, or in outright naval combat. Between 1613 and 1624, for example, Spain acquired 980 slaves from just 28 vessels captured in the Mediterranean. Initially forced to serve on Iberian galleys, some of these enslaved oarsmen were subsequently transferred to the Caribbean. [They] were far removed from their stated homes in areas corresponding to present-day Morocco, Algeria, Tunisia, Libya, Egypt, and Sicily (331–32).

Unfortunately, there is no systematic, comprehensive research on the later lives and destinies of the Ottoman slaves sent to the Caribbean basin. However, there were anecdotal accounts of Arab slaves, supposedly from the Mediterranean, in the American South. Two of the most interesting of these characters—"Selim" and "S'Quash"—were said to have been brought to this area in the eighteenth and nineteenth centuries. There is no indication in these accounts whether or not Selim and S'Quash passed through the Caribbean region; but their tales roughly approximated the hypothetical saga of Joseph Benenhaley.

Selim's story was reported originally in an article written by the Reverend Benjamin H. Rice for a publication on the Episcopal Church of Virginia ("History of Selim," 341–48). Selim said he was the student son of "wealthy and respectable parents." He had been captured in the mid-1700s by a Spanish man-of-war or privateer on his way from Algiers to Constantinople; and he was taken by a French trader to New Orleans. Thereafter, he told a rambling account whereby his captors "sent him up the rivers Mississippi and Ohio ... and left him a prisoner of war with the Indians." He claimed to have escaped and walked hundreds of miles to freedom in Virginia (342–46).

The equally dramatic tale of S'Quash was told by a medical doctor, Paul B. Barringer, who grew up in North Carolina during the Civil War era and served briefly as president of Virginia Tech, or what was known back then as Virginia Agricultural and Mechanical College and Polytechnic Institute (*The Natural Bent* 1949, 9–13). In Barringer's memoir, S'Quash was described as an educated Arab who "had been to Cairo and could read Greek as well as Arabic." His family ironically had been "long engaged in the slave trade." He was described as "extremely dark, like a Moor" and "obviously not a Negro." He had been captured by "Yankee traders," apparently while he was gathering slaves in West Africa in the early 1800s; and he was sent to Charleston and then to a plantation in North Carolina. Eventually, according to this document, S'Quash established himself as a strong ally of the plantation owner in keeping the other slaves under control; "such was his ability that he ultimately became head man on the plantation, succeeding in time the white overseer"(9-13).

The credibility of such stories is open to debate. Certainly, legitimate questions surround these and similar accounts of reputed North Africans who endured enslavement in America. The literature is sprinkled with captives who some speculate may have been of Arab descent or Moorish background and who were granted special status by white society. However, some scholars have criticized stories of such heritage. Indeed, historian Sylviane Diouf claimed that these tales reflected a functional effort to align these personal histories in accord with American bias against African humanity (*Servants of Allah* 1998): "Because the American system of racial classification did not recognize intermediate strata—the mulattos, for example—as the Latin system did, there could only be inferior blacks and superior whites. Within these limits, a particularly 'intelligent black' had to stop being black and become an ersatz white." According to Diouf: "He could be one by becoming an African white, that is, an Arab. The only Africans who could qualify for this co-optation were the Muslims, as their religion and their literacy in Arabic could be touted as tangible proofs of their Arabic origin. With the whitening of the 'elite' slave, the basis on which slavery rested was not threatened. Blacks were still subhumans and thus fit to be enslaved, whereas the Moorish princes, warriors, and fellow slave traders could elevate themselves to the highest positions within the boundaries of the rigid slave society" (100).

Despite the logic of the argument, this reasoning cannot be used for blanket dismissal of all such tales of Arab or Moorish slaves. These isolated cases—including Selim, S'Quash, the Barbary pirates, sundry Free Moors, and Joseph Benenhaley—must be judged on their individual merits and available evidence. Thus far, the authors have found no evidence contradicting the narratives of Selim and S'Quash; therefore, we consider the writings of Rice and Barringer credible accounts of Ottoman subjects from the Mediterranean area who labored as slaves in the colonies/states of the American South.

The most appropriate generalization to draw from these sources and anecdotes is that, while detailed, reliable data are scarce; various reports show that Ottoman captives from the Mediterranean area comprised a relatively small and different but definite part of the transatlantic slave trade. Millions of African slaves were brought across the ocean to the Americas; an unknown but significant number of Ottoman subjects made that same journey; and some, conceivably including Joseph Benenhaley, spent time in the Caribbean and ended up in North America.

Of course, it is not known how many Ottomans were sent to the Caribbean basin during the slavery period; and some of them eventually died or possibly melded into mixed ethnicities in the islands. However, based on what we had learned from extensive study and our own personal assumptions, they may have vanished, in part, because of the interplay among slave traders, slave buyers, financial considerations, and common contempt for people of color in the New World. A persuasive argument can be made that some of the Ottomans in the Caribbean "went away" via shady practices and hidden exit routes—as follows—in the intercolonial slave trade business.

We believe that the Caribbean traffickers of African slaves would have had no compunction against buying or stealing and selling and shipping dark-skinned Ottomans or any other prisoners of similarly toned appearance who happened to come their way. Furthermore, it is doubtful that many buyers would have turned down slave laborers due to their point of origin or the hue of their complexion, and there is at least one account on record attesting to such practice. In Paul Barringer's memoir (*The Natural Bent* 1949), he told how "S'Quash," an Arab, had been enslaved in a hectic raid on the Guinea Coast. He related that, as competing raiders scrambled to capture as many prisoners as possible before the 1808 termination of slave imports, they also grabbed a number of Arab traders and their families operating in the area. Barringer noted that it was obvious at the Charleston disembarkation market that S'Quash "was not a Negro"; but a prospective buyer said "I will take him." Then he asked, "What is his nationality?" The captain replied: "To tell the truth, I don't know. . . . This was our last trip, and we wanted no vacancies, so that when the last consignment was brought in we didn't ask questions" (12).

These suppositions, collectively, can be seen as a tentative proposition about how some Ottoman slaves situated in the Caribbean may have been ensnared in intercolonial trade operations; they could have travelled the same trade routes as did the African slaves to ports along the Atlantic coast of North America. This proposition led to a search for information about trade routes and shipments of "Africans" from the islands that might serve as a proxy indicator of Joseph Benenhaley's path to Charleston.

Historian Gregory E. O'Malley provided valuable new analysis of the intercolonial slave trade; and his research demonstrated that it was very common for slaves to be shipped from the Caribbean to colonial plantations in South Carolina (*Final Passages* 2014; "Beyond the Middle Passage" 2009). O'Malley explained that the Middle Passage across the Atlantic Ocean was just part of a chaotic transportation ordeal for African captives. After they arrived in a place like the Caribbean, they often would be transshipped somewhere else in the Americas. O'Malley characterized the business of intercolonial slave trading as a perverse function of crass merchants maximizing profits in a situation of demand exceeding supply. As he wrote: "In their eyes, the slaves were just another product. Understanding this helps explain the convoluted journeys of enslaved people, as they were swept into commodity flows alongside crops and trade goods" (2014, 25).

O'Malley also compiled detailed data and estimates for over seven thousand intercolonial voyages during the slave-trade period, providing for the first time a statistical and geographical assessment of those transactions; and, significantly, many slaves were transshipped to South Carolina. He calculated that 10,625 slaves were shipped from the Caribbean to the Atlantic coast between 1651 and 1710; and 2,900 of them went to South Carolina (2014, 121). Other data in his report indicated that, from 1701 to 1765, about 50,000 captives were transported along this route, with South Carolina receiving 11,250 of them (2014, 171, 176). All total, from 1619 to 1807, O'Malley estimated that about 72,000 slaves were delivered to North America from the Caribbean; and almost 22,000 of them were delivered to South Carolina (2009, 166). Background information could be compiled for about a third of these slaves; and it showed that most, or 92 percent, of them were "New Negroes" from Africa; however, 8 percent were described as "seasoned," meaning they had spent substantial time in the New World (2014, 21). Simple extrapolation suggests that almost six thousand seasoned slaves, who had spent time in the Americas, were shipped to North American ports and over 1,700 of them—which could have included our person of interest—went to South Carolina.

Interestingly, the intercolonial slave business described here was not the only scenario that might explain Joseph Benenhaley's journey to South Carolina. Certain historical developments and specific incidents suggest other transportational excursions through which both Africans and Ottomans might have accomplished this last leg of their transit; and, strangely, these excursions may have been a liberating experience for some of them. Most ironic was the common practice of slave plundering and illegal marketing. Sometimes, pirates and privateers simply stole other people's laborers in the Caribbean and resold them to ready buyers in the colonies of North America. In fact, South Carolina was a favored destination for rogue operators, especially in the early years of the slave trade era (O'Malley, "Beyond the Middle Passage," 2009, 143).

Obviously, these sea raiders and their outlaw excursions could involve all kinds of uncharted relocations and emancipating opportunities for enslaved personnel. Illustrative are the previously mentioned exploits of English privateer and slave trader Sir Francis Drake. Drake "liberated" four hundred captive laborers—including about three hundred Moors and Turks—from the Spanish or Portuguese during one of his southern expeditions; and, due to weather and logistical problems, he supposedly dumped most of them on an island along the North Carolina coast. Some suspect that they quickly went ashore and disappeared inland (Abd-Allah 2010; Kennedy and Kennedy 1997).

This incident reportedly occurred in 1586, well before Joseph Benenhaley's time; and this account has been contested by some scholars. The Melungeons have claimed for years that their origins stretch back to the Eastern Mediterranean, and they include as part of that theory the Moors and Muslims dropped on the Outer Banks of North Carolina by Sir Francis Drake (Kennedy and Kennedy 1997). A DNA study (Yates and Hirschman, "Toward a Genetic Profile," 2010) reported that the Melungeons represent an amalgam of Mediterranean, Middle Eastern, North African, Sub-Sahara African, and Native American ethnic groups. However, others deny such claims. For example, Estes and coauthors ("Melungeons" 2012) dismissed this theory as "widespread myth" with "no evidence, historical, oral, genealogical or genetic" linking the Melungeons to Turkish or Middle Eastern ancestry." (For a full background on this historical incident and controversy, see Abd-Allah 2010; Crain 2010; DeMarce 1996; Ertan 2002; Estes et al. 2010; Kennedy and Kennedy 1997; Quinn 1982; Thomson 1970; Yates and Hirschman 2010.) The Drake story illustrates the difficulty of drawing conclusions from what might have happened centuries ago. But numerous incidents of piracy and plundering occurred throughout the slave-trade era; so various versions of this tale could explain how "exotic ethnics" wound up in the southeastern region of this country.

In addition to the aforementioned developments and incidents in the Caribbean, there were several possibilities whereby slaves might terminate their captivity and perhaps end up in more hospitable environments; and we will close our speculation about Joseph Benenhaley's odyssey by mentioning two of the most likely possibilities. In the first case, there were legal procedures and financial arrangements whereby individual slaves might persuade their owners to grant them freedom—a practice known as "manumission"; secondly, numerous accounts attest that individual captives sometimes fled the plantation without formal permission, often joining other renegades, known as "maroons," in isolated camps beyond control of local authorities; and some of them reached the safety of foreign shores. (For detailed histories of manumission and marronage in one colony, see Handler, "Escaping Slavery," 1997; Handler and Pohlmann, "Slave Manumissions," 1984.)

Additionally, slaves might find opportunity for escape upon arriving at destinations along the Atlantic coast, since most of these prisoners then had to be taken from the port to backcountry plantations. O'Malley has noted that many African slaves attempted escape shortly after landing on the Southeast American coast (2014, 287–88); and, he said, the *South-Carolina Gazette* reported frequent such incidents in the Charleston area. No data was found indicating the success rate of these efforts; however, there is documentation of runaway "maroons" and their encampments in the Lowcountry swamplands of South Carolina. For example, historian Timothy J. Lockley has estimated that marronage was "comparatively common" here in the colonial and early statehood period (*Maroon Communities* 2009, 109).

Thus, New World history shows that it was very difficult but not impossible for enslaved individuals to unshackle themselves and pursue their destiny as free men and women. Perhaps the fabled Turkish patriarch had been one of the few who, somehow, secured his liberty and a new life in South Carolina.

Finally, a couple of questions that skeptics have often asked about Joseph Benenhaley and the Turkish narrative should be addressed. How could an Arab from the Mediterranean communicate with English-speaking South Carolinians? Also, how did this presumed Ottoman Muslim forefather a family and community of Christians in rural Sumter County? These issues were easily resolved, again by observing the experience of African slaves. According to linguistics professor Peter A. Roberts, African slaves in the English West Indies who had come from different parts of their home continent had to develop the ability to communicate with their masters and each other (*From Oral to Literature Culture*, 2000). "Each individual African had to go through the same language acquisition process which all who preceded had gone through. . . . They had to learn English for functional purposes . . . to communicate, no matter with whom" (72, 80). Also, as Herbert Klein has explained in his history of the Atlantic slave trade, slaves often converted to the ways and values of enslavers; and "African slaves readily adopted the culture, religion and education of their masters" (*Atlantic Slave* 2010, 13). In fact, there is clear historical evidence regarding that last matter—religious conversion—among Moorish captives. In his report on Muslim galley slaves in the Caribbean, David Wheat (2010) cited a report that "many of the Moors who came in the galleys have turned Christian, and have been baptised, having lost all hope of being able to return to their native land" (334–35). Similar reasoning can apply to our Turkish captive and refugee. Joseph Benenhaley could have learned to speak functional English wherever he landed in the Americas; and, it is equally rational that he might have felt inclined to raise his Carolina family in accord with the Christian affiliations and practices of his new homeland.

By this stage of our investigation, our minds were churning with curiosity and excitement. Could such transactions of history and circumstance really explain how Joseph Benenhaley (aka Yusef ben Ali) was born in the Ottoman Empire and ended up in Dalzell?

Certainly, the history and speculations recounted in these few pages suggest that there were a number of persons from the Mediterranean world who made their way to South Carolina way back when. There is no hard evidence tying Benenhaley with the Barbary soldiers, the sundry Free Moors, Sir Francis Drake, or the intercolonial shipments from the Caribbean; however, it seems reasonable that our mysterious Ottoman may have arrived here through kinship with these people or in a somewhat similar manner. He could have been the son of one of the Barbary soldiers, or a relative of the sundry Free Moors, or a descendant of Drake's liberated captives, or the residual product of numerous other such storylines. Maybe he came to coastal Carolina from the Mediterranean via the Caribbean in chains or as a runaway; or perhaps he arrived here as a freed man.

Maybe he disappeared into the wilderness on his own or under duress of some sort, where he began a new life among accepting backwoodsmen. Perhaps it was during such existence that he encountered and allied with Thomas Sumter in the Carolina backcountry.

Thus, initial efforts at determining Joseph Benenhaley's Turkish background in accord with oral history came to an end. There was no conclusive evidence of his epic journey from an Ottoman homeland, through the Caribbean, to military service and a familial settlement in South Carolina; but a historical case could be fashioned to show that it all was possible and credible.

~ Ottoman Origins and the Turkish Narrative ~

This probing inquiry accorded—conceivably and loosely—with the Turkish people's traditional narrative about the legendary background of Joseph Benenhaley/Yusef ben Ali. A mountain of documentary material showed that Muslims and Moors from North Africa journeyed to the New World during the 1500s, 1600s, and 1700s; and historical research and official records revealed Ottoman subjects in South Carolina in the latter half of the 1700s. Furthermore, despite ambiguities, Benenhaley's presence and settlement in the New World sounds reasonably rational.

Of course, one cannot read too much significance into specific situations or speculations regarding things that happened more than two hundred years ago. Nevertheless, these accounts provide cause to take seriously the possibility that the slave trade explains Joseph Benenhaley's experience in South Carolina at the end of the eighteenth century.

In order to appropriately and adequately address the exotic legend about Joseph Benenhaley's origins and journey from the Ottoman Empire to Dalzell, South Carolina, a draft of this above section was sent to Michael Gomez, professor of History, Middle Eastern and Islamic Studies at New York University; and Gomez was asked if the analysis made sense. Gomez is clearly qualified to comment on this topic, with a distinguished background in the ways that African Muslims negotiated slavery and freedom throughout North and South America. He has served as director of the Association for the Study of the Worldwide African Diaspora and as president of UNESCO's International Scientific Committee for the Slave Route Project. Also, he is the author of several books on this subject, including *Black Crescent: African Muslims in the Americas* (2005).

Gomez's response was succinct and affirmative: "I think you have done extraordinary work in tracking down information regarding Joseph Benenhaley/Yusuf b. 'Ali, and that you have clearly established the plausibility of his presence in South Carolina during this period.... Yusuf b. 'Ali could very well have been either Moroccan or a traveler from some part of the Ottoman domain who happened to get caught up in the slave trade."

However, nagging, legitimate questions remained. There was no real documentation of Benenhaley's role as founder and progenitor of the community—and that absence of evidence figured centrally in continuous controversy over the traditional narrative. In order to pass valid judgment on that narrative, it would be necessary to pursue Joseph Benenhaley harder and further and, if possible, find convincing evidence of his Turkish patriarchy in rural South Carolina.

~ *Chapter Four* ~

Documenting the Patriarch and His People

Up to this point there were few solid leads about Joseph Benenhaley's place in the traditional narrative. As already noted, there was no clear evidence of his Ottoman origins and serious doubts clouded his role, activities, and lineage in South Carolina. Questions about Benenhaley have been fundamental and persistent over the years. Did he actually serve in the American Revolution—or was that just romantic nonsense? Did Thomas Sumter give him property to settle and farm—or was he simply one of many squatters on the general's land?

Also, little was known for certain about Benenhaley's contribution to the history of this group. Was he really *the* founding father of the Dalzell community and *the* forefather of the Turkish people? Perhaps another person exercised greater paternal influence; or others could have served as cofounders or coforefathers?

To put this search for answers to these questions in perspective, consider how far removed the presumed patriarch is now, not just in years but in generations and kinship. The youngest Benenhaleys today represent the tenth generation of Sumter County's Turkish community. If these youngest descendants simply asked kinfolk to tell them about Joseph Benenhaley, that memory trail would have to go back, way back, to a grandparent's grandparent's grandparent—just to reach a child of their reputed patriarch. If they wanted to chart their full genealogy back ten generations, each would have to deal with a combined pool of 1,022 possible ancestors. Someone similarly situated in a normal population, assuming conditions of unrelated ancestral mixing, might "share" only about one thousandth of his or her blood with a specific ancestor so many generations separated. Benenhaley's origins are indeed a classic cold-case mystery in which one must prove a sketchy tale from long ago, with only suggestive lore, scarce evidence, and hearsay testimony. It would require a stretch of imagination to cover all the logical possibilities and wild speculations about the Turkish patriarch and craft a very wide and creative research net in order to solve the mystery of the Turkish community.

With only suspect leads, our pursuit of the elusive Turkish patriarch required traveling many miles, spending countless days in libraries, digging through piles of old papers, talking to an endless list of scholars and laypersons, and directing sensitive questions to the people of this community. This turned into several years of scrutinizing the Internet, governmental records, academic publications, media coverage, and whatever else seemed likely sources of information about the legendary leader.

A focus on special collections and private papers for arcane or hidden references to this mystical character was required as well. Included among these materials were the "Draper Manuscripts Collection," the "Anne King Gregorie Papers," the "Ellison Family Papers," the "Charles James McDonald Furman Papers," and the "Wes Taukchiray Papers." Furthermore, full access was gained to the papers, photographs, and information of Greg Thompson, who had married into a Turkish family and compiled significant material over the years (Thompson Collection and Interviews). This material had not been organized or processed for easy access. However, Thompson graciously shared his historiographical treasure, and his collection was the most useful single source in this research. Finally, an exciting course of genealogical research was undertaken, which included compiling a list of Turkish individuals and families who lived during the 1800s, an inventory of their burials at the local church cemeteries, and a small sample of DNA reports from living descendants. This research would provide very useful data and details about the early and evolving Turkish community.

All of these projects involved lengthy and laborious effort; but the payoff was critical new evidence. Each of several sequential steps led from questions to speculations, to possibilities, and eventually to the truth about Joseph Benenhaley and the Turkish community. The initial step in this assignment launched us into cyberspace, wandering hither and yon on the computer for possible clues or information about the life of the patriarch.

~ Searching the Internet ~

Searching the Internet was an elementary, time-consuming, often frustrating, but productive experience. For the record, an Internet search engine (www.google.com) produced about 1,250 items for "Joseph Benenhaley" and about 15,900 items for "Yusef ben Ali." Many of these documents were helpful in crafting a comprehensive picture of Joseph Benenhaley and the Turkish people. But most of these entries were duplicate listings of documents or irrelevant material for our project. For example, there seemed to be an excess of unconfirmed speculation about "Joseph Benenhaley" in endless discussion threads; and thousands of "Yusef ben Ali" hits reflected the universality and varied spellings of the three Arabic names.

Restricting search directions produced eighty items for "Joseph Benenhaley" + "Sumter County, SC" and these proved useful. There were only eight results for "Yusef ben Ali" + "Sumter County, SC," and none of these latter links contributed independently to the story of the Turkish community. A popular commercial research site (www.ancestry.com) produced thousands of documentary records and family trees for the name "Joseph Benenhaley" (with "Sumter County, SC" as an identifying term). Another popular free site (www.familysearch.org) showed similar information regarding documents and relationships for the same search. These records were helpful in constructing a rough genealogical history of the Benenhaley lineage. But none of them provided any real information about his background and family. Several sources stated, without documentation, that he was "born in Turkish empire on 1753" and "passed away on 1823 in Sumter, South Carolina, USA." There was no information about his father or his mother or any of his ancestors; and census records provided only clues to his descendants. Furthermore, the thousands of "Yusef ben Ali" items proved virtually irrelevant for our project.

As might be expected, the computer was a bounty of information, bringing huge and diverse treasures of publications and materials vital to our research and leading to useful offline sources. It was especially helpful in dealing with a basic question then roiling the community: Were Joseph Benenhaley and/or the Turkish people of Sumter County really Native American Indians?

~ Dealing with the Indian Issue ~

Anthropologists and archeologists have long speculated about possible linkages between European-Asian peoples and the American Indians. Some contend that the origin of Indians in North and South America stretches back to Eurasians crossing over the top of the globe thousands of years ago.

Thus, arguably, the Dalzell patriarch and his community may have had roundabout ties to both the New World Indians and the Old World Ottomans. This certainly would explain the common confusion among people of this area, some of whom consider the "looks" of the Sumter Turkish people and Native American Indians as being very similar. Debating that theoretical issue lay far beyond our concern. More pertinent was the fact that several analysts and activists contended that the Dalzell group was a spinoff from indigenous tribes of the Carolinas. Some locals—previously considered part of the Turkish community—dismissed the oral narrative and identified as Native Americans. They organized as a Cheraw Band about a decade ago, and they were certified by the state as the Sumter Tribe of Cheraw Indians in 2013. This "Turk-Indian" controversy posed specific and direct challenge to the traditional narrative of these people that had to be dealt with before proceeding on a pursuit of Joseph Benenhaley.

This author visited the South Carolina Commission for Minority Affairs in Columbia on several occasions to review the petition for tribal certification filed by the Sumter Band of Cheraw Indians. There were slightly over one hundred petitioners, including some whose surnames have been identified with the Turkish community (twenty Oxendines and seventeen Benenhaleys). After signing a Freedom of Information Act request, all 1,474 pages of material included in the application and certification were inspected, and pored over for months, which allowed a comparison of their claimed history and genealogy with personal research and the Turkish traditional narrative.

Eventually, we came to a simple and clarifying conclusion. These two lineages had different ancestors; but the Benenhaley crowd and some of the American Indians of Sumter County traveled an entwined, conjoined course in this area for almost two centuries.

~ Conjoined Lineages ~

United States Census records and various historical accounts allow us to trace these two lineages in rural South Carolina back to the early history of our nation. (For examples of these sources, see Bull 1986; Federal Writers' Project, late 1930s; Gregorie, 1954; Hodge 1912; McPherson 1915; Nicholes, 1975; Oxendine 1997; Sider 2003; Sumter, 1920; White 1975.)

According to these sources, Joseph Benenhaley, presumably from the Ottoman Empire, settled his family in Dalzell on land given by General Thomas Sumter after Benenhaley's service in the American Revolution. Obviously, this was not a purely Turkish endeavor, since both his first and second wives were white Europeans and their children married outsiders. Those early years have been chronicled by relatives of General Sumter, who grew up in the area and around the Turkish people (Bull 1986, 106–7; Sumter, 1920, 43–45).

Later generations established themselves as white people of Turkish descent in a secluded enclave with curious folkways. Some commentators cast them as backward people of uncertain origin (for example, Federal Writers' Project, late 1930s, 1–4). Later, they were described more compassionately as simple, law-abiding citizens who stuck together and clung to an unconfirmed narrative about their history (Gregorie 1954, 467–70; Nicholes 1975, 136–38).

At about the same time and continuing through subsequent decades, several families who claimed mixed Native American and white European ancestry began relocating from North Carolina to Sumter County and other locales in South Carolina. Some of the North Carolinians appear to have associated themselves with people of comparable background who lived in Privateer township, which was about twenty miles south from Dalzell. The Privateer Indians were known generally as "Red Bones," a term often used in a derogatory manner; they also were sometimes identified as the "Smiling" or "Smilings" Indians and the "Goins Family" or "Goins Community" of Sumter County. Their mutual association would not be surprising since, according to research for the US Senate and the

Smithsonian Institution, the Sumter Red Bones were "a similar people" and "evidently of similar origin" and shared some of the same names as the Indians from North Carolina, particularly those from the Robeson County area. Over time, there developed some contention among factions in the Privateer area, and that may have contributed to their ultimate dispersal and disappearance about the turn of the century. (See Hodge 1912, 365; McPherson 1915, 7; Sider 2003, 74–78, 171; also consult Oxendine 1997, "Furman Papers," and "Redbone Nation".)

The relationship between the Turkish and Indian people has always been unclear and debatable. General Sumter's great-grandson, Thomas Sebastian Sumter (1852–1934), grew up in the Stateburg area and he insisted that the two groups never mixed. "It has been unfortunately, but nevertheless true," he wrote in the early 1900s, "that on account of their inherited dark complexions, they [the Turkish people] have been confused with that class of people known as Red Bones, scattered about in North and South Carolina, but this is entirely a mistake. They have never made any alliances, except with white people, as all of us know who are conversant with their history" (*Stateburg, 71*).

Charles James McDonald Furman (1863–1904), a respected history enthusiast, spent his life observing the Red Bones, who lived near his plantation in Sumter County, and he claimed that the Indians also kept to themselves. Writing in the 1890s, he estimated their number at about seventy to eighty, with their own school and church. He identified Tom Gibbes as the "spiritual head" of the group, and he listed their names as Chavises, Gibbeses, Goinses, Smilings, and some others. He considered them a peculiar gathering, of uncertain heritage, and "worthy of ethnological research." He wrote that "while these people are classed with the negroes, their features and color as a race show unmistakable evidence of white or Indian blood, or both"; and "as a people, they are if anything, more apart to themselves than are the Hebrews of our State" ("Furman Papers").

The most complete inquiry into the nature of the reclusive Turkish group in Dalzell—until our project—was a compilation of material for the Smithsonian Institution by contract scholar Wesley DuRant White Jr., almost a half century ago (1975, n.p.). White struggled, just as had others, to understand these mysterious people; and he raised as many questions as answers. But his collection of documentary material proved to be a very useful resource for our study.

Most important, White concluded that "Benengeli seems to have been a native of Turkey, and of Arabic descent"; and he acknowledged that Joseph was founder of the Dalzell community. He identified some of the key Turkish families as "Benenhaleys, Hoods, Oxendines, Rays, Scotts, and others." The Benenhaleys accounted for an overwhelming majority of his references, which derived from census, legal, and journalistic documents, and the rest of his statements mainly cited Oxendines. White seemed just as uncertain as many other analysts about the geographical and cultural relationship between the Turkish settlement and the nearby Indians. In one section of his report, he wrote: "The two communities never had anything to do with each other, any more than if they lived on different planets"; but, as will be noted shortly, he observed in another section that some of the Privateer group provided "Indian ancestry" to the Turkish community (White, 1975 n.p.).

Specific information in White's collection may seem trivial and confusing; but his general observations were historically consequential, such as his findings of Benenhaley dominance and Native American presence in the community. Perhaps most important for our project was his characterization of those Indians as a peculiar ancestral phenomenon: "They were probably American Indians not belonging to any tribe and completely acculturated . . . the only group that I know of of that description in the United States today who have absolutely no tradition whatever of Indian ancestry." Instead, he said, they traced their origins to "founders of the community from Turkey" and called themselves "Turks" or "white Turk-Americans (White 1975, n.p.)."

Writing under his Native American name two decades later, Wesley DuRant Taukchiray and coauthor Alice Bee Kasakoff revisited the ethnic issue of the Sumter County community "Contemporary Native Americans"(1992), and these scholars decided to exclude the Turkish people from their study of American Indians in South Carolina. They explained: "We do not discuss groups that some outsiders have speculated have Indian ancestry, such as the Sumter Turks near Dalzell. . . . The Sumter Turks do not concur that they are Indian and have said that they consider themselves to be 'white Turk Americans'" (73).

Both the Indians and Turkish people in Sumter County had endured a world of unpleasant realities and they struggled to survive as isolated settlements. Considering their proximity—and passage of the Indian Removal Act in 1830—it seems logical that certain members of the Indian group began drifting toward Dalzell and eventually became part of the Turkish community, which had been recognized as white people decades earlier. (See discussions of this idea in Hobson et al. 2010, 4–9; Steen 2012.) Eventually, in the early decades of the twentieth century, most of the Privateer settlers dispersed with many returning to North Carolina, where they hoped to merge with the Indians there and attend Indian schools established by the state. (See Gross 2008, 118–25; Sider 2003, 69–90; Taukchiray and Kasakoff 1992, 76.) The Red Bone Indians faded away as a distinct community, and today there is little documentary or physical evidence, other than a few surnames and tombstones, showing that they ever lived in this part of the country.

This author could find no evidence of the most common Red Bone surnames (Chavis, Gibbs, Goins, and Smiling) in the first century of the Turkish community's existence. However, census and genealogical reports indicate that roughly a dozen Oxendines, mostly women, married into the Dalzell group, and a few other individuals with names sometimes associated with Native American lineage—such as Scott, Buckner, Lowrey, Deas, and perhaps others—entered that Turkish settlement in the 1800s.

~ Benenhaleys and Oxendines ~

Closer analysis of the forces that were at play generations ago also provides insight and specific details about how the Turkish community's two most prominent families—the Benenhaleys and the Oxendines—may have hooked up back then. This chapter confirms the Benenhaleys as a "home-grown" family in this part of South Carolina ever since the patriarch appeared in the late 1700s; and the following account focuses on how the Oxendines arrived here and became part of the Turkish community.

A variety of sources provide an overview of Oxendine history in this area. For example, census and genealogical records indicate that the Oxendines were among the families who began relocating from Robeson County, North Carolina, to the Privateer area of Sumter County in the late 1700s and early 1800s. A few Oxendines began mixing and marrying into the Turkish people in the 1830s and 1840s; and several Oxendine families were settled near Stateburg by the 1860s. Also, the previously cited McDonald Furman—who based his work on personal observation—mentioned Oxendines along with the Chavises, Gibbeses, Goinses, and Smilings among surnames of the Privateer group in the 1890s; and an undated, handwritten document in his collection showed a "Jessey Oxendine" as a member of the Bethesda Baptist Church, attended by the Red Bones, in that area ("Furman Papers").

Additionally, a 1915 North Carolina Supreme Court case included trial testimony placing Oxendines among the Privateer Indians back in South Carolina (Sider 2003). Most Sumter County Indians had left Privateer and gone back to the Robeson County, North Carolina, area in hopes of attending the new public school for Indian children; but officials there challenged their right to attend that institution. What is important for our discussion is an exchange during the trial in which one of the South Carolinians mentioned Oxendines in the Privateer settlement: "Upon the direct examination of W. W. Goins . . . counsel for plaintiff asked the witness . . . 'What did Dr. Furman (meaning the same Dr. Furman who was a [white] neighbor of the plaintiff while they were living in Sumter County, SC) do toward establishing the fact that you were Indian people?'" Goins replied: "He traced up our origin and found out that we—our parents went from North Carolina, some of the older ones, and there was a lot of names, Oxendine, Hunt, Chavis, and Goins . . . he having traced them up first give me a little light and that was what I found out about it" (75).

Finally, Wesley White—whose examination of various documents has already been referenced—concluded that some of the Privateer Indians, specifically the Oxendines, had merged into the Turkish community in Dalzell generations ago. Writing in the 1970s, he said: "Since the largest family today (after the Benenhaleys, who seem to constitute at least half of the group) appears as that of the Oxendines, I will consider the Indian ancestry among the Sumter Turks today to have come from them." White also noted that there were "no Indian customs left and no members of entirely Indian ancestry" among the Oxendines in the Turkish community (1975, n.p.).

These historical findings raised an interesting and important point for our investigation. The Oxendines had established their physical presence and an Indian identity in this area before a few of them merged with the Benenhaleys. Therefore, while some Oxendines went on to become a core family of the Turkish settlement, not all of the Oxendines of Sumter County could be considered, automatically, as Turkish people; and resolving this issue was a critical and complex challenge in our next assignment, attempting to identify Turkish individuals in this area during the 1800s. We decided that, during the first half of the century, it depended mainly upon if and when individual Oxendines married or were born into that community; however, due to extensive intermarriage and the vagaries of history and records, we included most Oxendine descendants mentioned in connection with this group who had birthdays in the latter half of the century as members of that community (likely exaggerating the presence of that surname in our compilation). Such determinations would prove to be an arduous task; but it made sense to us. For the record, we employed the same strategy for the Rays, Hoods, Buckners, Lowreys, and other surnames in that inventory; but calculations for those families were relatively simple compared to the situation with the Oxendines. Thus it seems reasonable that Privateer may have been the geographical pivot point from North Carolina to Dalzell for the Oxendines; and the Indian Removal Act could have been the historical impetus for some of them marrying into the Benenhaleys. Isolation and adversity likely forged these and other family groupings together as a communal society centered in the Dalzell area in the late 1800s. Ever since, the Benenhaleys and Oxendines have served as leading families among the Turkish people of Sumter County.

~ Enduring, Distinct Turkish Community ~

The idea of conjoined lineages helps explain the hazy history of the Turkish people, and various sources over the years have shown how some individuals of Native American descent merged into the Dalzell community. But readers should understand that these findings do not negate the legend of Joseph Benenhaley or significantly alter the Turkish traditional narrative.

It is understandable that some members of the Turkish community now question the traditional narrative and are proclaiming a new ancestral identity. In an interview with the *State* during the 2013 application process, Cheraw chief Ralph Justice Oxendine commented on the difficult history of his people: "We had to hide our identity—to be someone, to be able to own land, to be able to vote, to be a person"; and he stressed the importance of official recognition in a discussion during that time with the South Carolina Radio Network (Nov. 22, 2013): "We will be recognized as a real people. Not a tri-racial people, but one people. We know now. We have documentation. People can ask us and we can quickly pull out our records and show who we are and go way back all the way to 1500." Claudia Benenhaley Gainey, Cheraw tribal secretary at that time, who compiled most of the research for certification of the Sumter group, proudly announced this recognition on their website (Gainey): "On November 22, 2013, we were officially recognized as the 8th state recognized Native American Indian Tribe in South Carolina. The Sumter Tribe of Cheraw Indians."

Interestingly, as a result of their confusing background, some living members of this community now enjoy dual or multicultural ancestries. Most can continue to assert, with confidence, their Turkish identity; others are free to celebrate their Indian legacy; and some undoubtedly will argue forever about jumbled heritages. It would be helpful if scholars, journalists, genealogists, and activists were more careful to avoid undue partisanship; and partisans should adopt the prudent balance of loyalty and tolerance as expressed by two leaders in the Turkish and Native American communities. Former Long Branch pastor Eleazer Benenhaley expressed his sentiments thusly in 2008: "If an Oxendine can prove that his family came from North Carolina and wants to be called a Lumbee Indian, that is his right.... But as for me, I trust the oral tradition of my grandmother and those before her" (2008, 30, 36). On the other hand, Mandy Oxendine Chapman, a former chief of the Sumter Band of Cheraw Indians, observed in an interview with Robert Baker of *The Item (2006):* "While the tribe members are very proud of their culture, no one disparaged those of Turkish descent who might be living in the area. If there was any Arabic blood, I'm not aware of it. But if there is, I'm not ashamed of that. Our Indian heritage is the main concern in this tribe."

Despite the Cheraw Indians' newfound standing as a certified tribe, the voluminous documentation of historical evidence recounted in this book demonstrates that most members of the Dalzell community considered themselves a people of cultural commonality throughout their long existence in that area. They retained their identity as a people of Arabic descent and they went by the collective name of "the Turks."

In sum, different bloodlines mixed in Dalzell. The available record shows that some individuals of Native American ancestry subsumed—physically, socially, and culturally—into the Turkish settlement. But our reading and research of that record, along with the work of reputable analysts, clearly demonstrates that this group survived as an enduring, distinct Turkish community in rural South Carolina for almost two centuries. Thus these continuities—persistent identity as a people of Arab descent and prolonged existence as a social subculture—stand as both historical realities and central foundations of the traditional narrative, regardless of whether and when some individuals of different ancestry entered or exited the community. Having resolved the Indian issue, we began focusing on Joseph Benenhaley's life in Sumter County.

~ Discovering New Evidence ~

Fortuitously, early in our investigation, some startling new documents landed in our laps— that is, an early land plat signed by a hero of the Revolutionary War, and a surprising series of letters written by an intriguing and heretofore unacknowledged member of the Turkish community.

Thomas Sumter's Deed and Survey

According to conventional accounts, there was nothing to substantiate a relationship between Thomas Sumter and Joseph Benenhaley, and many skeptics had speculated that Benenhaley just squatted, like countless others, on the general's land. This depiction of Joseph Benenhaley as a squatter bears detailed discussion, because it undermines both his stature and the traditional narrative. It is based on a handwritten letter in the Draper Manuscripts Collection that referred to the relationship between General Sumter and his tenants (Draper Manuscripts Collection, "Thomas Sumter Papers," 2VV87).

On March 31, 1873, a Mr. Moody, aged 81, dictated his recollections to R. Thompson, who then mailed the letter to Lyman Draper for his collection. Moody said that he was a young man during the last fifteen years of Sumter's life, and he had no business or social intercourse of a special kind with Sumter, so he apologized for having so little to offer to Draper. However, based on what he "used to hear," the old-timer offered the following commentary: "The old General had many poor people living and squatting on his land to whom he was kind—never turning any off. He was good in giving money and medicine to them and was ready to do favors when approached in the right way. He had amongst his tenants a number of Indians, half-breeds, and indolent and unthrifty people—selling for liquor probably whatever they made." The elderly man went on to talk about General Sumter gathering and storing his tenants' crops in his barn because, in his recollection of Sumter's attitude: "Damn it, I shall have to feed them any how, and they would only waste it."

Unfortunately, some have related those remarks specifically to Joseph Benenhaley, John Scott, and the Turkish community. Never mind that the general owned several hundred thousand acres of land in South Carolina and North Carolina; and countless people—white settlers, Native Americans, and who knows who else—lived on that land. Inexplicably, for example, Robert Bass wrote the following in his biography of the Gamecock (1961), citing "Draper, 2VV87" as his only source for "the story of Sumter and his Turkish tenants": "After the revolution, John Scott and Yusef ben Ali squatted on his land near Home House.... But by tradition and training neither Scott nor Ben Ali was a farmer. In the fall Sumter would harvest their scattering crops and store them in his own barns. When a neighbor asked his reason, he replied testily, 'Damn it, they'd only waste it. I shall have to feed them anyhow!'" (237, 274).

A close examination of Mr. Moody's scribbled, seven-page document in the Draper Manuscripts reveals no mention of Scott, Benenhaley, or the Turkish people in that statement, which comprised the entirety of "Draper, 2VV87." Therefore, it was incorrect to direct the negative recollections of the old-timer to the Turkish community. However, that colorful tale has stuck around and is still repeated in historical conversations.

Family tradition is that Thomas Sumter originally and verbally gave property to his friend without a deed; but, as Sumter aged, Joseph Benenhaley became concerned that, should the general die, then white people would attempt to take the Benenhaley family's land. Hence, the story goes, Benenhaley asked and Sumter officially deeded the property to him. After Joseph Benenhaley's death in the 1820s, the "papers" were passed down among family members; however, according to our sources, those documents were lost somewhere along the line. Fortunately for our project, Greg Thompson spent many days searching files in the courthouse basement, and he found several documents and references that supported the traditional narrative.

The most convincing evidence was an 1815 land plat of a portion of Thomas Sumter's property. This plat, found in the Sumter County Office of Mesne Conveyances, consisted of a survey that was requested and signed by General Sumter and used in the conveyance of 219 acres sold by him to Julia Vaughn in that same year. "Josephs Land" was clearly marked near the bottom of the following enhanced excerpt, showing exactly where Benenhaley was supposed to have settled and lived near Long Branch (Deed Book DD, 35, 36).

Decades after Benenhaley's death, the Sumter County Probate Court corroborated the deeding of this property to him. Numerous family members had used the land in common after Benenhaley's death and desired to divide the property. The court summoned over a dozen heirs in 1874, and the record included reference to an 1815 deed conveying the land from Thomas Sumter to Joseph Benenhaley. That document described the homestead as "Real Estate of Joseph Bennenhally, deceased, situate in said County on waters of Black River, and containing thirty three acres (33) more or less, originally granted to said Joseph Bennenhally by Thomas Sumter by Deed dated November 1815" (Bundle 171, pkg 30, "Summons in Partition"). Thereafter, Benenhaley descendant right to this land was never challenged.

A third legal document of importance for our project was an 1869 land sale filing. Julia Vaughn's son, John N. Frierson, sold a ten-acre portion of the family's

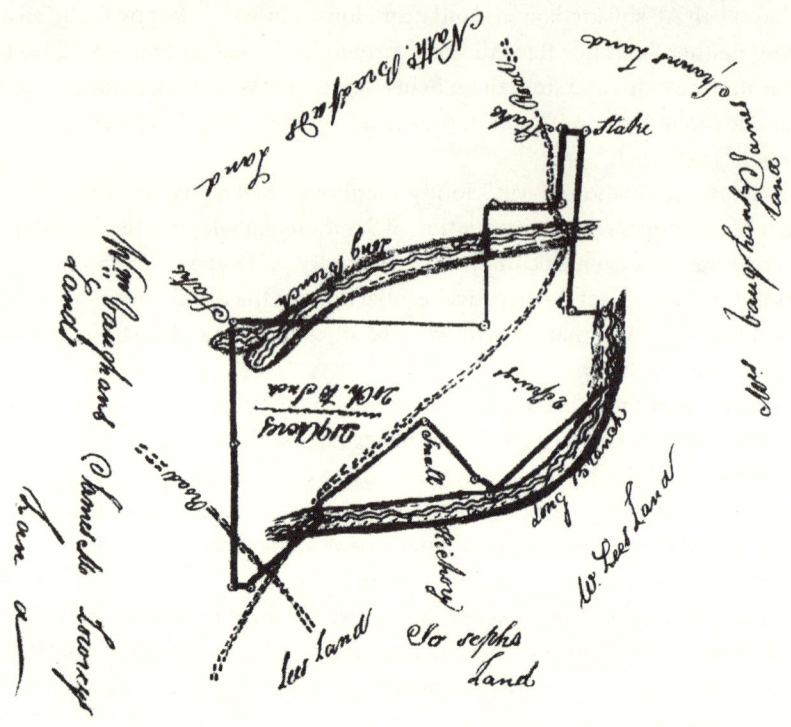

Excerpt of a survey plat dated 1815 that was requested and signed by General Thomas Sumter, with "Josephs Land" clearly marked in the lower part of the plat. Courtesy of the Sumter County Office of Mesne Conveyances (Deed Book DD, pp. 35, 36).

holdings to Jensey Ray, daughter of Joseph Benenhaley (Deed Book WW, 185). The significance of this registered transaction was its timing and location. The first "Turk School" and "Turk Church" were constructed on this tract, which lay adjacent to "Benenhali's Land" and the original Ottoman homesite.

Other court transactions substantiated Benenhaley and Turkish ownership of this property during the 1800s. For example, the original land was also resurveyed in 1833 and recorded in 1852 with the original "Josephs Land" designated as "Turk" property (Deed Book O, 413). Also, in 1871, another sale (Deed Book T, 550) depicted "Benenhaley's Land" in that location; and separate actions listed the property as "Benenhaley Land" in 1890 and owned by Benenhaley relatives in 1893 (Deed Book CCC, 522, 523).

These legal documents were critically important because they represented the only official public records that we had found—other than census lists—relating to Joseph Benenhaley, and they provided strong evidentiary support—historically and geographically—for the Turkish people's oral history. They suggested that Benenhaley enjoyed a special relationship with General Thomas Sumter, presumably from his service to the Gamecock in the Revolutionary War; and that friendship played a major role in the history of this settlement. They also designated Benenhaley as the central figure in the Turkish community.

Certainly, this was powerful corroborating evidence—that is, General Sumter's legal deeding of the property and his handwritten signature on a survey plat, plus other court documents attesting to Joseph Benenhaley's ownership of land precisely where and when the Turkish people were establishing their community. These official papers also provided strong precedent for more personalized documentation—Matilda Ellison Benenhaley's handwritten correspondence—regarding the Benenhaley saga.

Matilda's Letters

Matilda Ellison (1842–1936) is a vital character in the tale of Joseph Benenhaley and the Turkish people. She was the granddaughter of William Ellison—a "light-skinned mulatto" and freed former slave who was a prominent businessman and slave-owner in the Stateburg area from 1810–1861 (Johnson and Roark, *Black Masters*, 1984, and *No Chariot Let Down* 2001). The Ellison family had maintained a friendly relationship with both white and Turkish people; and Matilda, who was well-educated in Charleston and lived a young life of luxury, broke from her family and married into the Turkish community in the 1870s.

Matilda Ellison Benenhaley (1842–1936), granddaughter of a prominent mulatto slave owner, as a young woman. Matilda married Lawrence "Curly" Benenhaley (1848–1923) in the 1870s. She contributed no children to the bloodline, but her personal correspondence outlined the life of the Ottoman Turk in accord with the traditional narrative. Tintype circa the latter half of the 1800s. Courtesy of Greg Thompson Collection, donated to the collection by Isaac Benenhaley/David Peagler.

Matilda Ellison Benenhaley had no children and therefore never contributed to the community bloodline; however, she played an important role in the Benenhaley story because she wrote several letters of historical significance—the first one in 1870 and the last one in 1934. Her seven letters were kept among treasured items by Benenhaley relatives for generations.

Matilda was well-positioned to have gained information and insights from her grandfather, William Ellison, a close associate of both the Benenhaleys and the Sumters during the early 1800s. She would have been about nineteen years old when her grandfather Ellison passed away; and she would have known Joseph Benenhaley's wife Elizabeth and Joseph Benenhaley's daughter Jensey. Also, she grew up amid the children and other surviving members of both the Benenhaley and Sumter families.

Lawrence "Curly" Benenhaley (1848–1923), great-grandson of the patriarch and husband of Matilda Ellison Benenhaley (1842–1936). Tintype circa the latter half of the 1800s. Courtesy of Greg Thompson Collection, donated to the collection by Isaac Benenhaley/David Peagler.

Matilda's correspondence added original and authoritative testimony to the traditional narrative—complete with references to the progenitor's Ottoman background, his enslavement in the Caribbean, his alliance with General Sumter, his service in the Revolutionary War, and his settling in rural Sumter County. In short, as will be related in the next few pages, she provided convincing testimony to the tale of the original Turk in her personal written communications.

The first of several emotional letters was dated May 5, 1870, when the twenty-eight-year-old Matilda wrote to confidant Sarah Oxendine Buckner that Lawrence Benenhaley, her secret Turkish suitor, should not ask her father for permission to call on her: "Do tell Mr. Lawrence I received his inquiry, however to be called upon would never be permitted. Please advise discreetly as father must not be made aware of his intentions for he is displeased with any who simply labour." Subsequently, the two married and her father cut off Matilda from their family circle and financial support. Her life with Lawrence—who was known as "Curly"—was far removed from her privileged upbringing in the Ellison mansion and cultured environs of mulatto society in Charleston.

A half century later, in 1923, Curly died, and Matilda wrote a desperate plea to one of her late husband's relatives and friends, Noah Benenhaley. At eighty-one years of age, she begged to be allowed to live her last days among friends. She had realized a financial and property benefit—including Keith Hill plantation—from a settlement of the Ellison estate; and she offered to pay for her keep in Noah's household:

Mr. Noah,

I humbly beg your consideration of my earlier proposal. I respectfully request your making allowance for my care. Since Curly passed I have none left to attend me in my time of need. You have always presented yourself as an honorable and Christian man and your testimony speaks greatly in regards to your character. You were one of the few to stand present at our union. You accepted me without reservation and provided assistance during Curly's last breaths. I make only a few requests, that you promise to use your stature within the church to secure a final resting place next to my beloved Curly and also that you make the provisions for my care. . . . My life I know is almost at an end and I pray for your care on the balance.

Respectfully,

Matilda Benenhaley

Noah and Rosa (aka Rose) Benenhaley accepted Matilda into their home and treated her with compassion as one of their family. About a decade later, in 1934, Matilda wrote a final, heart-wrenching letter that rightly belongs among the classics of romantic and historical literature. The ninety-two-year-old Matilda, then close to departing this world, addressed the following farewell message to Noah's children and grandchildren, with whom she had found refuge in old age. Readers should recall that "my grandfather" was William Ellison, the former slave; "Mr. Noah's grandfather" was Joseph Benenhaley; "Frenchie" was John Scott; "She and Old Eliz" were Joseph Benenhaley's wives; and "Old Mrs. Jensey" was Joseph Benenhaley's daughter. Also, the "tins" mentioned in this letter were an early type of photography that had been arranged and paid for by Matilda so that future generations of Turkish people might know something about their ancestors; therefore, we have available the portraits of Matilda and the Benenhaley family presented in this book. Here is her final letter, written in 1934:

Dearest Children:

I pen these words for Mr. Noah's keeping. Time will recall not the ramblings of an old woman but pieces of a life for preservation. I have witnessed much in my day and lived on both sides of the Old Hills beginning in finery at my Hall and passing in homespun on anothers. I bore witness to both field days and wars and to the destruction of my beloved Charleston. There are none left to claim me save the good Lord as my relations turned long ago. You dear ones are my family now and to your grandfathers patience and generosity I am much indebted. As my final gifts to you I wish to give you these words and tins. As my grandfather was once bonded by the overseer and kept from freedom on a plantation also was your Mr. Noah's grandfather an Ottoman bonded by the Spanish at sea and kept from freedom in the Indies. Both persevered a trade and were made free which brings me to my current words. Hold close these words and the stories told by the others under the Old Oak. Mr. Noah knows these stories well having heard them many times. Old Mrs. Jensey told how he and Frenchie came to old Charleston from the Indies. He was a tradesman and agreed upon service with General Sumter in the War or Revolution in exchange for a homestead as he had no other. Serving well as his wheelwright he returned with the Old General after the war and was given the Home Place on the Branch where your grandfather keeps his grave to this day. Your namesake was a wainwright freed by the Spanish after bonded. He married twice to fair women the first passing as barren as I. She and Old Eliz. are both buried on the Home Place. Eliz and relations came across the ferry from Columbia. Old Joes Ottoman features passed down to your grandfather and to your Maybelle and Murray. Fret not the words of the neighbor for they have received their due as all have fallen planter and field hand alike. . . . Ample times such as the early days ended with the war of Secession. Forsake not your studies to toil in the fields. Apprentice a trade as my grandfather and Mr. Noah's grandfather before us. Rely not on the good fortunes of others as they too may dwindle. Love the Lord and your Church and not be dissuaded by the goings as of late. I leave you with these papers and tins to keep and remember. Hold fast to my image young and old alike and keep these words close. I know not my final resting place, but do promise to keep my grave as your grandfather keeps the graves of the elders. With fondest memories I will always be,

Aunt Till

A year or so after writing this last letter, Matilda passed away. Noah and Rosa waited until nightfall; and, in keeping with her request, they secretly buried her next to Lawrence Benenhaley in the cemetery of Long Branch Baptist Church. Their two graves were unmarked, due to strong feelings of the time. Most in the community still don't know the full story; but those who do accept this tragic woman's right to rest in peace beside her "beloved Curly."

Noah Benenhaley (1860–1939), grandson of the patriarch. This charcoal portrait likely was sketched in the 1880s by an unknown traveling artist. Courtesy of Greg Thompson Collection, donated to the collection by Isaac Benenhaley/ David Peagler.

That final chapter in Matilda Ellison Benenhaley's life was related almost a century later by Isaac Benenhaley, a great-great-grandson of the original Benenhaley and one of the "Dearest Children" to whom the last letter had been written in 1934. Known as "Big Ike," Isaac was the last family member entrusted with this treasure of letters, photos, and other keepsakes. He was a World War II veteran who had gone often as a child with his grandfather, Noah Benenhaley, to help tend the gravesite of the forefather and his family. Isaac shared his memories and mementoes with Greg Thompson, who had married into the family and hoped to write their history. Fortunately, he allowed Thompson to photograph Matilda's letters, which could not be found among other treasured items in his home when he died in 2011 (Thompson Collection and Interviews).

Rosa Benenhaley (1857–1937), great–granddaughter of the patriarch. This charcoal portrait likely was sketched in the 1880s by a traveling artist. Courtesy of Greg Thompson collection, donated to the collection by Isaac Benenhaley/David Peagler.

Our recounting of the story of Joseph Benenhaley and the Turkish people would be woefully deficient without acknowledging Matilda's contributions to the effort. For example, besides the letters cited in this section, she was responsible for the tintypes of Turkish people displayed in our photo section. Keen viewers might notice that two of the male descendants wore the same new suit. The explanation, as related to us by Thompson, is that Matilda arranged and paid for that suit and those images so that future generations might appreciate her friends and adopted family. Matilda's letters represented dramatic new revelations and potent testimony about the Ottoman origins of Joseph Benenhaley, his relationship with Thomas Sumter, and his revered standing in the early history of the Dalzell settlement.

The newly discovered land plat and letters thus added essential information and validity to the Benenhaley saga and led to the next and most difficult aspect of this project, investigating Joseph Benenhaley's life as founder and progenitor of the Turkish community in Sumter County.

~ Compiling the Genealogical Record ~

Unlike other founding fathers of history, Benenhaley kept no diary or personal writings, and no other contemporaneous sources chronicled him as progenitor of his community. If we were ever going to know the full story, we would have to recreate the genealogical record as best we could, as a retrospective indicator of his role in the origin and lineage of the Turkish settlement. Thus we attempted to compile documents and data validating Joseph Benenhaley as founder of the community and forefather of the Turkish people.

Isaac Benenhaley (1927–2011), who served in the US Navy during World War II. Known as "Big Ike," he provided valuable information and other material used in this book. Courtesy of the Greg Thompson Collection. Photograph donated to the collection by Isaac Benenhaley/David Peagler.

~ Founding and Forefathering ~

Validating Benenhaley's historical role was a time-consuming but straightforward process of stating our assumptions, reviewing available literature, researching limited sources, developing new data, and assessing evident history. We had discovered and discussed important documents—such as General Sumter's legal papers and Matilda's letters—clearly pointing to him as the single candidate for this honor; and ancestral analyses of varying nature presented throughout this manuscript substantiate his primordial place in the family tree.

The remaining task here was simply elaborating the chronological how and why of Joseph Benenhaley's prominence as the group commenced in rural South Carolina. The authors had started with Joseph Benenhaley, John Scott, and their wives as the first generation during the waning years of the eighteenth century; but historical, census, and genealogical records shifted our attention to Joseph Benenhaley early in the investigation.

Benenhaley and Scott apparently married white European sisters surnamed Graham and settled in the Dalzell area. Benenhaley's first wife died without bearing any children, and he then married Elizabeth Miller, another white woman, from Columbia, South Carolina, who eventually had as many as nine and possibly eleven children. The litany of immediate family names, spellings, and dates of birth, as best as can be estimated from census records and other sources, was as follows. Joseph Benenhaley was recorded as a resident of Sumter District in both the 1810 and 1820 censuses. He was listed as head of a household of seven persons in 1810, most likely himself, his wife Elizabeth Miller Benenhaley, his mother-in-law Mrs. Miller, a son Francis (1802), a daughter Sophronia, or Sophonia (1804), a son Joseph II, or Joseph Jr. (1805), and a daughter Catherine, or Katie (1808). He appeared again in 1820 as head of a household of twelve persons, which likely included the original seven plus a daughter Leo Cadeo or Cadia (1810), a daughter Jensey or Jency (1817), a son Lyrander or Lysander (1819), and two unidentified daughters born about 1813 and 1815 (however no evidence has been found specifically confirming the last two births or what may have happened to those two children). Later censuses—1840, 1850, and 1860—indicate that Joseph and Elizabeth then had a daughter Isabella (1824) and a son Ferdinand (1825). Although oral history dates Joseph's death as "about 1823," it seems that he probably died sometime later in the 1820s. Certainly, available records are problematic; and these names, spellings, and dates are speculative. However, this is a reasonable approximation of the original Turkish family. We detected no listing for Yusef ben Ali in any official report; and we believe that the census presence of "Joseph Benenhaley" was due to the fact that this was the name he used in everyday life in Dalzell.

Readers likely are wondering about our decision to focus on Benenhaley instead of the man called Scott, since they show up in the traditional narrative as a team, first as recruits for Thomas Sumter's militia then as recipients of the General's personal blessing as "white men," and finally as original settlers in the Turkish community. Therefore, we will deviate from Joseph's saga and try to explain why we chose Benenhaley and what we know about Scott. This decision was based mainly on the fact that our key definitional proposition established Joseph Benenhaley's lineage as the basis of the Turkish community. That was a simple, logical presumption based on our understanding of the traditional narrative. Also, there was nothing in the available record attesting to John Scott's background and role in the evolving Turkish community.

There are reports that Scott was of French descent; however, his claimed name and ethnicity have always been viewed with suspicion by historians. He, like Joseph Benenhaley, may have been a victim of Old World conflict, perhaps also an Ottoman, who landed among the white Europeans, black Africans, and Native American Indians of the New World. Indeed, Thomas Sebastian Sumter described Scott, like Benenhaley, as a dark-complexioned man of unclear background (*Stateburg* 1920, 43–44); and Matilda Ellison Benenhaley wrote in her 1934 letter that both individuals "came to old Charleston from the Indies." Historian Robert Bass referred to the two recruits as "corsairs . . . from the Barbary Coast" (*Gamecock* 1961, 78), and historian Charles Bracelen Flood described them as "Arabs" and "North Africans" (*Rise and Fight Again* 1976, 312).

The following is an unconfirmed account of the immediate family of the man called Scott. Reputedly, he married a white European named Graham, the sister of Benenhaley's first wife, and the couple had three daughters. Two of them supposedly married into the Benenhaleys; the third daughter was rumored to have had a child who was not named or raised as a Scott in this community. Apparently, Scott's suspect surname "daughtered out" and his bloodline quickly flowed into the Benenhaley family lineage. Some have attempted to link the man of our interest to Scotts who were residing in Sumter County of that time; and census records indicate that some Scotts married into the Turkish settlement in later years. However, no evidence has surfaced credibly tying any of these people to the legendary individual who called himself Scott. It is also interesting to note that a sworn deposition by a Turkish plaintiff during the 1950s integration case states that "All Scotts have long since departed from the community in which our group lives" ("Hood v. Board of Trustees" 1953).

In sum, John Scott's story is masked in uncertainty and intrigue—much more so than that of Benenhaley. Aside from the few references recounted here, no other documents have been found that provide authoritative information or shed further light on him as the person who paired with Benenhaley in the early years of this community drama. Perhaps there are documents somewhere that might enlarge the story, and those records would be welcomed. Until then, it must be noted that John Scott's uncertain surname has not been accorded core family stature in the early history of the Turkish people.

As will be shown in the next few pages, we had more reliable markers for Joseph Benenhaley as the originating personage in this community. We also can affirm from federal censuses and genealogical reports that several additional surnames—the Oxendines, Rays, Deases, Hursts, and Taylors—entered the mix in the second generation, and others thereafter. However, according to various historical sources reported in this manuscript, the Benenhaley brand continued its prevalence in the group; and the members of the Turkish community—including those who "married in"—considered Joseph Benenhaley their ancestral leader, identified themselves as people of Turkish descent, and lived apart from white and black people. Many in the outside world called them, collectively, "the Benenhaleys" or, simply and often derisively, "the Turks."

~ Master List ~

The next step was evidencing Joseph Benenhaley's role—more precisely and quantitatively—in the lineage and expanding population of the Turkish community. The authors ambitiously attempted to assemble a "master list" of Turkish persons who lived during the 1800s so that we might trace and assess Benenhaley's paternal impact. It was thought that the first century would give a useful profile of the early group and provide insights into the formative generations of this community. Many months were dedicated to diagramming the growth of this settlement, and the US Census was the primary source in this effort. Getting the right information was tedious and time-consuming; but these decennial counts provided the standard source of information about Joseph Benenhaley and his expanding communal family.

Family histories—accessed through websites such as www.ancestry.com and www.familysearch.org, online discussion forums, and conversations with members of the community—also proved a valuable source of information about the Turkish people's genealogical tree in the formative century. Despite a clutter of baseless claims and constant bickering, these records helped sketch Joseph Benenhaley's place in the lineage of this community. Once becoming proficient in mining census and family data, we began combining these and other sources, such as legal reports, historical accounts, and vital records, into a master list of Turkish people in Sumter County during the 1800s.

The first several decades and generations involved few people, but the lineage was hard to document, because the census count of that time showed only the name of the head of household and did not list the names of other family members. However, by consulting later censuses and private records, details for the young family tree were filled in. The inventory got more complex in the fourth generation because of the increasing population of the group and the aforementioned lack of documentation. Fortunately, the US Census began listing all individuals by name in 1850, making it somewhat easier to trace the community lineage thereafter.

Joseph Benenhaley's household of seven persons was the beginning of the line in the first decade of the century, and John Scott's family quickly merged with the Benenhaleys in the early years. Records indicate that the other prominent surnames married into the group in staggered manner. First came the Oxendines in the 1830s, then the Rays in the 1840s, the Hoods and Lowreys in the 1870s, and the Buckners in the 1880s. Among the specific individuals who married in and contributed significantly to the lineage during that century—as best as can be determined and with some uncertainty regarding exact names—were the following people, listed in rough chronology: Catherine Scott (Joseph Benenhaley II/Jr.), Sarah Scott (Francis Benenhaley), Thomas Oxendine (Catherine/Katie Benenhaley), Sarah Hurst (Lyrander/Lysander Benenhaley), Washington Oxendine (Isabella Benenhaley), Elizabeth Scott (Ferdinand Benenhaley), Charles W. Oxendine (Eliphare Benenhaley), James Ray Sr. (Jensey/Jency Benenhaley), Reese Hood Sr. (Martha Ann Benenhaley), Robert Columbus Lowrey (Alice Benenhaley), Charles Wilson Buckner (Blanche Benenhaley), and Samuel Buckner Sr. (Virginia Benenhaley).

Decennial US Censuses and other records showed that the group absorbed well over a dozen surnames during the 1800s and the community's numbers increased steadily. A rough estimate—based on calculations from available documents—indicates that the settlement grew by six people in the 1810s, three in the 1820s, about fifteen in the 1830s, about thirty in the 1840s, about twenty-five in the 1850s, about twenty in the 1860s, about forty in the 1870s, about fifty in the 1880s, and about sixty in the 1890s. It was not possible to determine dates of birth for all individuals, so everyone could not be plugged neatly into this chronology, and some of the early individuals passed away or left the area during those decades.

Eventually, 270 individuals were identified who were confirmed or were likely to have been born or married into the Turkish community of Sumter County during the 1800s. Most of them were identified conclusively in more than one reputable historical document (such as census reports, vital records, obituaries, and cemetery interments), and some were sufficiently likely as indicated by one of these documents and/or other acceptable sources to have been part of the extended Turkish lineage during the studied period. The authors believe that this list includes almost all Turkish people who lived in this community during that formative century. Additionally, we attempted to compile family relationships for as many persons as possible; however we had less confidence in the accuracy of that compilation.

Admittedly, this community list has its faults. The normal problems of census and genealogical research always require caution as mentioned previously. It is impossible to devise an exact recreation of any community stretching back two centuries. This was particularly true of the Turkish people of that era, whose common surnames and repetitive use of given names obscured precise tracking and whose dynamics of intermarriage, remarriage, and reclusive ways defied full deciphering of their lineage. Such connections among individuals were complicated and represented informed speculation in many cases, due to unclear records. Also, this "piecemeal" inventory may have missed some households; and some people may have left the area and settled elsewhere. Finally, this list (drawn mainly from US Census reports for Sumter County rather than limited to the Dalzell area) probably included some individuals who shared names now considered part of the Turkish community but who actually were not part of the targeted group. We can assume that any Benenhaley in Sumter County during the 1800s was a member. However, individuals of other surnames commonly associated—such as Oxendine, Ray, Hood, Buckner, and Lowrey—could have been members of unassociated families who happened to reside in Sumter County during those times. Consequently, it was necessary to sort out these other individuals; and our master list may have overcounted or undercounted these names. In sum, it is not a perfect compilation. But it approximates the totality of the group in numbers and names and we consider it a true representation of the familial community during that century.

Analysis of this master list conveyed a clear conclusion. Joseph Benenhaley exercised original, continuing, dominant influence on the lineage throughout the first century. In fact, according to simple birth surnames, the Benenhaleys represented slightly over half (51 percent) of the individuals identified in the 1800s, followed by the Oxendines (21 percent), Rays (8 percent), Hoods (5 percent), Buckners (4 percent), and Lowreys (2 percent); and these six family surnames accounted for 92 percent of the list.

Family and relatives of Noah Benenhaley (1860–1939). Noah was a grandson and his wife Rosa was a great–granddaughter of the patriarch. This photograph was taken at their farm home in 1903. *Left to right:* son, Jesse Noah/Noah Jr. (1896–1960); father, Noah; his daughter Maybelle (1898–1972); his wife, Rosa Benenhaley (1857–1937); his nephew Joseph W. Benenhaley (1882–1921); and his daughters Alberta (1886–1972), Florence (1882–1954), and Etta (1889–1961). Courtesy of Greg Thompson Collection, donated to the collection by Isaac Benenhaley/David Peagler.

Martha Ann Benenhaley Hood (1855–1919), granddaughter of the patriarch, and her niece Martha Jane Oxendine Benenhaley (1866–1951), great-granddaughter of the patriarch. Photograph circa 1914. Courtesy of Greg Thompson Collection. This copy of the photograph was donated to the collection by Isaac Benenhaley/David Peagler.

John Benenhaley (1853–1923), great-grandson of the patriarch. Tintype circa the latter half of the 1800s. Courtesy of Greg Thompson Collection, donated to the collection by Isaac Benenhaley/David Peagler.

The family of William Joseph Benenhaley (1858–1920) and his wife Cathreen Oxendine Benenhaley (1863–1934). William was a great-grandson and Cathreen was a great-granddaugter of the patriarch. This photograph was taken in 1905 at their family farm. *Left to right:* William Jr. (1884–1942), Martha (1888–1917), Annie (1898–?), Katie (1899–1965), Mary Magdalene (1894–1971), Dolly (1900–1992), baby Nora (1902–1970), father William Joseph Benenhaley, William Moses (1895–1950), Edward (1891–1952), mother Cathreen Oendine Benenhaley, baby Soloman (1904–1967), and Aaron (1891–1929). Courtesy of the Greg Thompson Collection, donated to the collection by Isaac Benenhaley/David Peagler.

The two youngest children born to Noah and Rosa Benenhaley. Jesse Noah/Noah Jr. (1896–1960) on the left and Maybelle (1898–1972) on the right. Photograph circa the early 1900s. Courtesy of Greg Thompson Collection, donated to the collection by Isaac Benenhaley/David Peagler.

Great-great-grandchildren of the patriarch: Isaac Benenhaley (1927–2011) and his sisters Leah (1931–2008) on the left and Lillie (1933–2005) on the right, circa 1940. Courtesy of the Greg Thompson Collection, donated to the collection by Isaac Benenhaley/David Peagler.

~ Cemetery Records ~

In addition to charting the Turkish population for the 1800s through census and related reports, we decided to examine paternal influence for the 1800s and 1900s through an alternative research strategy. Our thinking was that a different and perhaps truer grasp could be obtained of the Turkish community and we culd determine Joseph Benenhaley's impact on the lineage of the Turkish people by visiting church cemeteries in the area. This was a close-knit community; the church was the most important social and cultural institution for them; and interment in the church cemetery was a mutual matter of personal affinity for the group and group embracement of deceased individuals. Therefore, what better definition of the community existed than an inventory of individuals who deemed to be buried and were accepted for burial where the Turkish people attended religious services and interred their loved ones? And what better indication of Joseph Benenhaley's paternal role could be fashioned than the measured presence of his surname on the headstones in those cemeteries?

Of course, early generations of Turkish people usually buried their dead at isolated home sites or in family plots that have been forgotten with time. In fact, the patriarch himself rests in an unknown grave. Ironically, there is no written documentation regarding the death of Joseph Benenhaley; nor is there a grave marked with his name in any cemetery in the area. Apparently, he was buried near his family home, the exact location of which has faded over the years. His final burial ground thus has been as much a mystery as the origins of the man himself.

However, readers will be interested to know that we think we have found the general area of his final resting place. According to Greg Thompson, an older Turkish friend—Isaac Benenhaley—then in his eighties, stated that he used to hunt the area as a boy and was always told that the land was "hallowed ground" due to Joseph Benenhaley being buried there. Years later, Isaac Benenhaley also reiterated stories—congruent with the words of Matilda Ellison's letter—that his grandfather, as a child, saw and helped others tend to the gravesite in a field on the Benenhaley property. Isaac's grandfather, Noah Benenhaley, continued to take care of the gravesite until the property was lost at a tax auction in the early 1900s.

On one of our visits to the community, the authors explored the historic area with Greg Thompson, and he took us to the site where, as related by Isaac, Joseph Benenhaley was buried. The property location matches the 1815 survey plat on record at the Sumter County courthouse that references "Josephs Land." Unfortunately, bulldozers involved in the construction of Shaw Air Force base's "5000 Housing Area" would have obliterated any signs of the original patriarch's grave and that of early Benenhaleys buried there. Now, all that one finds on that land is a base convenience store and a military housing maintenance facility at the front of the property and a forested area on the back of the field. Having chased Joseph

Benenhaley through cyberspace across several continents and centuries, we experienced a personal sense of satisfaction and reverence in visiting and taking some photographs at the unmarked burial ground of this mysterious gentleman.

Eventually, the Turkish people established church graveyards for deceased relatives. So the authors focused on cemeteries of the two churches that have served as principal houses of worship for the Turkish people—Long Branch Baptist Church, founded in 1904, and Springbank Baptist Church, founded in 1971—where burials included departed relatives with births dating from 1841 through recent times. Another church in the area, the High Hills of Santee Baptist Church, was a predominantly white congregation that had accommodated some black and Turkish people during the 1800s; but membership rolls and cemetery headstones there revealed very few Turkish names.

The cemetery behind Long Branch Baptist Church is filled mainly with the graves of Turkish family members. Photograph provided by Glen Browder.

Wandering through the Long Branch and Springbank cemeteries provided an impressive visual display of headstones—with "Benenhaley" inscriptions here, there, and everywhere. More statistically impressive was the detailed enumeration of graves, precisely documenting Benenhaley's paternal dominance over many generations. A computerized file of cemetery interments (www.findagrave.com) covered almost all the graves at the two churches; and it included the names of close to five hundred deceased individuals—369 at Long Branch and 122 at Springbank. Therefore we had a good list of Turkish people who were born and died in the 1800s, 1900s, and 2000s, mainly individuals from the fifth and later generations, most of whom had stayed in the area for the entirety of their lives.

Many familiar Turkish family names can be found in the Springbank cemetery. Photograph provided by Glen Browder.

This survey of interments closely paralleled—in numbers and family patterns—our previous research for the master list; and these data bear further testimony to Benehaley's paternal dominance in the community from the beginning through contemporary times. "Benenhaley" was engraved as the primary surname—that is, the last name at time of death—on 42 percent of the headstones, followed by Oxendine (15 percent), Ray (11 percent), Hood (11 percent), Buckner (6 percent), and Lowrey (1 percent); and, together, these six families comprised 86 percent of the markers.

A more impressive indicator of patrilineal influence can be discerned through examination of both birth names and married names. This analysis of mixed surnames revealed that Benenhaleys accounted for slightly more than half (51 percent) of the individuals buried in these two cemeteries, followed by the Oxendines (18 percent), Rays (15 percent), Hoods (13 percent), Buckners (8 percent), and Lowreys (1 percent). The proportion of "others"—whose birth and married names differed from the six major surnames—dropped to 9 percent in this analysis; and many of these individuals could be connected with those six families, particularly

Who Are the Turkish People of Sumter County?

Some gravesites in the cemetery behind High Hills of Santee Baptist Church have been disturbed and eliminated over time; however, a few markers for deceased Turkish persons can be found among the graves of white congregants. This headstone marks the grave of Eliphare Oxendine Benenhaley (1839–1894). Photograph provided by Glen Browder.

the Benenhaleys. These calculations mounted to over 100 percent, reflecting the double-counting nature of intermarriages among families; however, what this scrutiny tells us is that a majority of the deceased people in these two graveyards had either been born Benenhaleys or had married Benenhaleys.

This website (www.findagrave.com) also revealed other interesting patterns for the two local cemeteries. For example, there was a surprising lack of Scotts buried at the two local sites. Of course, we are aware that the "man who gave his name as Scott" was part of the community in the early years; and Scotts of a different family line would join the group in later years. However there was no record of interments for that name—except for one individual who lived during the late 1800s and another in the late 1900s. The original Scott was a cohort of Joseph Benenhaley in the beginning; but, for some reason, he and his surname seem to have faded as a significant factor in this community during its formative century.

Also interesting is that, other than the Benenhaleys, Oxendines, Rays, Hoods, Buckners, and Lowreys, no other family names accounted for any significant proportion of the graves in these two cemeteries. There were several dozen such surnames on headstones (most of whom had some ties to the six main families); and the only families of those surnames that had multiple grave listings were the Amersons (4), Carpenters (3), Griffins (3), Jacksons (3), Sackets (3), Bolsers (2), Browns (2), Carters (2), Deases (2), Edgeworths (2), Erbs (2), Horns (2), Pinkhams (2), Scotts (2), Simses (2), and Vanovers (2).

Additionally, we found few graves in the other local church cemeteries with surnames matching the six basic families of the Turkish community. For example, High Hills of Santee Baptist Church (the original home of white, black, and Turkish worshippers) listed only eleven headstones with these surnames among 177 identified graves. The Church of the Holy Cross (Thomas Sumter's home church and still an active Anglican parish in the Episcopal Diocese of South Carolina) listed only one grave among four hundred for any of the Turkish names. There were nine listings similar to the Turkish names among over six hundred graves at the four churches mainly serving Black residents of this area (High Hills AME Church, High Hills Baptist Church, Hopewell Baptist Church, and Wayman Chapel AME Church). We also found no evidence of Turkish-sounding names among the few readable headstones in the cemetery at Bethesda Baptist Church (that likely served the Privateer Indians in early times). Also interesting is the fact that Sumter Cemetery and Evergreen Cemetery, the county's two main area burial sites with a combined total of over seventeen thousand graves, showed only forty-seven listings for the six surnames commonly associated with the Turkish community.

Of course, readers should keep in mind that these online inventories were less than complete and could include mistaken information. However, the findings attest to Benenhaley predominance; and they reveal the striking isolation—however one might explain it—of the Turkish people in Sumter County.

~ Death Notices ~

The same basic patterns were apparent in death notices—as recorded in vital records and newspaper articles—for this group during the 1900s and early 2000s.

Helen Team, a Turkish relative who lives outside Sumter County, has compiled an extensive file of death certificates and published obituaries for the common family surnames as part of a genealogical project; and this collection—fastidiously gleaned from local newspapers, regional archives, and the Internet—included 389 items about deceased Turkish persons with ties to this community who were laid to rest, not just at Long Branch and Springbank but also at more than a dozen other locations in South Carolina. The notices essentially covered the past century in patchwork fashion. For reasons relating to administrative/legal restrictions, the death certificates (about half of the collection) were dated from 1915 to the 1960s; and the obituaries (the other half of the collection), for a variety of technical reasons, mainly covered the period from the 1960s to the present.

This file of death notices from various locations in the state closely tracked the local cemetery inventory. Of the notices in the file, organized by reported surname, the Benenhaley family accounted for a majority (51 percent), followed by Oxendines (18 percent), Hoods (8 percent), Rays (7 percent), Buckners (5 percent), and

Lowreys (2 percent); and "other names" totaled less than 10 percent. Obviously such data are partial and subject to error, but the patterns were definitely similar and supportive of our previous research.

~ "First Family" ~

In addition to these findings, several online sources of national demographic information soundly support designation of Joseph Benenhaley and his descendants as the "first family" of the original and continuing Turkish community.

To illustrate, the census count of 1810 listed Joseph Benenhaley as the head of a household in Dalzell; and additional data, as compiled by www.ancestry.com, showed no other households anywhere else in the country by that name at that time. Also, www.ancestry.com reported that, about a century later, in 1920, the census showed that 95 percent of Benenhaley households nationwide were located in South Carolina, almost all in Sumter County. Interestingly, too, www.locatemyname.com reports that, currently, 76 percent of Americans named Benenhaley are located in the Palmetto State. Even in death, the Benenhaleys have demonstrated loyal ties to their cultural home. Our accounting of national interment data, at www.findagrave.com, shows that 89 percent of Benenhaley graves are in Sumter County, mainly at the two local church cemeteries; and only 4 percent of deceased Benenhaleys are buried outside South Carolina.

One could quibble with specific aspects of these data sets. Census methodology has changed over time, and reported results differ slightly from one website to another. But their overall patterns are consistent; and, collectively, they affirm that the American Benenhaleys originated, for the most part, in this rural community; Benenhaley progeny grew up and settled here for many decades; a large majority of living Benenhaleys still reside in this area; and most deceased Benehaleys are buried near their birthplace.

By comparison, the other five core surnames entered the Turkish community in later decades from family lines that were widespread and still are dispersed elsewhere. Census and genealogical records indicate that the Oxendines joined the group in the 1830s, the Rays in the 1840s, the Hoods and Lowreys in the 1870s, and the Buckners in the 1880s. An analysis of demographic data (www.ancestry.com) indicates that more than 95 percent of all these family groups resided outisde South Carolina at the time their surnamed relatives married into the Turkish community; and, currently, fewer than 6 percent of the country's Oxendine households, fewer than 4 percent of the Ray households, fewer than 4 percent of the Hood households, fewer than 3 percent of the Buckner households, and fewer than 2 percent of the Lowrey households are located in South Carolina (www.locatemyname.com). Also, a national cemetery count (www.findagrave.com) shows that few deceased Oxendines (4 percent), Rays (<1 percent), Hoods (<1 percent), Buckners (<1 percent), and Lowreys (<1 percent) are buried in Sumter

County; and huge majorities (ranging from 94–99 percent) of these families are interred out-of-state.

This is not to suggest that other individuals in this community were less "Turkish" than the Benenhaleys; as we will demonstrate later in this manuscript, these surnamed families fully merged into the Turkish people and assumed leading roles in the group. The relevant point in citing such data is to demonstrate broad genealogical compliance with our analytic model and to emphasize just how much Joseph Benenhaley exercised paternal influence on this community.

In fact, available data indicate that Benenhaley is still impacting the extended lineage, to a less but significant degree, into the twenty-first century. The swamp of names and dates and relationships among Turkish people has become deep and murky over time. However, Benenhaley's continuing mark is indicated in the genealogical history submitted by the Sumter Cheraw Tribe in their application to the South Carolina Commission for Minority Affairs. As has already been shown, these two lineages began merging in the 1830s and became integral parts of the Turkish community in the latter half of that century; and the Cheraw Tribe's submission conveys, at least partially, the interplay among Turkish, Native American, and other lines during the twentieth and twenty-first centuries. That application includes a genealogical chart with over 150 family surnames spread far and wide; and a simple eyeball survey revealed frequent Benenhaley references throughout the fifty-page document.

To summarize, census reports, vital records, cemetery interments, and demographic patterns solidly support the central tenet of our analytic model: Joseph Benenhaley and his namesake descendants fully qualify as the genealogical core of this subcultural community. These varied data sets show that the Benenhaleys have constituted the predominant group in Dalzell from the beginning and for later generations. Half of the Turkish people who lived and died in this small community over the past two centuries were either born Benenhaleys or married Benenhaleys. Just as important, these records show that, historically, the Benenhaleys, Oxendines, Rays, Hoods, Buckners, and Lowreys have comprised the vast majority of Turkish people. These six families accounted for about nine of every ten persons in this community until the recent past.

~ **Assembling a Genetic Profile** ~

Fortunately, we also have acquired critical evidence of more recent and scientific nature; and this evidence neatly complements the aforementioned research. Genetic analysis, as presented in the following pages, suggests a collective profile pointing to Joseph Benanhaley as the ancestral Ottoman and as the progenitor of the Turkish community. Of course, genetic analysis can never provide perfect depictions of ancestry and it is fraught with limitations and uncertainties. However, it can be helpful when used in conjunction with other information as part of a comprehensive investigation. Such was the historically significant case of ancestral squabbling among Thomas Jefferson and Sally Hemings descendants. As noted by bioethics professor Carl Elliott in a *Wilson Quarterly* essay, the "slender thread" of genetic information provided what was needed in that situation; and the claims of the slave descendants "are now widely treated as valid" ("Adventures" 2003, 16).

~ DNA Reports ~

There is great reluctance among the Turkish people to even talk about genetic testing; however, we were successful in accessing reports—either the full documents or relevant results—for eight members of this community who are descendants of Joseph Benenhaley. Our eight individuals provided a small sample for generalizing about the Turkish people, and we are certain that we would see somewhat different results if we were able to test a larger number of subjects. But we are confident that the genetic data of these descendants, combined with the results of our previous research, provide valid insights into Joseph Benenhaley's role in the history of this community. We also doubt, based on close examination of census and genealogical records, that a full and perfect testing of all Turkish people living today would appreciably alter our assessment of the traditional narrative.

The most pertinent results came from a male Benenhaley who is the great-great-great-grandson of the original progenitor; he can trace his lineage as "the son of the son of, etc." all the way back to Joseph Benenhaley. Geneticists tell us that male descendants make especially useful subjects for research, since they can reveal paternal lineage straight to the targeted ancestor. This individual submitted to DNA analysis as part of our investigation, and his report should be indicative of the origins of Joseph Benenhaley. This DNA sample showed predominantly Mediterranean/Middle Eastern/North African ancestry—with slight European markers, and no evidence of Native American or Sub-Sahara African blood. These data provided clear support for the traditional version of Joseph Benenhaley as a "Caucasian of Arab descent."

We then found online, publically available DNA results for two females, a mother and her daughter. We are uncertain about the technology used in these cases; but their maternal line involved only Benenhaleys and Oxendines, as far as could be determined, back to the mid-1800s. The tests mainly showed links back to Mediterranean/Middle Eastern/North African areas, with some European and Native American matkers and no matches for Sub-Saharan Africa.

We also obtained the reports of three DNA analyses from a male and two females whose Benenhaley ancestor (one of the progenitor's daughters) married outside the community, to an Irishman, and the family left the state in the mid-1800s. Their reports covered all ancestral and/or maternal DNA, and their connections to the core family obviously were meaningful from a different perspective. Their genetic profiles give us an idea of the Benenhaley lineage, along with their "married out" lines and absent any other lines that joined the Sumter Turkish community in later generations.

The male subject's report showed mainly Western European ancestry (reflecting several generations of European lineage), with secondary Mediterranean/Middle Eastern/North African links, indicative of the Benenhaley line. The report of the second subject, a female, showed primary links to European and significant links to North African Berber populations. The test for the third subject, another female, produced similar European and Mediterranean connections. None of these analyses showed any Native American or Sub-Sahara African markers for their lineage.

The six reports cited thus far suggest varying but significant connections to the Middle East or Mediterranean area; and, apparently, no Native American or Sub-Sahara African blood flowed through Joseph Benenhaley's or his European wife's veins. As one of these descendants said: "I'm linked directly to Joseph Benenhaley; and my report indicates that he was exactly what he claimed to be—a Turkish man."

Two other individuals are descendants of the progenitor; but they employed genetic methodology that excluded, minimized, or obscured Benenhaley's ancestry. Therefore, these results were interesting mainly because they give us a glimpse into their non-Benenhaley lineage. Both showed predominantly European ancestry and revealed a sprinkling of Native American markers.

Obviously, as mentioned previously, this is a limited number of respondents. However, these results allow us to assess the Benenhaley line (the core family of this group); and, combined with our other research, they provide suggestive insight into the origins and lineage of the Turkish community in its formative century.

∼ Origins and Lineage ∼

We examined these reports of genetic data for possible insights regarding the ancestral origins of Joseph Benenhaley and the primary lineage of this community—both of which objectives were achieved. To generalize, these reports comply with hypothetical origins from a Mediterranean/Middle Eastern/North African progenitor, with substantial white European admixture, some evidence of Native American contribution, and no significant Sub-Sahara African linkages among the early generations.

We should acknowledge that these results were derived from reports of varying nature with different testing technologies. Also, several of the reports for our living respondents included minor or "trace" markers for various other geographic regions—including "Africa," "Southeast Asia," "the Arctic," and elsewhere. Such traces are not surprising considering the fact that our DNA respondents are so distanced, genealogically, from the founding families. Virtually everyone who submits to DNA analysis evidences such trace linkages, which genetics professionals consider as statistically insignificant and unreliable for determining regional origins. That is why all reports include a version of the standard explanation for these markers: "There is only a small amount of evidence supporting the regions as part of your genetic ethnicity. Because both the estimated amount and the range of the estimate are small, it is possible that these regions appear by chance and are not actually part of your genetic ethnicity."

This summary generalization about origins and lineage constitutes an especially notable conclusion when compared with conventional presumptions about the history of the Turkish community. For the most part, previous analysts—whose work we covered earlier in this section—have dismissed the Turkish narrative and categorically lumped the "Sumter Turks" among the many tri-racial isolates of this region. They have usually described these settlements as deriving from clustered remnants—usually poor white settlers, disassociated Indians, and fugitive or freed African slaves; or, sometimes, they have depicted these people as products of indistinct, unknown alliances. Often, critics belittled the idea of Turkish ancestry and called the traditional narrative a racist scheme to hide African origins. But our collection of DNA reports has contradicted those presumptions. This research sustained the idea of a cultural group distinctly different from other settlements in this part of the country. These data were congruent with the narrative of the Turkish people's origins as beginning with an identified Ottoman founder/progenitor and continuing through the evidenced admixture of white Europeans and Native Americans.

Some are uncomfortable talking about this aspect of our investigation—because of racial sensitivities and history in this part of the country. But this project was not about race. Our investigation was about how early and successive analysts have distorted the historical ancestry, ethnicity, and character of the Turkish people. Their presumptions not only were unfounded and insulting; they also have hindered the Turkish people in understanding and celebrating their own cultural heritage.

Therefore, it was important that we determine—through thorough investigation—whether oral history or outside presumptions should prevail in the case of the "Sumter Turks;" and our DNA research was consistent with the traditional narrative. Since this was such a sensitive and significant result, we decided to seek professional input from experts with solid credentials and with whom we had no previous relationship. We submitted our genetic conclusions to James Bindon, former chair of the Anthropology Department at the University of Alabama. He is a biological anthropologist whose distinguished career includes research among South Pacific Samoan, Mississippi Choctaw, and Alabama African American populations. He responded thus: "I think the report of the DNA results is well-stated and certainly is consistent with the Turkish hypothesis.... You have clearly done a great deal of work to untangle this mystery" (e-mail message, October 10, 2014).

We also contacted Donald N. Yates of DNA Consultants in Phoenix, Arizona. Yates is principal investigator, owner, and founder of DNA Consultants. One of our Benenhaley descendants had been part of a 2010 study by his company, and that individual's report, presented online, showed strong links to the Mediterranean/Middle Eastern/North African area, slight Native American association, and no matches for Sub-Sahara Africa. Yates confirmed those findings; he also added the following comment about the skin tone of the Turkish people of Sumter County: "I think the Benenhaley case ... demonstrates that dark, exotic looks often have nothing to do with African heritage" (e-mail message, February 13, 2014).

To summarize, the genetic reports for Joseph Benenhaley's descendants provided support for that narrative, by reasonable evidentiary standards, on two critical counts: first, they vouched for his ancestral connection to the Mediterranean/Middle Eastern/North African area; and, second, they affirmed his paternal impact on the lineage of this community.

~ Proclaiming the Patriarch ~

The history of war, piracy, and slavery, combined with official reports of people from the Mediterranean/Middle Eastern/North African region present in this colony and state, buttressed with Matilda Ellison's handwritten letters about his Ottoman origins and slave experience, and capped by General Thomas Sumter's deed/survey/signature certifying "Josephs land"—all these documents strongly support a rational scenario whereby Joseph Benenhaley ended up in the Carolina backcountry, joined the Revolutionary War effort, and founded a communal family at Dalzell. Just as important, our census, genealogical, genetic, and vital records clearly demonstrate that he was the founder/forefather of the Sumter County community. His progeny dominated the early families of the Turkish people; his bloodline figured prominently in subsequent generations; and his name disproportionately marks the graveyards where his people rest in peace.

Ever mindful of previous doubt and skepticism, we again sought professional counsel regarding the total package of findings about Joseph Benenhaley. We were able to locate perhaps the only expert who has examined the histories of both the Turkish people of Sumter County and the Native Americans of South Carolina. Ethnohistorian Wesley DuRant Taukchiray (previously known as Wes White Jr.) is a legendary character with singular qualifications in this area. (See "Wes Taukchiray Papers" at the University of South Carolina; "Wes Taukchiray Collection" at the University of North Carolina Pembroke; "Wesley D. White Papers" at the South Carolina Historical Society; Hicks and Taukchiray 1998; Taukchiray and Kasakoff 1992; White 1975.) An anthropologist by education and a genealogist by experience, he has spent his lifetime researching the backgrounds and ways of interesting peoples. He has worked as a contract scholar with numerous organizations (such as the Native American Rights Fund, the Lumbee River Legal Services, the Indian Museum of the Carolinas, and the Smithsonian Institution); he also has consulted with Native American groups throughout the country.

Most pertinent for our project, Taukchiray gathered valuable documentary material on the Dalzell community in the 1970s for the Smithsonian's Center for the Study of Man, and he produced a 1975 report entitled *A History of the Turks Who Live in Sumter County, South Carolina, from 1805 to 1972*. That project represented the most impressive collection of historic information available at that time. Also, to his credit, he has revised the report periodically to add new information and interpretation to the story of the Turkish people.

After weeks of investigative tracking, we located Taukchiray by cell phone on a secluded mountain in rural North Carolina. We mailed him a hardcopy of our draft manuscript so that he could examine the evidence and conclusions, and we engaged in mail and phone conversations about the project during December 2014 through December 2015.

Taukchiray wholeheartedly endorsed our research and findings. Most important, he said that the collected evidence resolved important questions that have long haunted these people: "You have proven Benenhaley was the Turkish progenitor and you have validated the oral history of that community." He also was impressed with the compilation of information explaining the relationship between Indians and Turkish people in Dalzell and the early connection between Oxendines and Benenhaleys. "This all makes sense," he repeated throughout our conversation.

Finally, we can confidently and conclusively proclaim Joseph Benenhaley as historical patriarch of the Turkish people.

~ *Chapter Five* ~

The Turkish Traditional Narrative Is Confirmed

This assignment necessitated an exceptionally broad and creative strategy, intense research, and constant processing of disparate documents and data; and it produced results—the mystery is solved.

When we started this investigation, we doubted that we would be able to resolve questions about Joseph Benenhaley and the history of the Turkish community. We were very aware of the doubts and disparagements expressed in other forums and throughout many years; and we wondered whether we would find anything of value for today's Turkish people.

But we had confidence in our analytic model and personal commitment. If there were anything out there that could confirm or deny the traditional narrative, we had a plan for resolving the issue and we were driven to do so. We devised logical propositions about Turkish history and culture, and we employed sound strategies in exploring and testing those propositions. We diligently gathered and systematically scrutinized countless historical documents; we discovered previously unknown or unavailable material; and we conducted innovative analyses of data from public and private sources. Equally important, we interviewed real, live Turkish persons of all ages. As is demonstrated in this manuscript, they substantiated our research about Turkish history; they made available important documents that they had treasured among themselves for generations; and they talked, personally and passionately, about the human side of the Turkish experience. Each of these efforts contributed to an increasing feeling that we were on the right track.

We hereby absolutely endorse the traditional narrative as passed down through generations. Of course, that narrative has been amended and embellished along the way. However, our judgment is that the body of evidence presented in this section weighs in heavy favor of the long-cherished story of the Turkish people.

Who Are the Turkish People of Sumter County?

We base this judgment on seven points that we consider collectively convincing.

1. Historical Documentation. In the first place, colonial and state governmental documents show that some individuals of Mediterranean/Middle Eastern/North African origins found themselves in strange circumstances in South Carolina during the latter half of the 1700s, just as did Joseph Benenhaley. US Census documents certify his presence in the Dalzell area in 1810 and 1820; and Thomas Sumter's 1815 deed and survey plat confirm Benenhaley's ownership of land where and when the Turkish people began their community. Finally compelling, authoritatively and emotionally, are the letters of Matilda Ellison, who was well positioned to have learned about his circuitous journey from the Mediterranean, to slavery in the Caribbean, to service in the American Revolution, and to settlement in the Carolina backcountry. These historical documents lend circumstantial plausibility, official certification, and powerful personal testimony to the narrative of the mysterious Ottoman Turk.

2. Benenhaley Patriarchy. Dramatic new evidence supports our designation of Joseph Benenhaley as patriarch of the Turkish people. Matilda's letters and General Sumter's legal documents point to Benenhaley as the founding father of the communal family; and just as important, our genealogical research shows his strong and sustained role as progenitor of the lineage. Benenhaleys comprised slightly over half (51 percent) of the individuals on the master list of Turkish citizens who lived in the community during the nineteenth century; and, similarly, a slight majority (51 percent) of deceased persons in the graveyards of Long Branch Baptist Church and Springbank Baptist Church—which have been attended by congregants who were born and died in the nineteenth, twentieth, and twenty-first centuries—bore the Benenhaley name at some time in their lives. Joseph Benenhaley clearly predominates over any other figure in the history of this community.

3. Turkish Ancestry. We are especially impressed with recent scientific data indicating Turkish lineage in this community. We have acquired DNA reports for several of Joseph Benenhaley's descendants, including descendants of direct paternal linkage, descendants with blood of both the patriarch and outsiders who joined that community, and descendants who left that area without mixing their blood with that of later members of the Turkish community. These subjects allow us to consider ancestry from several different perspectives. Most important, this genetic analysis is congruent with the notion of varying but significant Mediterranean/Middle Eastern/North African origins among six of the eight reports of

living descendants. This was never a family of singly sired consanguinity; other groups—particularly white Europeans and Native Americans—entered the community over time. Overall, however, genetic analysis complies with the claim of Mediterranean ancestry; and the Ottoman Turk's bloodline demonstrably impacted these people throughout the period of the traditional narrative.

4. Subcultural Ethnicity. A fourth supportive factor is that extensive historical reporting and a few personal writings—such as Eleazer Benenhaley's biography about growing up in Dalzell—have authenticated this ethnic subculture. Our investigation has documented that the community of mainly dark-skinned people was founded by the Ottoman Turk, and it was nurtured by a nexus of patriarchy, blood, marriage, color, isolation, discrimination, and identity. The Benenhaleys began their secluded existence at the beginning of the 1800s and others joined them over the years. These huddled families—mainly the Benenhaleys, Oxendines, Rays, Hoods, Buckners, and Lowreys—assumed a common identity as an outcast group, and they kept to themselves for many generations in rural South Carolina. The Turkish people neither blended openly and prominently into mainstream society nor dissipated in the shadows as scattered refugees. They sustained themselves as the single clear case of an ethnic community that went its own separate way toward cultural isolation for almost two centuries. The community numbered about five hundred at its peak in the mid-twentieth century; and only in the past few decades have they begun assimilating into broader society.

5. Outside Testimony. Additionally, numerous accounts, news reports, academic analyses, and journalistic profiles by outsiders attest to the narrative with stories about the history of the Turkish people. For example, two knowledgeable observers—Thomas Sebastian Sumter and F. Kinloch Bull, who lived and spent considerable time among Turkish people in the 1800s and 1900s—related the tale of Joseph Benenhaley and reported events, traditions, and folkways of this unique society. Their writings indicate that, in many ways, Turkish lives, days, and activities were like those of other southerners in rural areas; but in everything they did or hoped to do, there was always the reality that Turkish people were different and precluded from the full blessings of American democracy.

6. Self-Identification. Of special importance as an argument for the traditional narrative is the matter of self-identification and self-definition. The Turkish people themselves have provided witness to who they are and were over many years. They have consistently asserted themselves as Caucasians of Arab descent, or white people of Turkish background, to past writers and to us in recent, in-depth interviews. Some now

are reconsidering their origins; however, as demonstrated in numerous documents and public statements, the members of this community generally considered and still consider themselves as the Turkish people of Sumter County (and they have always been singled out as such by other segments of the broader society). It is hard to deny a people's right to claim their own cultural identity, especially if that group has suffered isolation and adversity throughout most of our country's history.

7. Absence of Convincing Contradiction. The final point in favor of the traditional narrative is simply that no solid evidence has been presented convincingly contradicting that narrative. Some early critics faulted the oral history; but their criticisms were based on inappropriate presumptions and incomplete information. Others have offered interesting, alternative notions about the community, supported by their own sentiments, oral traditions, and various records; but their notions and sentiments and records, when scrutinized, supplement the story of Joseph Benenhaley and his descendants. Points one through six of this discussion depict a community of "the Turkish people" that existed for two centuries; and that narrative is a fact of history that stands without serious challenge.

Therefore, our opinion—based on the aforementioned documents and other solid evidence—is that we have compiled the true history of the Turkish people of Sumter County and their traditional narrative has been validated.

To summarize, we now know—based on solid evidence, reliable sources, and logical reasoning—that Joseph Benenhaley was a dark-skinned Caucasian of Mediterranean origins, an Ottoman subject most likely from North Africa. Somehow—arguably through the slave trade—he made his way to the New World. During the American Revolution, he served General Thomas Sumter, perhaps as a scout or maybe as a wheelwright, in South Carolina. After the war, Sumter gave Benenhaley some land near Stateburg, and the general vouched for his status as a white man. Benenhaley was the patriarch of the familial enclave and his bloodline dominated in that community. Other surnames and bloodlines entered the established family of "Benenhaleys"; however, they considered themselves, collectively, as Turkish people. For many generations, they charted a difficult course, marked by isolation and adversity, in the Carolina backcountry.

It is true that the narrative has evolved and this community has changed over the years. In fact, as the following chapters will demonstrate, their assimilation into the broader society of our county, state, and nation illustrates the dilution of that history and lineage. The "Turkish people" are becoming a mindset of heritage as much as a genealogical and geographical subculture. However, the results of this investigation show that the early designation of this community's origin—a misinterpretation based on faulty conjecture—led some analysts to deny the history of

The Turkish Traditional Narrative Is Confirmed

the Turkish people; and it has been wrong—in retrospect—for critics to disparage their culture as "so-called Turks."

Considering the experience of this community over the years, it seems appropriate here and now to state their ancestry and ethnicity in timeless terms of cultural identity. They are what they have always said and will always believe. As they proudly declare in the next section of this book: "We are the Turkish people of Sumter County."

~ *Part Two* ~

We Are the Turkish People of Sumter County

~ *Chapter Six* ~

Our Voice

A Family Discussion

We are the Turkish people of Sumter County in the state of South Carolina. Our story has never been told fully and accurately. We have roots that extend all the way back to the Revolutionary War, and we served in the Confederate army during the Civil War and fought for America in World Wars I and II. However, for two centuries our rich history has been overlooked or misrepresented, our cultural identity has been questioned, and we were denied equal access to education because of the tones of our skin. We persevered; and we prevailed. Now, though our spirit endures, the Turkish community faces new and different challenges, as a fading ethnicity, in the twenty-first century.

Our history was documented in the previous chapters; now it is our responsibility to discover our voice and tell our story as living Turkish persons. Perhaps I should alert readers that my part of this effort is more personal and passionate than that of my coauthor. Unlike Browder's academic study, I will pursue our family mystery mainly as a descendent of Joseph Benenhaley and as one of the Turkish people. Besides expressing my own ideas and feelings, I will get my relatives to relate the inside story of life among the "Sumter Turks." I will ask them to share what it was like growing up and living in this area during the past century. They will provide real-life memories and information that confirm the Turkish experience as proposed in our analytic model and documented in the first half of this book. They also will help anthropologists, sociologists, historians, educators, and curious readers better understand unique ethnic groups. These stories will move you, unnerve you, and encourage you to make a positive difference in this world by seeing the beauty in others, regardless of their differences.

In the past, the history of the Turkish people of Sumter County has been written by non-Turkish people. While these accounts may have been accurate from their perspectives, they were missing one key component that could have strengthened and validated their findings. They never let the Turkish people tell their own story. Some will argue that this was the fault of the Turkish people; and I admit that our community has always been reluctant to talk about themselves to outsiders. But the reality is that recorded history is incorrect and needs to be corrected.

Turkish beliefs about history are based on the oral traditions and conversations that have been passed down from generation to generation. On the other hand, non-Turkish people have formed their own conceptions of this community, based on written records and conventional theories of a different nature. Through it all, someone had to make judgment calls regarding which events and people were important enough to remember or record and how they would be analyzed. In many cases, the dominant culture has had the strongest voice in these decisions; those in power have taken precedence over the voices of less powerful people.

Is it not important, though, to seek out other voices, perhaps voices from non-dominant cultures? On the chance that we might happen upon a different story regarding the way things were from those who lived through it, should we not record it, analyze it, and reveal it for all to hear? For example, who better to explain the Integration Movement and how it affected the Turkish people of Sumter County in the 1950s than those who lived through it and still remember specific details about it as if it had happened yesterday? Therefore, I call upon the Turkish people to discover their voice, and, together, we will tell our story, in order to fill a gap in history and enrich the lives of today's Turkish people.

~ Wisdom and Woe at the Dinner Table ~

Through the years, I have listened to the stories of my grandfather, grandmother, uncles, aunts, cousins, and mother around the dinner table. We talked about their interactions with other Turkish people as well as with non-Turkish people. I have learned what it means to be part of a community that is set apart from the rest of the world. My role in this study is to help give honest and compassionate voice to those stories—their versions of family wisdom and communal woe—so that others might understand the true experiences of the Turkish people of Sumter County. I think this research went especially well, because it was like our everyday conversations around the dinner table; we simply wanted to tell our own story fully and accurately.

To illustrate, one of my first interviews with a Turkish informant was actually over dinner at a local restaurant. Readers will meet Boaz later in this section, but what is important is that he and his wife wanted to share a meal of chicken, vegetables, and biscuits before he agreed to participate. Boaz specifically asked whether my intentions were "pure"; and only after I assured him that my purpose was to "uplift" rather than "demean" did he agree to help with this project. Throughout the rest of that meal and afterward in their home, we developed a "family" relationship and a solid plan for telling the story of our people.

Each interview with my four primary respondents was structured to cover a set agenda of topics; but I also tried to conduct the interviews as personal discussions about their lives. I tried, as often as possible, to find some things that were important to them as real human beings, such as memories, anecdotes, pictures, report cards, tickets to a fair, newspaper articles, and census records. I used these mementos to engage them; and they usually would respond with heartfelt tales of what life was like for them. For example, I found an old picture of several girls in a school play, and one of the participants in the study told me that she was in that play when she was only seven years old. She had never seen the picture before and was amazed that there was evidence of her participation. Needless to say, this picture triggered a warm and rich interview.

Most of the time, I recorded the interviews; but, when I sensed discomfort, I turned off the audio recorder and simply took notes. I also kept a journal—with entries written after certain interviews—to capture the emotional aspect and human setting of those conversations. Of course, these "family discussions" wandered far and wide; and they revealed things—tearful dramas—that had never been revealed before. For example, the following is an entry from my journal after spending some time with one of the participants, Tonie. She and I went to her neighbor's house to visit. Her neighbor was an elderly black woman who was born and raised in Sumter County.

Journal entry: Wednesday, April 4, 2007.

Tonight Tonie and I went to her neighbor's house. We sat outside in the neighbor's front lawn chairs and just chatted about all kinds of things. Regarding this study, one thing the neighbor told me was that if "one of the Turkish people likes you, they all like you." This attests to the unity of the Turkish people.

We listened to crickets, were bitten by mosquitoes and witnessed a child being chastised across the street. We talked about gardens and how to make flowers grow. Tonie's neighbor said that she can break a little piece of a plant off of a living plant and simply put it in the dirt, water it, and it will grow.

I observed the participants as they spoke and took field notes regarding their emotions, gestures, voice tones, facial expressions and body language. I noticed that the two women treated each other as sisters. Though not related, their intimate relationship warmed my heart. The neighbor had recently lost a loved one and Tonie was comforting her with a listening ear, frequently looking down and moving her feet in the sand. They both wore nightgowns and were comfortable with their appearance. I watched as the neighbor showed Tonie where the preacher had come by to spray wash her house. She told Tonie, "He won't take any money. He just wants to help." The neighbor seemed comforted to know that so many people, regardless of ethnicity, cared about her.

After the walk around the house, Tonie marveled at her neighbor's garden. She called me over so that I could also admire the various plants. What I really admired, though, was the close bond of friendship that I had observed in the two women. This friendship might not have been so intimate 60 years ago because of the great social distance that existed among the ethnic groups in Sumter County.

Earlier today, Tonie took me to the site of the old Hillcrest School. It is another school now. We walked through the halls and I took pictures of the building of the old school that refused admittance to Tonie in the late 1950's. One day, when she was younger, she was allowed to go to this school to register. The next day none of the white students came to school because they were boycotting. Only the Turkish students showed up for school that day.

After an informative tour of the school, we left. When we were back in the car, Tonie's eyes started welling up with tears. She looked out the passenger side window as we were leaving the school. As I watched the image of the school diminish in my rear view mirror, Tonie said with a muffled voice, "Sometimes I wonder why God didn't let me get an education." She then wiped the tears from her eyes and did not say another word during the ride back to her house. It was obvious to me, from this experience, that she is still very affected by the neglect of the school system and the people in charge from when she was a child. While she has moved on and become a successful adult, her painful childhood memories have not been forgotten.

These interviews covered some difficult territory—ancestry, ethnicity, isolation, discrimination, life at the "Turk School," relationships with white and black people, and their memories of the Integration Movement—and my journal notes were very helpful later on as I tried to communicate the tone and environment of these conversations. Before presenting these family discussions and tearful dramas, allow me to introduce myself.

~ My Story ~

I was born to an Italian-American father, Daniel Ognibene, and a Turkish-American mother, Pearl (Ray) Corcoran. My father met my mother while he was stationed at Shaw Air Force Base in Sumter County. They married in Sumter when they were teenagers but did not settle there. They soon moved to England, where my mother became pregnant with my brother, Michael. She wanted him to be born in the United States, so she came back until he was born. When he was just a toddler, my family moved back to England for a few years until my dad was once again sent to the United States, where I was born in St. Charles, Missouri. As my father was in the Air Force, we did not stay in Missouri very long either. We soon moved to Georgia where I grew up in an all-white neighborhood and attended an all-white school.

I remember the first time a black person moved into the neighborhood and attended the elementary school. I was in the sixth grade. He was accepted in our class, but not in our neighborhood. I did not understand the tension that evolved in the neighborhood when we suddenly had black neighbors. One day his house burned down, some believe by arsonists, and the family moved. It was my first memory of racism.

Years later, a strange experience caused me to think more seriously about my ethnic background. I was sitting in Randy Fair's cultural diversity class at Georgia State University. I did not have the best attitude about going to class one day, because I was not particularly enthused with the book that we were reading. The book was *Teaching to Transgress: Education as the Practice of Freedom* by bell hooks (1994). I said something in class that day that I regret saying, but I'm glad I said it because my eyes were opened afterward. I said, "I'm tired of reading the same thing over and over again. I wish that the author would stop belly-aching about the oppression that she went through. Yes, it was horrible, but it is over now, and it is time to move on." The students in the class were appalled. You could have heard a pin drop. How dare I say, "belly-aching" and "move on?" I would never forget the words of a student across the room. She said, "That's easy for you to say. You come from a privileged background." I had never even heard of a "privileged background," and I sure did not feel that I came from one.

Now I was the one who was offended. That student did not know my family's history. "How dare she judge me?" I thought, not recognizing that I had similarly judged the author of the book we were reading. While I suppose it is true that I do come from a "privileged background," it is only because of the ones who came before me who fought for my rights to receive an equal education and other equal opportunities that I have grown up privileged. They, themselves, did not have a privileged background, and this includes my own mother. I was ignorant that day in class. I wish I could take the insensitive words back, but at least my eyes were opened to the way that "privileged" people think. Because they have not experienced oppression, they do not realize that they are privileged. Myself included.

After telling my family's story to the class that day, Fair challenged me. He said, "There is a story that needs to be told here, and you are the one who needs to tell it." I had not even realized that my family's story was so unique. I guess there really is something to that saying, "You can't see the forest for the trees." I decided to change my dissertation topic and follow my heart. I was on a mission to tell their stories; and, in the process, perhaps discover my own identity. Over the next few years, I was able to interview my relatives in Sumter County and complete my doctoral dissertation at Georgia State University. I thought that was the end of my mission until Browder and I began corresponding and decided to try, as a team, to tell the full story of the Turkish people of Sumter County.

This all started because someone in a class challenged me about my privileged background. That discussion had caused me to think differently about my life, and it triggered troubling memories of my mother. My mother never enjoyed such privileged status as a young person. She was not able to graduate from high school, mainly because of how she was treated during the integration turmoil of the 1950s. That experience stuck with her the rest of her life. However, the humiliation of those years instilled in her the vision of a better life for her children. My mother wanted me to have the education that she was denied because of her ethnicity. She pushed me to break through barriers and let my voice be heard. She had a vision for my future. It mirrored that of Martin Luther King Jr.'s dream (1963). I have always known that my limitations would be established by my own lack of zeal, not by the limitations imposed on me by society. When I was growing up, she would often encourage me to get a good education because she was not allowed to get one. After dinner, she would excuse me from the table, and she would say, "I'll clean up. It's more important that you do your homework." So I became a pretty good student.

She once told me the story of waiting for the bus to pick her up for the first day of integrated school. She was fourteen years old. As she watched the bus approach, of course she was nervous and anxious about finally getting to attend the white school, but she was not prepared for what actually happened. As the bus approached, she watched as it sped up and left her behind. The students on the bus were hanging out of the windows and waving at her. She walked home, defeated. When she actually made it to school, she sat down at a table in the cafeteria to eat her lunch. Everyone at the table told her that she was not welcome, and they asked her to leave. They shouted at her, "We don't eat with Turks."

This humiliation continued to follow her throughout her high school career. She often felt as if everyone were against her, even her teachers. They would sometimes point to the Turkish students in their classes and say, "You people over there need to speak up" instead of addressing them by their names. My mother did not realize that she was any different from anyone else until she was allowed to attend the high school for white students. Her childhood experiences were similar to those of Lenny, a character in Bapsi Sidhwa's novel, *Cracking India* (1991), when she first noticed that people were different. Lenny states, "And I become aware of religious differences. It is sudden. One day everybody is themselves—and the next day they are Hindu, Muslim, Sikh, Christian. People shrink, dwindling into symbols" (101).

I have often heard that children are colorblind, and to some extent, this is true. As a young child, I was unaware of how ethnic backgrounds had any bearing on people's attitudes toward each other. Having grown up in Georgia, I was sheltered from many of the harsh realities that my family members experienced in South Carolina because of being Turkish. I also remember the first time I thought about what it really meant to be Turkish. I was spending the night at my cousin's house, which was a real treat that usually ended in tears when it was time to go home. She was telling me how some students at her school in Sumter County had made some derogatory comments about her being Turkish. I could not comprehend what she was saying. I could not see any difference between them and us, and I did not know that others could. And even so, what difference did it really make? I wondered if people thought that some groups were better than others. Even with our differences, were we not all still a part of the human race? She literally had to explain to me that according to them, we were different, and that our parents had it even worse than people our age did, back in the "good old days." I began to analyze myself. Was I different? I never thought so, but did other people see something that I did not?

I am a Turkish person who is living in a different time period, in Atlanta rather than Sumter County, with different rules, and a whole new set of freedoms. I am free from historical and racial segregation, and I am grateful to those who came before me and fought for my rights. I would not be who I am today, indeed, society would not be what it is today, without these pioneers of change. I, like Sandra Cisneros's character, Esperanza, in *The House on Mango Street* (1984), will not "forget who I am or where I came from" (87), but at the same time, I will not let my past dictate my future. While I am mindful that past social and educational injustices occurred through segregation, I am hopeful that the oral histories of the participants of this project will benefit future generations. Investigating the lives and experiences of the Turkish people of Sumter County was a difficult, yet rewarding, process. Both before and during my fieldwork, I spoke with family members to help me decide how to proceed.

I was surprised when some of them cautioned that it might not be a good idea to stir the pot. Several clichés came to mind: "That's water under the bridge;" "Let sleeping dogs lie;" and "Don't fix what is not broken." Two family members, in particular, cautioned me. One asked why I "wanted to bring all that up again?" and the other told me that she would not do this investigation if she were in my position because "some people might get mad."

Most people who have experienced segregation are very cautious when speaking about it. They are afraid that their talking about the past will only make the pain resurface, and that it can not possibly have a positive effect. Their opposition to this project was more than likely based on the fear that it might bring negative attention to our ethnic group and that it might cause them to have to remember suppressed hurts inflicted by outsiders in Sumter County.

Regarding those outsiders, I want to explain in my own way why Browder and I use various words—such as "white," black," and "Indian"—to refer to other ethnic populations in this area. We will not use divisive or degrading terminology to refer to any person or group, but these words will appear in our discussions. While we agree that to differentiate among ethnic groups can be divisive and seemingly racist, this project analyzes ethnicity issues that are unique to this region; and it will, therefore, distinguish among various ethnic groups. Our definitions are not exhaustive, and they by no means should be interpreted as suggesting anything negative about those populations. They are simply our own working definitions, not perfect but based on our experiences and research of what the words mean for the purposes of this manuscript.

For example, as we have already mentioned in our introduction, the phrase "Turkish people" is difficult to define because of the sensitive nature of the term. Just the mere mention of this expression or especially its alternative version, "Turks," may cause group members to become very angry because of the racist way in which some people have used this term in the past. Turkish people, while proud of our heritage, do not like for outsiders to hint that we are different in any way. In the past, the word "Turks" was used to refer to groups of people who had specific family surnames or to refer to people whose complexion ranged from very light to very dark.

I have heard many times that the only true Turkish people are the Benenhaleys because of their ancestor, Joseph Benenhaley. Some believe that other Turkish people with different surnames were labeled as such because of their marriages to the Benenhaleys. Some common surnames among those who claim to be or who are labeled as Turkish are Benenhaley, Ray, Hood, Oxendine, Buckner, and Lowrey. Other surnames also may be representative of the Turkish ethnic group but will not be discussed in this study. We choose to use the term "Turkish people" because they themselves refer to themselves as Turkish people. Many Turkish people claim to be white of Turkish descent, just as Italian Americans claim to be white of Italian descent. Some who have been labeled as Turkish people actually claim to be Native American and have worked to get the Cheraw Indian tribe formally recognized by the state of South Carolina. Others challenge both of these claims and suggest that through the years, we may have intermarried and mixed with other ethnic groups.

I greatly appreciate my family members loving me enough to approach me regarding the sensitivity of this project. Their advice to approach the situation with humility and respect guided me through each interview. My intention was not to belittle, demean, or hurt anyone in any way, but rather to celebrate and document the bravery of my predecessors through an oral history project. Without their efforts and the efforts of similar segregated groups, I, too, might have had to attend a three-room schoolhouse for Turkish students. Now that I am an adult, I strive to stand up for the brokenhearted and neglected, and I will speak of them only in terms of respect.

~ Our Storytellers: Boaz, Helen, Jean, and Tonie ~

The interviewed participants were in their sixties and seventies, and they were born and raised in Sumter County. All four had attended the Dalzell School for Turks as children and participated in the Integration Movement as teenagers. Only one of the four graduated from high school. Two of them married Turkish spouses, while two married non-Turkish white spouses. Three of them have moved around to other cities, states, or countries. I am related to all of them in some way.

Initially, I wanted to confine this part of the study to my close relatives, and my reason was threefold. First, I believed that my immediate relatives would be more willing than extended relatives or nonrelatives to allow me to interview them regarding such a sensitive topic. Second, I believed I would be able to earn their trust sooner than I would be able to earn the trust of extended relatives or nonrelatives because they already knew me. Third, I wanted to offer this project as a gift to them for sharing their oral histories with me. I viewed this project as a way that I might honor my immediate family as well as those in our family who have passed away.

However, after researching the history, documents, and artifacts of Sumter County and talking to some members of my immediate family, I changed my mind. I began to think about how this study might affect the relationships I have with my immediate family members. I knew that some members of my family had mixed emotions regarding whether or not this study should be done, and I thought that involving them might cause unnecessary strain on our relationships. I would no longer be just "Terri." For some of them I would be the unwanted researcher, too. Also I already knew a great deal about their lives, and I believed that the familiarity that we shared might interfere with the quality of the interviews. I believed firmly that I could collect the information I needed from other participants, who actually wanted to participate, without my becoming too emotionally involved. This is why I chose to branch out and meet other Turkish people whom I had not known very well before.

Of course, I sought advice from my mother, who still lives in Sumter County. She was a vital part of this study, because she served as a mediator between the Turkish community and me. She was an insider, whereas I was merely the daughter of an insider. While I am part of the family, I do not live in Sumter County and could have been perceived by some to be an outsider. She also was very familiar with the history of the county and knew many Turkish individuals. She grew up with many of the Turkish people and knew who might want to share their stories as well as their photographs. She gave me advice as to whom she thought I should interview.

I carefully searched for participants who were willing to share their stories so that I might learn a great deal about the life experiences of Turkish people who grew up here during the early part of the twentieth century. I was confident that my mother would be able to lead me to information-rich participants, and that they, in turn, would lead me to others. They did, in fact, lead me to other people who had stories to share and who were interested in participating.

The names of my four primary respondents—Boaz, Jean, Helen, and Tonie—are pseudonyms. The Turkish people are still very private people, and some are especially reluctant to speak openly about their history. We decided to use other names for these persons in consideration of this sensitivity. I conducted three separate sessions with each of them, with each session developing a greater sense of trust and probing more forcefully their memories and attitudes. Most of the interviews were recorded; in the others, I took notes and the sessions produced rich and revealing information.

Boaz

When I first met Boaz, I was intrigued by his story. His parents were separated before he was born, and he was raised by his mother and other extended members of his family. He grew up in a humble home that was full of love. His mother believed in him from the time that she gave birth to him. He told me, "I was born in Sumter County, close to Wedgefield. I grew up on a farm. Mom raised me, and she had to work in order to provide for me. We lived with her mom and dad. Mother had very limited schooling. When I told her I was going to drop out, she said, 'You can, but you're going to work.' And so she had a job for me the next day." Boaz's mother emphasized the importance of getting an education. She did everything in her power to help Boaz either continue his studies or face the hardships of earning a living. Her belief in her son pushed him to overcome many obstacles that he would face in the school setting.

As an adult, Boaz is a natural leader among the people of South Carolina. He is highly regarded and is a very wise and loving man. He is also very well educated. He used to be a teacher and a football coach. Called by God in the early 1950s, Boaz served as pastor in several churches in the southeastern part of the United States, including one church in Sumter County, until he recently retired. He now serves as interim pastor of a church on Sunday mornings. Boaz has held several leadership positions in schools, colleges, churches, missions, conventions, associations, and conferences. He has also authored two books. I first became familiar with Boaz after reading one of his books, twice. In his book, he discusses some of his childhood experiences of growing up in Sumter County as a Turkish boy. I was naturally drawn to him as a possible participant for my project, since I had read his work and connected with it. When I approached him, he was very supportive. He wanted to get to know me, so he and his wife met with me in a restaurant to discuss the project. I have already mentioned this meeting briefly in an earlier chapter, but I think it worth further elaboration to let our readers know more about the character of this amazing individual.

After ordering our meal, he asked the blessing, and we discussed the purpose of this project. He wanted to be sure that my intentions were pure. I assured him that they were, and I expressed that I would do my best to uplift the Turkish people and their efforts to end segregation. He then invited me to his home to talk. He said, "The only thing I ask of you, Terri, is in your report, anywhere you quote me, is that it's to elevate the people, not in any way to demean." I responded, "Yes, sir. That would be my purpose." He then said, "Right, and nothing in any way to hurt somebody." I assured him that I was in accord, and that I would do my best to honor our people.

Over the course of this project, we became very close. He and his wife were exceedingly hospitable, cooking for me, inviting me to stay for a weekend, and making it a point to introduce me to other family members. Boaz also gave me the names and phone numbers of other people whom I should contact for the purposes of this project. He gave up many hours of his time to tell me about his educational experiences both before and during the Integration Movement. He also took me under his wing and mentored me during this whole process, leaving encouraging messages on my voice mail and sending an uplifting note through the mail. His participation proved to be of paramount importance, and I am forever grateful to this man and the other three participants for agreeing to share their stories with me.

Helen

Helen grew up in a large family. Having several brothers and sisters may be the reason that she is so humorous and quick-witted. She asked me if I had read anything from the *Ebony* magazine. The title of the 1957 article was "South Carolina's Raceless People." When she held it up, I asked, "What does that mean? What's in there?" She said, "Just hold your horses, girl. This den is so dark my friend says, 'Why don't you paint your den white?' I say, 'Why don't you paint it for me?'" Once she stopped in the middle of one interview to tell me a joke. She said, "Did you hear about the letter that Chelsea Clinton wrote to that general? She asked him to explain why he didn't do something. He replied that he was afraid. She said, 'With all of those medals that you wear on your uniform, I wouldn't think that you would be afraid of anything.' He said, 'I'm afraid of three things: Osama, Obama, and yo' mama.'" We both laughed heartily and then continued with the interview.

Helen is vibrant and full of life. She used to work with young children in an educational setting. She attended school until the eleventh grade and then decided to get married. During our initial meeting, she insisted that I not use her real name, videotape her, audio record her, or take pictures of her. She wanted to remain completely anonymous. After we chatted for a while and became acquainted, she offered to take me on a tour of the Sumter/Dalzell area one windy afternoon, so we jumped in the car and she pointed out areas of interest. We ended up at a cemetery where many members of our family are buried. Several headstones share common family surnames that are representative of Sumter County's Turkish families. As we walked through the cemetery, she gave an account of the lives of various people who had passed away. We came upon the recent gravesite of a young man in his twenties. Helen admired the flowers, carefully pulled a weed or two, and commented that the family had really taken good care of his gravesite. She also was filled with great sorrow at the passing of such a young person. Helen loves passionately and feels pain deeply. She told me that she had come to know me and love me, and that she wanted me to continue to visit her. I assured her that I would, as she was family, not only by blood but also now through a relationship.

Helen is also feisty. She has always had a very strong will, standing up to those who sought to keep her down. She said that when she was in school, people used to refer to her as the "mean white Turk." She confronted students (male and female), bus drivers, school teachers, administrators, and even community leaders. She believes firmly in equality and is quick to speak her mind. She said that she has always wanted to write a book or appear on Oprah, and that this is probably the closest she will come to it. Helen had a plethora of documents that she shared with me, including birth certificates, court documents, magazines, newspaper articles, and pictures. She treasures these documents and keeps them in a large plastic bag with a zipper in a very safe place. When she showed them to me, I was amazed at the number of documents that she has kept throughout the years. Many of the papers had yellowed over the years, but they were still intact. She even had some of the items laminated for safekeeping.

Helen's stories are heartbreaking. She recalls with detailed precision events that happened over fifty years ago as if they had happened yesterday. Her internal conflict regarding the way she feels about the people who demanded segregation is a constant battle. She desperately wants to forgive but has difficulty forgetting the way she was treated. Through it all, she tried to make sure that her children's and grandchildren's educational experiences were better than her own. Her participation was extremely important in many ways, but mostly because her reaction to segregation was different from the other three participants. Her personal anecdotes offer our readers a unique perspective on how some people fought segregation at the time.

Jean

Jean is and always has been brave. She is also steady and grounded. During the time of our interviews, she underwent surgery that would keep her off of her feet for a while. She faced that, just as she faced daunting events when she was a child, with extreme courage.

Our conversations were more serious than some of the conversations that the other participants and I had. When she was younger, Jean was an inspiration to other Turkish students in that she was one of the first two Turkish students to graduate from Hillcrest High School. During our interviews, she was very open about many sensitive topics. She discussed the fact that Turkish people often had to sit in other areas of churches, theaters, buses, and hospitals. During one interview she explained, "I remember one occasion when I, I think I told you once before that we used to go out, and we'd ride to town on public transportation. They would make you go to the back of the bus." I asked, "So did you ever, did you automatically go to the back because you knew that that's what you were supposed to do?" She responded, "Oh, they would send you to the back." I questioned, "They would send you back there?" She replied, "Yes, they would tell you to go to the back, yes."

Since Jean was one of the first Turkish students to attend a white high school, she probably endured more resistance than most. We conducted our interviews over the phone because we do not live near each other. Jean met her husband at a summer camp. While there, she heard about an employment opportunity and inquired. She was hired and moved away from Sumter for a period. She and her husband have served in several churches, and Jean even worked in a college for a while.

Jean earned the right to attend Hillcrest High School when she was in the eleventh grade. As expected, she faced great opposition, being one of the pioneers of social change in the community. Jean is a very sweet person. She has moved on with her life, in spite of the way that others treated her when she was young. She is very open to learning about the history of the Turkish people, and she thirsts for more information regarding our genetics. She hopes that this project will help her to understand more about our history and who we are ethnically.

Jean is the one participant who graduated from high school. Boaz, Tonie, and Helen quit for a variety of reasons. They either did not feel prepared, decided to get married, or chose to avoid the resistance that they faced while attending the white high school. In spite of leaving high school early, two of the three took the General Educational Development (GED) test and passed, and one even went on to receive a doctoral degree.

When I asked Jean to comment on earning the right to attend high school with non-Turkish white people, she stated, "I hated even getting on the bus. It was a burden to have to go to school. They never accepted us in anything. They rejected us. Any class activities, you weren't a part of it. Some quit. They couldn't handle it. My friend and I stuck it out, though."

Tonie

Tonie has a very small frame but a huge heart. When I arrived at her house, she took me on a tour of the yard. She likes to garden and is very knowledgeable about plants and flowers. She was raised in a very large family and told me, "Back then, we didn't have TV and things so we spent a lot of time at home. We had all of our meals together, morning, noon, and night, where the blessing was always asked." While family was of paramount importance to her parents, education was not. Tonie's parents had limited schooling but were still able to raise several kids and provide for all of them. While times were tight, Tonie said that she was unaware that they were poor. They always had food on the table, and they were never in need of anything.

Tonie has a very healthy sense of self, in spite of her childhood educational experiences. She does not allow those experiences to affect her self-esteem today. The last year that she attended school was the ninth grade. She stopped going to school because of the pressures of school and home. When she approached her parents about taking a correspondence course in order to take the GED test, they were not supportive. She married a man in the military, had children, and then traveled all over the world. She was a stay-at-home mom and worked occasionally when her children were older. As an adult, she rarely thinks about being Turkish. She identifies herself as being white and does not like to be thought of as being any different. She also has a vivid imagination and a sharp memory. When recalling memories from her elementary school years, she was able to describe things meticulously. When I asked her if the Dalzell School had a graduation ceremony, she responded, "Yes. I went to an eighth-grade graduation. I wore a dress that was pulled off of the shoulders and fitted in the bodice. It had ruffles all the way down and had a hoop under it. It was light green."

Tonie is compassionate. She has forgiven those who demanded segregation and even occasionally visits the gravesite of one of the boys who was the least accepting of the Turkish students when they attended the white schools. I was with her on one occasion. She called me over to the gravesite and made a point to let me know that she had forgiven him. It was almost as if she were trying to say it in his presence. She told me that in spite of the way things used to be, she was not bitter. She was truly saddened by his death. She said that the past is in the past and that there is no point in harboring ill feelings toward those who were unaccepting of the Turkish people. She regrets that she and others had to endure segregation at the time, but she knows that she cannot change the past. She only wishes that things could have been different. Tonie, like Boaz and the other participants, was vital to this project. She shared newspaper clippings, books, photographs, and documents that she thought might aid me in this project. Tonie called me often to check on the status of my work and to encourage me over the phone. Without her help, this project would not have been complete.

Up until now, Turkish people have always been reluctant to share their lives and stories with the outside world. For the most part, they do not talk publically about their heritage, their dreams, their mistreatment, and the ordeal of integrating the white schools of Sumter County. All four participants agreed that most people—including their own young family members—have little comprehension of what happened during the past two centuries, and they have a difficult time believing it. Helen explained in one of her interviews that she could not talk about this issue with her grandchildren. They dismiss her stories because they sound so foreign to them. Likewise, Tonie made a comment that there are few people, even in South Carolina, who are aware of the Turkish people and what they experienced during the Integration Movement. When she chooses to confide in someone and tell them about her educational experiences, the reaction is always one of shock. Jean also said that her children have difficulty believing her stories. Boaz encountered disbelief in his own church. The members found out about their minister's educational experiences by reading one of the books that he wrote about growing up as a Turkish boy during the Integration Movement.

So I probed my participating informants about why they decided to speak up in this project. I specifically asked: "What do you hope this study will accomplish?" Boaz stated, "I think it's good for some of those who have their ideas so to speak about the 'Turks' to understand our feelings. We're proud of who we are. I think it will be educational to a lot of people; and it will blow the minds of some of them. They may not like it, but I say they need to know it." When I asked Jean what she hoped the study would accomplish, she replied, "I hope it will help us know more about the Turkish people, and I hope that it will help us to understand their experience." Helen said, "The truth needs to be told. I hope people who read this will learn a lot about the way things were, and the injustice that the Turkish people endured." Perhaps Tonie said it simplest and best: "I think the world needs to know what happened back then."

~ The Setting for Our Story ~

The setting for our story is Sumter County, South Carolina. Sumter County and its county seat, the City of Sumter, are named after General Thomas Sumter, the "Fighting Gamecock" of Revolutionary War fame (and friend of our Turkish ancestor, Joseph Benenhaley). Although Sumter County reflects much of the culture of the historic Black Belt (the stretch of plantations, dark soil, and African slaves from Texas to Delaware), it is geographically located in the midlands of South Carolina, about an hour and a half from the Atlantic coastline in one direction and the Blue Ridge Mountains in the other.

The 2010 US Census lists Sumter County's population at 107,456, of which 50 percent is made up of white individuals, 48 percent is made up of black individuals, and the rest is a mixture of other races. The county seat is Sumter, a city of 40,524 people, with 47 percent white people and 50 percent black people. (Census data presented in this book are drawn from US Census Bureau publications for 1790–2012, such as the "Decennial Census" and "American Community Survey."

The Census Bureau has changed its methodology and reporting style over the years. Therefore, such information and percentages may vary slightly, reflecting the different publications and tabular presentations. In most cases, we will simply identify the source as the "US Census.")

During the 1950s, the period of my focus on the Turkish people's push for entry to the white schools, both Sumter and Sumter County numbered about half their current population. The city of Sumter was about two-thirds white people and Sumter County was about three-fourths black people in those days. The "others" category has never been a significant proportion of the total population.

The rural areas that served as the locus of this project and the traditional home to most of the Turkish people—Dalzell and Stateburg—are in some ways the same today as back then, just more populous. The immediate area of much community activity (such as the church and cemetery) has been developed commercially, a result of the creation and expansion of Shaw Air Force Base since the 1940s. The 2010 census estimated Dalzell with slightly over three thousand citizens and Stateburg numbering almost fourteen hundred citizens. White individuals predominate over blacks in both areas, with only a handful of "other" races.

The highway leading eastward from the state capital, in Columbia, into Sumter County is lonely. Except for a cemetery that divides the lanes, a pair of old cement bridges that mirror one another across the Wateree River, and a picturesque blackwater swamp, the view is limited to road signs, a few stores, and many trees. Historical Sumter County family surnames can be seen repeating themselves on road signs, businesses, and schools. One does not need to travel far to find a beautiful sunset at Swan Lake, old plantation homes, or the ruins of forgotten buildings. The remains of homeless chimneys and porches suggest that brutal times have come and gone.

This area is quaint enough that a visitor might happen upon sandy roads out in the surrounding countryside and tour a downtown that reflects yesteryear. Like most small metropolitan areas, there are various restaurants, parks, educational institutions, libraries, a mall, a hospital, a museum, and even an air force base. In downtown, one can find the old courthouse, the old opera house, and most of the old commercial and business operations of the area. The people of Sumter often cruise along Broad Street Extension to find a multitude of modern stores, schools, businesses, and small shops. While Sumter County is more rural than urban, the city has a growing number of new business establishments that have brought many shopping and employment opportunities to the people.

Spanish moss haunts many of the older trees, and muscadine vines can be found along neighborhood roads in late August. Children can be seen walking their dogs without leashes as they head to the fireworks stands. Some of the more agricultural residents set up fruit stands along the sides of the roads to sell their hot boiled peanuts and fresh produce. The sound of roosters crowing can be heard all throughout the day. Mobile homes are readily available, as are older brick houses. Newer subdivisions have begun sprouting up in the outskirts of Sumter.

The people of this community are friendly, and it seems that everyone knows everyone else. One seldom goes to town without running into a familiar face. The words "sir" and "ma'am" are common in the mouths of young and old alike, and conversations often revolve around the passing of someone or ailments common to all. Sumterites are generous with their time and with their possessions. One rarely goes to a neighbor's house without bringing something from the garden, and when it is time to leave, someone always asks, "What's your hurry?"

In August of 2006, when I drove from Georgia to Sumter to start gathering information and material about the Turkish people, the field research for this book began. I had visited the area many times previously, since my mother and many relatives live there; but this was different. I returned to Sumter in 2006 and 2007 on "official business," exploring the history of my Turkish ancestors.

I began my academic investigation with a meeting with a prominent member of the community establishment of Sumter County. I had begun to research the history of Sumter County in the library there in town. An employee of the library directed me to "Mayor Bubba." W. A. "Bubba" McElveen Jr. had served as a city councilman and mayor during the 1970s and 1980s. He had been a very popular politician; and, afterward, he assumed the role as purveyor of goodwill and historical information for the community. Apparently he was well-liked by most. He agreed to an interview and we met and talked several times. I wrote down some of my thoughts and impressions after my interviews with this man, and they reveal a lot about him, his community, and the history of the Turkish people in this area. Here are a few excerpts from my notes about those sessions with McElveen:

> He is a very kind, southern man. He searched through his files and pulled out a file surprisingly labeled "Turks." He flipped through a green file folder, about an inch thick, and told me that the articles that he has collected over the years were in no particular order. He said I could take the folder to the table outside of his office and read, but we talked for at least 30 minutes before that....
>
> When I asked him where he thought that the Turkish people came from, he explained that either General Thomas Sumter or Thomas Sumter's son married a French woman and that she may have brought some Moroccans with her to Sumter County. He also said that another possibility would be that since the Ottoman Empire (Turkey) was so powerful at one time, that anyone who looked foreign was simply referred to as being a Turk, regardless of where they really originated. This group of Turkish people in Sumter County would not actually be Turkish (from Turkey) but referred to as Turks because of the Ottoman influence in the

world. He did state that the Turkish people were not Red Bones. If so, we would be allowed to accept money from the government for being Native American. Since we are not allowed to do that, we are not Native American....

He told me that the best thing going for my people (regarding our status as whites) was that Thomas Sumter himself stood up in a court room and recognized them as being white. Because of Thomas Sumter, my people were allowed to vote, which gave them great political power in the county....

He said that he will never forget a lesson he learned through politics. Apparently, during a past election a politician had taken the Turkish vote, about 300 people. It seems to him that the Turkish people vote as a block, so a candidate who has the Turkish block has 300 votes right off the bat. He told me that the Turkish people pick the county's officials—they have in the past and they still do. This was a valuable lesson for him to learn....

He said that some of my people are very particular about being referred to as being different. They believe that referring to them as a distinct group, other than white, is denigrating. They do not like to be called "Turks." They also do not like the attention....

He also told me that his boss is Turkish. He said that he holds the Turkish people in very high regard. He explained that they are attractive people with good skin tone that everyone wants.

I'm sorry to report that "Mayor Bubba" passed away after only a few of our meetings. I am very grateful to him for what he shared with me. His words during our sessions validated Sumter as a place that, like most southern communities, has been through difficult times over the years; but it has tried to move forward.

Similarly, the Turkish people of Sumter County have endured difficult times, but we are still standing. The stories of those who lived during the period of this investigation will be told here, using their own words, in an effort to represent them as authentically as possible.

In the rest of this section, I will relate the story—based on my own research and as told in the words of my relatives—of our ancestral Turkish culture. Chapter 7 covers the journey of the Turkish people—from isolation to assimilation—from a historical perspective. Chapter 8 reveals my respondents' reflections about their ancestry, ethnicity, community, relations with white and black people, and oppression by the system. Chapter 9 describes their days at the Dalzell School for Turks and their integrating Edmunds and Hillcrest High Schools. Chapter 10—based on interviews with younger respondents—shows what the Turkish community looks like today. Finally, chapter 11 concludes this section with my personal reactions and feelings about the Turkish experience in this area.

~ *Chapter Seven* ~

Our Journey

From Isolation to Assimilation

Sadly, the Turkish people of Sumter County seem to be fading away. The older generation is passing on; most Turkish people today marry outside the Turkish circle; and many of the younger crowd seem disinterested in their cultural history. Moreover, contemporary forces threaten to dilute or contradict our heritage in this community. Some groups would like to absorb the Turkish people into a broader society of mixed-blood ancestry, that is, the Melungeons. Other activists argue that our founders were actually American Indians. Already, some Turkish families of Sumter County are reconsidering their historical identity or drifting away from their traditional legacy. My point is that, after two centuries of adversity, our people—and our culture—seem to be assimilating into broader society; and we must tell our story before time and evolving forces erase our cultural history.

One of the main things I hope that readers will recognize as they follow this story is my earlier point that history generally has been recorded by the privileged about the privileged. Many gaps exist in historical text, because the voices of the underprivileged have been ignored and forgotten. When gaps such as these exist, and they can be bridged, historians should seek ways to offer various perspectives on the way things were. I sought to search and find the voices of those who had been ignored in historical texts. Their voices deserve to be heard and recorded for all to hear.

Browder documented the "true history" of the Turkish people in the first century of their existence, covering their origins and growth during the 1800s. The key to his success in solving the mystery of Turkish history was the fact that he secured the confidence and cooperation of the Turkish community in this investigation. However, there is more to our history than Joseph Benenhaley and the early years of the Dalzell settlement. The traditional narrative of the past led into an evolving narrative of the contemporary community and that journey must also be shared. Now, again with the assistance of living Turkish persons, I will attempt to tell the Turkish historical experience of the past century, the 1900s, from our perspective. I will combine my own historical research with interviews among the Turkish people of Sumter County to demonstrate our journey through isolation, segregation, discrimination, oppression, integration, and assimilation.

~ Isolation and Segregation ~

Whatever one concludes about ancestral origins, our investigation shows that the Turkish people have faced many struggles in the past two centuries because of the tones of their skin. They were not light enough to be considered white people by broader society nor were they dark enough to be considered black by that society. Consequently, despite continuous patriotic service to their state and country, the Turkish people lived and were set apart, as a unique, distinct society for most of the twentieth century in rural South Carolina. For generations, the Turkish people maintained their own institutions, such as churches and schools; and they lived their lives separated, in important ways, from the rest of regional society.

There is considerable confusion and disagreement about the "who" or "how" or "why" related to the isolation of the Turkish people of Sumter County. Some believe that there are two explanations, or at least a mixture of mutual preferences, for this isolation: Turkish people chose to isolate themselves; and society pressured them into isolating. Sumter's *The Item* reported an anecdote about a specific situation from the 1930s as part of a retrospective feature ("Yesteryear," July 5, 2009), and this account suggested that both sides embraced separatism:

> An announcement that appeared as an ad, "To Whom It May Concern," and placed by Henry Benenhaley Sr., stated that "a false report" was being circulated that Superintendent W. O. Cain was trying to put the Turks in the Hillcrest School. However, in a meeting with Cain, Benenhaley said he was told that placement of the Turk students in the school was a matter for the Hillcrest trustees to decide. Benenhaley added that he had met with Hillcrest trustees last year and a high school teacher was provided to the Turks' school, "and as far as the trustees and the Turks are concerned," Benenhaley stated, "both are satisfied with the arrangement. We have our own church and our own schools and all that we ask is that we be given the right kind of school of our own and we believe that Mr. Cain will see that this is done for us."

William D. Workman, a *Charleston News and Courier* reporter who interviewed people from the community before the integration of schools in the 1950s, wrote several articles about the Turkish people of Sumter County. In one of these articles

(December 17, 1950), he offered the following commentary about their clannishness: "Their forefathers made a mistake by building a wall about themselves. That clannishness, manifested also by a patriarchal type of leadership only now fading away set the Turks up as a group separate and distinct from their neighbors. But it is easy to understand why they stuck together in their associations. The distinctive appearance of the Sumter county Turks kept them from general social association with their white neighbors, although they have always had business, legal and other dealings with them."

High Hills of Santee Baptist Church, founded in 1770, was an early center of the Stateburg community. The pictured structure was built in 1803. White congregants sat on the right, Turkish congregants sat on the left, and black congregants occupied the balcony. Photograph provided by Glen Browder.

Numerous other stories written about the Turkish people likewise have implied that they chose to isolate themselves from the rest of the county. What these authors did not mention is that the Turkish people had been segregated for many generations and faced discrimination throughout all aspects of community life. So, certainly, the Turkish people were quiet and kept mostly to themselves. However, their separation was not a simple matter of subcultural choice. Many of them sought to be accepted into the dominant culture but were denied access by white society.

Regardless of who instigated Turkish clannishness, it is unsurprising that segregation would pervade social relations in this area for a long, long time. Perhaps nothing conveys the dynamics of southern segregation like early interactions among the congregants within the High Hills of Santee Baptist Church, also called High Hills Baptist Church and commonly known as High Hills Church. This house of worship was located in the home area, Stateburg, of their champion, General Thomas Sumter; in fact, General Sumter provided the lot of land on which it stands. The High Hills Baptist Church was founded in 1772 with Richard Furman, for whom Furman University was named, as the pastor. The current structure, built in 1803, is still a place of worship ("High Hills of Santee Baptist Church").

James Ray (1878–1929), great-grandson of the patriarch, and his wife, Nellie Benenhaley Ray (1879–1952), donated the land on which the original Long Branch Baptist Church was built in 1904. Photograph circa early 1900s. Courtesy of Greg Thompson Collection, donated to the collection by Mertis Ray Benenhaley.

At one time during the mid-1800s, all three groups attended this church, with the white worshippers sitting on the right, Turkish worshippers sitting on the left, and black slave worshippers in the gallery (Gregorie 1954, 469). Although it might be surprising that this church was made up of three ethnic groups, it is not shocking that they were separated inside. After the Civil War, in 1869, the black ex-slaves decided to establish a separate church. The exact history is unclear, but it appears that, in the 1870s, they set up several churches, all within the same general area. These churches are now known as: High Hills Baptist Church, which is separate from the older church of the same name ("High Hills Baptist Church"), High Hills AME Church ("High Hills AME Church"), Wayman Chapel AME Church

("Wayman Chapel AME Church"), and Hopewell Baptist Church ("Hopewell Baptist Church").

Similarly, in 1904, the Turkish people built their own church—Long Branch Baptist Church—on land donated by James and Nellie Ray in nearby Dalzell (White 1975, n.p.). This church continued as part of the Santee Baptist Association and the South Carolina Mission Board ("Long Branch Baptist Church"). Then, in 1971, some of the Turkish community established another, independent congregation—Springbank Baptist Church—about a half mile away ("Springbank Baptist Church").

Nellie Benenhaley Ray (1879–1952), great-granddaughter of the patriarch and wife of James Ray (1878–1929). Nellie had applied a powderaed makeup for this photograph, circa 1930s. Courtesy of Greg Thompson Collection. Photograph donated to the collection by Mertis Ray Benenhaley.

The first minister for the Turkish people of this area was Joseph H. Mitchell, a white man who helped Long Branch Baptist Church increase its membership dramatically in his few years there, from 1904–1908. Toward the end of his long career, Mitchell reflected on his Dalzell friends: "Looking back over my forty years of ministry, I find some of my warmest friendships were among the Turks. I think especially of Uncle Tom, William, Noah, and Henry Benenhaley. Henry was and is as true a friend as any preacher ever had" ("Long Branch Church" 1943). This personal reflection suggests that some people were willing to come together in worshipping their God. However, for the most part, the mainstream populace in this area did not seem interested in socializing anywhere and anyway with their Turkish neighbors. Isolation and segregation of the Turkish people would continue for generations in Sumter County; and, unfortunately, that separatism would take a pernicious toll—in the form of discrimination and oppression—on the Dalzell settlement.

The first minister and deacons of Long Branch Baptist Church, founded in 1904. The church was built next door to the original school, near the patriarch's homesite. Left to right: Herbert Ray Sr. (1853–1924), William J. Benenhaley (1858–1920), pastor Joseph H. Mitchell (who served 1904–1908), Henry Benenhaley (1867–1950), and Noah Benenhaley (1860–1939). Courtesy of Greg Thompson Collection, donated to the collection by Isaac Benenhaley/David Peagler.

~ Discrimination and Oppression ~

It is clear that General Thomas Sumter's early voucher for Joseph Benenhaley as a white man did not extend to full equality for the Turkish people in either the 1800s or the 1900s. The Revolutionary War hero had been a defender of white status for his Turkish friends; but they were not really accepted by white individuals for most of their history. The Turkish citizens were allowed to vote when voting was limited to white people; and they fought alongside white soldiers in the Civil War, in World War I, and in World War II. Yet, for many years, they were not appreciated for their sacrifices and they were ostracized from white society. While such separatism was not legalized as strictly and harshly as was the case with black people, the Turkish people endured increasing abuse as routine segregation tended toward rampant discrimination.

We heard countless comments and anecdotes about discrimination as we moved around the area. Most incidents reported to us were mundane slights. One informant told us that a white child was instructed by his mother to "stop playing with me." Another said that white teenagers warned their friends to "stay away from the Turks." There also were incidents of snobbish treatment in businesses; a Turkish mother said she was refused lay-a-way privileges at a department store; another said that a beauty parlor operator refused to cut the hair of her darker friend; and one community member remembered the cynical bulldozing of Turkish gravestones at a cemetery. There also were scary moments, such as everyday fights between Turkish and white students during the integration years, a teenager's horror at seeing a burning cross in her Turkish family's front yard, and the whispered tale of a Turkish man's beating and death.

Actually, though, our informants told us that what hurt most was learning what their white friends and neighbors in that area really thought and said about them. They felt betrayed by the folks with whom they had worked in the fields and factories, played ball, gone fishing, and hunted deer. One incident in particular stands out as an example of heartfelt pain. According to Greg Thompson (who married into the Turkish community), one of the old Turkish men defended a white friend for years, even when other community members told him that person was working against them. "No, no," the older man said, "He's trying his best to help us." Years later, the old Turkish man was shown a document confirming the

The Long Branch minister and leadership burned the mortgage note in the early 1950s, signifying they had paid off the loan for building their church. Left to right: Ray Buckner, holding the burning note (1916–1999), Henry Benenhaley (1889–1960), Jacob Oxendine Sr. (1895–1979), Herbert Ray (1892–1975), Julius Benenhaley (1891–1987), Marion Hood (1907–1979), Hammond Ray (1914–1990), Ernest Benenhaley (1923–2006), Wallace Benenhaley Jr. (1930–), Vernon "Chic" Buckner (1929–2011), Pastor Doyle Burgess, and Jacob Oxendine Jr. (1920–2010). Courtesy of Long Branch Baptist Church.

The congregation of Long Branch Baptist Church celebrated paying off the debt of their church in the early 1950s with a mortgage-burning ceremony.
Courtesy of Long Branch Baptist Church.

white friend's involvement in the continued segregation of "Turks" in that area. Our informant told us that the old man broke down and cried (Thompson Collection and Interviews).

Most cited experiences were tied to specific situations of disrespect and exclusion. However, mistreatment of the Turkish people went far beyond personalized discrimination; public power was exercised commonly and unjustly to proclaim the message that the "Sumter Turks" needed to stay in their place in rural Dalzell. Even by the presumed standard of "separate but equal," this subculture experienced systemic oppression.

The pattern of official offense was most evident in the schools. For many decades, the Turkish students attended their own segregated schools in the area. A historical photo collection showed that, in 1913, one school was called Benenhaley and had twenty-eight students and one teacher (Woody & Thigpen 2005, 96), and a 1928 article in the *State* reported that there were about one hundred children and three white teachers in two schools, one located in Dalzell and the other in Stateburg ("Sumter Colony Locally Called Turks").

The Turkish families asked for admission to the white schools in 1934 but they were refused. The next year, the county constructed a new building, the Dalzell School for Turks, which served those children until the 1960s. The Dalzell School was not accredited for college entrance as it only went up to the eleventh grade; and, upon finishing the eleventh grade, students were awarded a certificate instead of a diploma.

Long Branch Baptist Church in Dalzell. The Turkish people split from High Hills and built their own church in 1904, and a larger church was constructed in 1921. Pictured: the third and current church building on Peach Orchard Road, which dates from 1960. Outsiders used to call Long Branch "the Turk church"; however, worshippers of other ethnic groups are members and attend services. Courtesy of Long Branch Baptist Church.

Springbank Baptist Church, formed in 1971 in Dalzell. Pictured: the church and its Family Life Center on Fish Road. Members include both Turkish people and other diverse groups. Courtesy of Springbank Baptist Church.

Known as the "Dalzell School for Turks," this building served the community from the 1930s until 1961, when integration with the previously white schools shut it down. Courtesy of the South Carolina Department of Archives and History.

Students and their teacher at the Dalzell School, circa 1930s. Courtesy of the Greg Thompson Collection.

More Dalzell students and their teacher, circa 1940s.
Courtesy of the Greg Thompson Collection.

Three grades posed for this photograph at Dalzell School, circa late 1950s.
Front row, first graders; second row, second graders; third row, third
graders. Courtesy of Vickie Buckner Underwood.

It is clear that Turkish education was not a priority of the white establishment; and Turkish children constantly were slighted and shortchanged. In a situation reeking of incongruous drama, these families—originally championed by a Revolutionary War hero as Caucasians, acknowledged since then as white people, and routinely allowed to participate in restricted white Democratic Party primaries—eventually would have to go to the federal courts and plead for equal educational opportunity.

The pattern of discrimination and oppression against the Turkish population also could be seen throughout the rest of public life in Sumter County. For example, most of the rooms in the local hospital were reserved for white patients; a smaller number were reserved for black patients; and two were designated for Turkish patients (according to W. A. "Bubba" McElveen in a 1996 column, "Our Town," for *The Item*). In fact, arbitrary social differentiation was a critical part of the beginning and ending of life for Turkish citizens. Designations in the space for "race" on birth certificates and death certificates were left up to the individuals filling out those forms; and we found that many Turkish people had been labeled as "Turk" or some other description rather than "white." We even found that some siblings born of the same parents had been categorized differently (one as "white" and another as "Turk").

It is very probable that the various groups either chose or accepted some of this separation early on, for a variety of reasons; however, with time, discriminatory practices became more pervasive and oppressive in Sumter County. This situation bred special stress and turmoil, particularly in the middle decades of the twentieth century.

World War II—or more specifically the activation of Shaw Air Force Base in the 1940s—brought many outsiders into their quiet, rural community, and that community changed forever. The US government bought much of the land that the Turkish people had farmed for generations; federal jobs at the base opened up to them; and military personnel from other parts of the country became part of their families and lives. These changes directly challenged historic arrangements among the various ethnic cultures in Sumter County. Most importantly for the Turkish people, the time had come to demand equal educational opportunity for their children, and school integration would break down historic barriers for this community.

~ The Integration Movement ~

A clear illustration of the setting and plight of the Turkish enclave was their fight for educational opportunity midpoint of the twentieth century. Fortunately, the traumatic Integration Movement paved the way for integration and assimilation into broader society. The Turkish people of this area again asked to attend the white schools in the late 1940s, relatively ignored by a nation fixated on the more prominent and much celebrated civil rights movement in places like Little Rock, Montgomery, and Selma.

~ Second-Class Citizens ~

Sumter County had provided the Turkish people with limited public education for many years, perhaps as far back as the late 1800s; but their children generally were treated as second-class citizens in secondhand institutions.

Historian Anne King Gregorie noted the situation at mid-century in *History of Sumter County* (1954): "Until recent years, the Turks had their own separate schools, one near Stateburg with a white teacher, and the other near Dalzell with two teachers, thus adding to the racial and financial problems of Sumter County. Apparently, these two schools were consolidated into one in the outskirts of Dalzell, with three white teachers. This school made some effort to prepare pupils for high school, but was not accredited for college entrance" (469–70). Another news article—which appeared in 1928 in the *State*—hinted at the prevailing attitude in a report that two schools were given over to "Turk" children, both "good frame buildings left vacant by the recent consolidation of the white schools of the community"("Sumter Colony Locally Called Turks").

An interesting and revealing view of Turkish education earlier in the past century was conveyed in 1916 in the local *Watchman and Southron* account of a special program concluding the school year at Benenhaley School in Stateburg. After praising Miss Katie Ray, apparently the principal, for her organization of the event, J. C. Dunbar wrote: "Miss Ray is a conscientious young woman who has spared no labor and pains in trying to instruct those under her tutorship, that they can become useful men and women, when they grow up. The exercises inspired the writer with the thought that these people have natural ability, which can be cultivated and developed into a power for good to themselves and those by whom they are surrounded. They are a quiet and inoffensive people, who attend to their own business; they are industrious and have an ambition to build themselves up in a moral and intellectual way and should have the sympathy and encouragement of all right-thinking people"(3).

Older Turkish citizens have expressed many warm thoughts about their days at the Dalzell School for Turks. However, it is clear that not all their memories are pleasant. Eleazer Benenhaley recounted some of those mixed feelings in his biography (*Moulded Clay*, 1983, 14–17). He fondly related tales of recess among the schoolboys: "Playtime at Dalzell was something. . . . we played ball, the older boys played cowboys. . . . The brave boys would participate in boxing" (15). He also noted the importance of moral instruction: "Thank God for those teachers who taught the Bible" (15). And he appreciated the efforts of his teachers: "My first grade teacher was a lovely lady and I think she did her best for us" (15). However, he also was adamant about the lack of resources at the school: "There were no research books and the only microscope at the Dalzell School was a picture in the science book.... As I look back over those years and realize how much I missed, it is hard not to be bitter" (17).

Sara Jernigan, at ninety-two years of age, is likely the last living teacher from the Dalzell School; and, in an interview on June 20, 2014, she recalled vividly the good and bad of those days. "I taught the first and second grades; and I thoroughly enjoyed my work. I adored those children. I especially remember making outfits for them to wear in a play about 'Tom Thumb'; and I still see and talk with some of my students here in Sumter." Jernigan said she did not know where the Turkish people came from. "They were slightly darker than white people; but they certainly were not Indians or blacks. They mostly kept to themselves." She also said that they were not treated right by the people of this area; and they resented not being able to go to Hillcrest School. "I remember one lady from here in town asked me why I wanted to waste my time at the Turk school; and I told her I was proud to teach there. There was not a thing wrong with them; and they didn't get involved with murder and other bad things that we read about in the paper."

A single incident conveyed rising tensions regarding Turkish education in the 1940s. Greg Thompson told us about the case of his mother-in-law—Leah Benenhaley Peagler—a 1949 valedictorian at the Dalzell School for Turks, who had prepared her brief graduating comments as presented here: "We are grateful for having been born and brought up in a country which does so much for the education of most youth. As we leave our school we are grateful for the basic training we received. However, we know we are not prepared well for a future of opportunities as we received a lesser education than what we deserved. We leave our school without a true education. We do feel fortunate for the basic training we received, but know that our hopes and futures rest not with that training but with our own desires to succeed in life."

Leah was instructed that the speech was inappropriate, and she was required to write another one of more positive nature. The chastened teenager wrote another speech under close direction: "We are grateful for having been born and brought up in a country which does so much for the education of the youth. As we graduate from high school, we are grateful for a country which has furnished the opportunity for such good basic training. We leave high school feeling that we are exceedingly fortunate. The training we have had makes possible a future of interest and excitement." According to Thompson, when the valedictorian delivered the latter speech at the school's commencement exercises, the audience response was total silence. "Not a single person clapped because they all knew about the speech being rewritten." However, at Long Branch Baptist Church on Sunday, where Leah gave the original version after the regular service, "She got a standing ovation" (Thompson Collection and Interviews).

The Turkish people had long been aware of segregation among themselves, black people, and white people in Sumter County; and, eventually, they grew tired of the impact on their children. These parents reached a turning point; and they united to achieve equal educational opportunities.

~ **Decade of Trial and Triumph** ~

The 1950s would prove to be a time of continuous legal challenges and maneuvering for the Turkish people of this area (*Hood v. Board;* 1953, 1956, 1961, and 1961).

Rarely does anyone recite the names of those brave souls who stepped forward to challenge the system by filing a federal lawsuit—so here is the official list of litigants, in alphabetical order: Heyward Nathaniel Benenhaley (1914–1966), Myrtle Benenhaley (1925–), Nell Benenhaley (1933–1997), Raymond Benenhaley Sr. (1912–2005), Stella Miller Hood Benenhaley (1920–2015), Wallace Levore Benenhaley Sr. (1903–1998), Connie Carolyn Benenhaley Buckner (1930–2013), Samuel Lewis Buckner (1923–2002), Peggy Ann Benenhaley Hood (1920–2010), Woodrow Wilson Hood, Jr. (1918–2002), Henry W. Lowrey (1915–2002), Ruth Annette Ray Lowrey (1917–2012), Eugene Ray (1908–1986), Irma Buckner Ray (1912–1999), Lever A. Ray (1910–1973), and Viola Hood Ray (1909–2001). They had little support, except for their attorney. But, in 1961, for the first time, all their children—from first grade to high school—took their classroom seats alongside white students.

The struggle began in 1949, when some of the Turkish leaders of the community sought to have their children admitted to the white high schools so that "they might enter college with a better standing than they can now have," according to reporter William Workman. In an article written for the *News and Courier, (Dec. 17, 1950)* Workman wrote:

> The Turks of Sumter county, who live about here and Stateburg, have their own school on the outskirts of Dalzell, but until now have not had opportunity to attend a local accredited high school.
>
> High school work of a sort has been conducted at the three-teacher Turk school, but the only accredited high school in the area is the Hillcrest school. Hillcrest serves white students from the four school districts in northwestern Sumter County and is a consolidated high school.
>
> This year the Turks tried to have some 12 to 15 of their children admitted to the Hillcrest high school. It would have been financially and educationally unsound to build a separate high school for that limited number of Turk children. The Hillcrest school board turned them down, and the Turks hired a lawyer and took their case into federal court.

A series of Sumter lawyers (including Ramon Schwartz, Ramon Schwartz Jr., Augustus Merrimon, and Ira Kaye) handled the Turkish appeal to federal law.

Attorney Kaye explained the situation, retrospectively and with some exaggeration, in a 1996 interview (Jewish Heritage Collection). Sumter County had a "white system, a black system, and technically, the Turks were in the white system, but it was a three-room special school that only Turks went to with teachers, none of them from the county. None of the white teachers would volunteer to teach there. So they got an extremely inferior education. Their kids were being screwed" (18–20).

Their fight paid off quickly in the City of Sumter, where the schools accepted a few Turkish students in 1950. However, the situation was different in the rural area of Dalzell, where most of the Turkish families were concentrated and tensions ran high. A US district judge issued a temporary order in favor of the Turkish children, and the local school acceded. However, white parents started a school boycott, and the county board then stopped the integration process (Kaye 1963).

The legal struggle for entry into Hillcrest High School proved to be difficult, lengthy, and entangled in the "mystery" of Joseph Benenhaley. Here is a 1953 account of the situation as reported in the *Lubbock Evening Journal ("South Carolina Colony")*: "A federal judge must go back to revolutionary War history Wednesday to settle a school segregation dispute over a mysterious colony of 'Turks.' The 'Turks,' a colony of some 300 persons, have petitioned the federal court of the eastern district of South Carolina for admittance to the Hillcrest School for white children in Sumter county. The colony, which up to now has had its own schools and churches, has been called 'as much a mystery to their neighbors as the mound builders,' by one historian and no one seems certain of its background."

The trustees of Hillcrest High School, citing the legality of segregated schools at that time, mounted a defense based on the history of the Turkish people as a reclusive and different race. For example, a member of the board asserted, in sworn testimony, that "the Turks" had always attended the separate school near Dalzell and had their own church and burial ground. He also said that "there is no social relationship between the white people of the community and the so-called 'Turks.'" A County Commissioner swore that the Turks were "clannish" and "dark-skinned and having features that are different from the white people of the community" ("The Evolution of a Government"). Curiously, after years of skirmishing, the Hillcrest trustees relented without a final decision in the courts; and Turkish students entered Hillcrest High School in 1954.

Unfortunately, their younger brothers and sisters remained segregated at the institution reserved for the Turkish community. These elementary students were at an extreme disadvantage when permitted to attend white high schools. Because they had not been granted a strong educational foundation in their early years, they were not prepared to be placed into classrooms with their White peers who did have access to proper educational facilities. The frustration that these Turkish students experienced in not being able to keep up with their classmates forced many of them to drop out of school, through no fault of their own.

Attorney Kaye, who handled this phase of their legal struggle with support from the American Civil Liberties Union and the Southern Regional Council, stated in a 1961 ACLU publication that "only local prejudice, ignorance, and superstitions are keeping these children from the main stream of American life." He described the Turkish students' elementary schooling this way in a later interview (Jewish Heritage Collection): "With the right to attend high school, the Turks now discovered that their children's inferior elementary schooling made high school very difficult for them. Its educational facilities were extremely poor. In an age of consolidated school districts with good libraries, laboratories and classroom aids, the Turks struggled on in a three room school for eight grades with no libraries and other equipment, local school teachers would not teach them and teachers were imported from another county." Kay also noted that this situation "meant that most of the children did not receive decent instruction which was reflected in poor grades in high school for most of them and a large number of drop-outs" (12).

Kaye therefore filed another lawsuit against the school board; and, again, without final disposition of the court, the county school trustees yielded. The legal obstacles collapsed on February 15, 1961, and news reports that same day chronicled the close of the long struggle for educational equality. The *Charlotte Observer* reported that "South Carolina's 'Turks' Tuesday won their seven-year battle to attend white elementary schools." In the fall of that year, all Turkish students were admitted into the white schools of Sumter County

Eleazer Benenhaley, who attended the old Dalzell School, still thinks back about what might have been: 'When I am in Sumter County, there are times when I pass by the spot where the old Dalzell School for 'Turks' once stood. I often wonder how it would have been, not only for me, but for those before me had we been given our rights to a decent education in the public schools of the area" (*An Analysis* 2008, 33).

When I think about that period of history, I am struck by the difference between the situation in Dalzell and what happened with the more prominent and national civil rights movement of that period. Several local school systems in southern states—including Clarendon County, South Carolina—had joined in a class action lawsuit that culminated in the landmark 1954 decision of *Brown v. Board of Education*. Most South Carolinians and other Americans were unaware that other underrepresented groups, such as these Turkish children in Dalzell, suffered just as blacks did before the US Supreme Court in 1954 ordered the racial integration of schools.

The local *Sumter Daily Item* had provided regular coverage of the integration effort; the state media periodically reported on the situation; and a few out-of-state news outlets carried wire stories about the legal bickering between plaintiffs and defendants in various forums of the federal judiciary. Here, to illustrate, are some selected examples of that coverage: "'Turks' Seeking Educational Opportunities," *News and Courier,* December 17, 1950; "S.C. 'Turks' To Attack School Law," the *State,* January 10, 1951; "South Carolina Colony of 'Turks,'" *Lubbock Evening Journal,* September 9, 1953; "Carolina 'Turks' Lose School Plea," *New York Times,* October 6, 1956; "Turks Win School Battle," *Charlotte Observer,* February 15, 1961; and "'Turk' Case Is Closed," *Sumter Daily Item,* February 15, 1961. But most often, the outside world focused on this case as a quirky twist of southern segregation (as did *Ebony Magazine* in "A Raceless People," 1957); and one newspaper even covered that litigation as a source of legal amusement ("Turkish Children No Longer Segregated, Thanks to the NAACP," *Pittsburgh Courier,* March 4, 1961).

By comparison, media from all over the country meticulously captured every aspect of every moment in 1957 when black teenagers—the "Little Rock Nine"—were escorted to Little Rock Central High School by the Arkansas National Guard. Furthermore, the world was fully aware of the black students' personal stories, which resonated with drama and compassion. But few Americans outside of Sumter County noticed, prior to Little Rock, when a handful of Turkish teenagers integrated Hillcrest High School—or, a few years later, when Turkish kids were finally admitted to the white elementary school. There was no national celebration of this subculture's struggle for equality. No one asked these young people about their dreams, or what they endured in that environment. And there has been no effort, since then, to commemorate the Turkish triumph several years before the integration of white and black students in the schools of Sumter County.

Thus ended, rather quietly but still painfully, a traumatic period in the history of this unusual community. A deeper discussion—covering both the drama and torment—of integrating the white schools appears in a later chapter. That was an emotional trauma for my four respondents, but it also ushered in a process of assimilation and a different, better life in the twenty-first century.

~ Assimilation in the New Century ~

During the last half of the twentieth century, the Turkish people of Sumter County traveled a transformative journey. Their Integration Movement opened the doors not only to the schools but also, eventually, to the world of a new century. Most Turkish youngsters began marrying outsiders, many moved to other areas, some changed their ancestral affinities, and, in many ways, the Turkish people now fit comfortably and well in the local environment.

A later discussion elaborates on how the Turkish community currently is adapting to the new world. However, the next two chapters present the results of my interviews with some of the teenagers from the 1950s, who now are elder citizens living in a better environment. Those conversations will tell us how they feel about their history; also they will relate what life was like for them when they were young, how it has changed, and what they hope for the future.

~ *Chapter Eight* ~

Reflections on Our Ancestry, Ethnicity, Community, Race Relations, and Systemic Oppression

Obviously, historical ambiguity has kept the Turkish people from understanding their origins and celebrating their heritage. I can personally attest to the fact that figuring out the history of the Turkish people has been a difficult and sensitive topic. Prior to the current project with my coauthor, I had little to go on other than oral tradition and genealogical records on the Internet. Most discussion had always gone back to the mysterious Joseph Benenhaley—and it had always ended in speculation and argument.

The great-grandson of General Thomas Sumter wrote that Joseph Benenhaley was a "Caucasian of Arab descent" in a 1917 newspaper article ("An Interesting People"); but even this description left room for individual interpretation. He also wrote about General Thomas Sumter's defending the white status of the Turkish people (*Stateburg and Its People* 1820). But without proof of our forefather's origins, the Turkish people of Sumter County have had to piece together skimpy tidbits and oral traditions that have been passed down from generation to generation.

I had never found any written documentation that explained precisely where Joseph Benenhaley was born, what his life was like, or where he was buried. I recently was told about the general vicinity of his suspected burial, in a wooded area adjacent to Shaw Air Force Base; but the exact location of his burial site cannot be determined. That area, which was part of the land that Thomas Sumter deeded to Joseph Benenhaley, had been bulldozed for a base maintenance facility many years ago; it simply looks like undeveloped land now. On a cold rainy afternoon in 2014, Browder, Greg Thompson, and I went there, and my coauthor walked behind the maintenance facility and took a picture of the overgrown area. However, the exact burial site of Joseph Benenhaley, our progenitor, may never be identified or memorialized.

Readers should keep in mind that the initial interviews in this project were conducted before we knew the results of Browder's research. So, neither I nor my respondents had any solid information about our true history during those conversations. We believed the traditional narrative, but we could cite no real evidence to support our beliefs. It was simply a matter of faith on our part.

Therefore, our focus in this chapter is how Boaz, Jean, Helen, and Tonie coped with these issues regarding their uncertain place in history and society. Most of the time, we discussed their vague Turkish origins, what it meant being Turkish in an unfriendly environment, and how Turkish people related to white and black residents in Sumter County. Also, some may have difficulty—as did my relatives—with the discomforting questions and dialogue in these pages; and academic types may find fault with some of the blunt language. However, I am proud of this discussion. It is an honest account of how the Turkish people have struggled to survive and make sense of their curious history.

~ Questions about Where We Came From ~

The first thing I wanted to know was what my relatives thought about where the Turkish people came from—that is, did they believe the traditional narrative? As might be expected. Our discussions rambled considerably, owing to the fuzzy interplay of ancestry and ethnicity. Like most people, they have not had any anthropological or sociological training; and I believe they were uneasy talking about such aspects of their history.

The four participants differed in how they answered my question about ancestry. But they all stated that they were of Turkish descent. Generally, they related their origins to General Thomas Sumter having brought their ancestors to Sumter County. Boaz stated the situation very well for the group. "Going back to the Benenhaley name and studying Thomas Sebastian Sumter's history of Stateburg, and Robert Bass's book, which is titled, *The Gamecock*, and then Anne King Gregorie's book, all three of these point out the fact that the first Benenhaley, Joseph Benenhaley, was a scout for Thomas Sumter during the Revolutionary War. So for as being able to pinpoint when the first Benenhaley came to South Carolina, to America, it's been hard to describe."

Jean repeated the basic element—a Turkish ancestor—of the story. "I was always told about General Thomas Sumter and that the Turkish man came over or a couple, or whatever, and that's the way it got started. But I don't know anything. They'll say, 'Have you ever been to Turkey? Were you born over there or what?' And I'll say, 'No. It goes way back.' That's what I tell them. 'It goes way back.' I don't know how far back. I wish I did, though."

Helen answered indirectly, but I am is confident that she identifies herself as a person of Turkish descent. For example, when talking about her grandparents, she stated that "the white comes from my grandfather. My grandmother was full-blooded Turkish."

These discussions led naturally into the issue that was running pretty hot in our community at that time—the idea that we were really Indians rather than Turkish people. Some individuals who used to identify as Turkish descendants are now claiming that they are descended from Native American Indians, that the old crowd had to pretend to be "Turks" to keep from being prosecuted and forced to relocate out West. Some have even argued that the Dalzell School was really an "Indian school." When I asked the participants if they believed that they were Native American or if they knew anything about the Dalzell School being called an Indian school, Boaz responded, "I'd never heard that. In fact, I don't believe that. There may be something I missed along the way, but as I told you, I spent ten years of my life at the Dalzell School and I never heard such a thing,"

I then asked, "What would you say to someone who asked you if you were Native American?" He seemed agitated by the question and said with great authority, "I'd tell them in no uncertain terms, no." I did not want to push the subject but was curious, and I believed that Boaz and I had established a strong interviewer/participant relationship. So out of curiosity I asked, "How do you know?" He raised his eyebrows and gave a very thought provoking response. He stated, "How do I know? How does everyone else know who he or she is? They take somebody's word. They read it in a book. Somebody's passed it down, your parents, or your grandparents. This is who we are. This is where we came from." He had a point.

Helen's responses were similar. She stated, "Indian school? I've never heard of that. The old people don't put any stock in that. Who were these Indian children?" I explained to her that the people who refer to the Dalzell School as being an Indian school are assuming that the Turkish people were the "Indian children." She suddenly had a disgruntled look, and just shook her head no.

Tonie based her belief that she is not Native American on her physical characteristics not being typical of Native American and on her never having heard the Dalzell School referred to as an Indian school when she was attending the school. She said, "I don't believe we're Indians because we don't have Indian characteristics. When I was a little girl, I had light hair and beautiful green eyes. I still have beautiful green eyes." She then blushed and laughed.

I pursued the idea of the possibility of the Dalzell School being an Indian school. I asked, "Do you think that if it had been referred to as an Indian school that you would have known back then?" Tonie responded, "All I ever heard was that it was a Turk school." Since she did not answer the question directly, I specifically asked, "Was it an Indian school?" Her answer was a confident "No." I wanted to understand more, so I asked, "How do you know it wasn't an Indian school?"

Her response was directly to the point. She stated, "There weren't any Indians there when I went." Tonie, like Helen, seemed confused as to why some think that the Dalzell School was a school for Indian children when many of the ones who attended this school did not claim to be Native American.

In her first interview, Jean had mentioned that she would rather be Indian than from Turkey. I asked her to elaborate on that. She said, "I don't know. I would just like to know that I would be an American Indian rather than from Turkey, you know, the Middle East. If I had known that we might be Indian, we would have applied for assistance." She laughed and said, "We joke about it." Jean also told me that her kids say "'We'd like to be Cherokee Indian.' I really don't know. I really don't. My daughter, she said, 'Mom I always liked Indian people.'"

I also asked a couple of my resource people of Turkish descent who do not live in this area about the Native American issue. Helen Team, who lives in another part of the state, is a genealogist and descendant of Joseph Benenhaley. Team acknowledged that some of the Turkish people of Sumter County identify themselves as Native Americans from the Cheraw Indian Tribe. While she did not discredit this claim, she added this comment:

> It has not been proven on the Benenhaley side. The Oxendines might be. I do not believe that the Benenhaleys are Native Americans. There is no proof that I can see from all of my research that they are Indians. What I've seen that says that they are Turkish, I don't know about that either. What I've read is just what people have written. Others may have proof that I have not seen. What I have gotten is just through research. It is just what somebody else has said, but I do not believe everything I have read. I personally don't believe that the descendants of Joseph Benenhaley are Native Americans. I have not seen the physical features of an Indian. I don't see the facial features or the muscular build either.

Likewise, Sue New, who lives out of state but also can trace her lineage back to Joseph Benenhaley, has written online that "we will never have all our questions answered, but we cannot tack Indian blood on the Turkish people with no proof, whatsoever. Joseph Benenhaley was not Indian" (New, "Joseph," 2005, 2).

I was not surprised at these comments about ancestry. My people have always believed the traditional narrative. They had no evidence to back up that narrative; but they were certain that they were of Turkish descent.

~ Thoughts about Who We Are ~

I next asked the participants about their ethnic identification. I anticipated, correctly, that ethnicity questions would be tough for them. Sometimes the way we identify ourselves is determined by our genetics, and sometimes the way we identify ourselves is determined by the context in which we live. I know that being a person of Turkish descent and living in Georgia does not have the same meaning as being a person of Turkish descent and living in Sumter County; I also recognize that being a person of Turkish descent and going to school during the second half of the twentieth century does not have the same meaning as being a person of Turkish descent and going to school during earlier times.

So, our conversations again rambled in many directions and about all aspects of their Turkish identity. Boaz said, "My ethnicity is Turkish, as far as I know," but he also laughed, and with a twinkle in his eye he said, "That's a good question because so many times I've had people come up to me and say to me, 'What's your nationality?' and I'll just laugh, and I'll say, 'American.'" He then became a little more serious and stated that his ethnicity is Turkish, as far as he knows. When Boaz stated that his ethnicity is Turkish, as far as he knows, he was basing that on his research, not simply on a guess. He has read the works of several historians and he has examined census records. All of the evidence that he has collected over the years has led him to believe that he is a direct descendant of the original Joseph Benenhaley, whom he believes to be "Caucasian of Arab descent." He gave me a copy of a letter that Thomas Sebastian Sumter left with Boaz's grandmother so that future generations would know a little about their ancestors and how they fought and died for their country.

In a later interview, Boaz elaborated on what it meant to him to be Turkish. He explained, "I assume I accepted it just like anyone else who would have been from whatever ethnic background they were from. That's who I am. I'm proud of it. I have no reason not to be. God gave me the same abilities, and I have the same rights that anyone else has, and I hold my head high." When Boaz made this statement, I could not help but notice that this statement was not simply a figure of speech. He was literally holding his head very high as he spoke, and he had a solemn look on his face.

When I asked Tonie the same question, she exclaimed, "I'm Caucasian of Turkish descent." She went into detail about how her maternal grandmother was not all Turkish, but her maternal grandfather was. When she was a child, she recalled, "We couldn't go to the white schools. They didn't think we were white, and they treated us as such. I only have an eighth grade education because when we graduated from the eighth grade, we had to go to another school, but there was not another Turkish school to go to." Tonie, who had been mild-tempered during most of the interview, raised her voice when she made that statement. I could see that the memory of others not accepting her as a white person was still a sore topic of conversation. Later in the interview she stated, "I hate saying that we had to go to a white school. I hate saying that because I consider myself as white." She would rather not distinguish herself from non-Turkish whites because she identifies herself as "Caucasian."

That is not to say that Tonie is ashamed of being Turkish. In fact, she mentioned several times that she was proud to be Turkish. She attributes her olive complexion and green eyes to her Turkish ethnicity. But this same olive complexion that is coveted by many today caused her problems when she was younger. During her interviews, Tonie told me many stories about her educational experiences. She usually did so with a look of sadness in her eyes. Based on Tonie's composure during some of the interviews, I believe that she experienced pain and trouble when she was younger because people chose to distinguish among ethnic groups. She does not wish to see those lines drawn anymore.

When I asked Helen to define and identify herself, she dodged the question with a joke. She has a great sense of humor, even when talking about a sensitive subject, such as this one. So I asked her how she would feel if someone asked her about her ethnicity. She stiffened in her chair, leaned forward, looked me in the eyes, and responded, "How would you feel if someone asked you that? I would ask why they wanted to know. I wouldn't be insulted. I used to be offended about it, but not now."

Helen explained to me that her grandfather was white. He married a Turkish person and their children were then classified as being Turkish. She even had a question for me. She asked, "Your daddy's white, right?" I replied, "Yes, ma'am." She became inquisitive and asked, "Why is it that your daddy is white, your mama is Turk, so why would you be labeled as a Turk? If you lived around here, you'd be classified as being a Turk. Can you explain that to me? If you lived here, and you had gone to school here, you would have been classified as a Turk. Why is that?" Helen was clearly unsettled at the injustice of being labeled. She made it a point to reiterate that had I grown up in a different place, at a different time, that I, too, would have been labeled. She enlightened me with those words, because I had never thought about someone labeling me that way—I did not like the thought of it and it made me uncomfortable.

Jean was very interested in learning about her background. She relied on the oral traditions that have been passed down through the generations; but she was very open-minded to any new information regarding her ancestry. When I asked her about her ethnicity, she hesitated for a few moments. She then stated, "That's a hard question." She then went on to say that a lot of people have asked about her ethnicity. "Well, I just tell them I don't know that much about it and they will say, 'Well what nationality are you?' And I would say, 'Well I've always been told that I was Turkish.' And I'm not ashamed to tell them that. Like I used to get down on the word, 'Turk' or whatever, but that doesn't bother me, doesn't phase me anymore."

I decided to change the conversation somewhat and asked the four participants to tell her how they felt when someone called them a "Turk" in the old days or used the word "Turks" around them now. I also asked them to elaborate on what it means to be Turkish today. Boaz became pensive and said, "For someone to call me a Turk, I didn't like the expression, the way it was used because it was used out of derision. I did not know enough about the history of Turkey to appreciate my ancestry until I did go back to school and study history. I'm very proud of my Turkish ancestry. But at that time, when someone used the term, it was a term out of derision, and I did not like it at all. Now it's different because the mentality of people has changed. The younger people coming along, many of them do not have the same attitudes that their grandparents or even their parents had because when they used the term 'Turk,' at the time, they used it in a condescending manner as if to say, 'We're better than you are.'"

Boaz elaborated about what it meant to be a "Turkish person." He said, "To me, a Turkish person is just like an Englishman, a German who came to America and made America their home . . . no one to be set apart any different than anyone else, Jewish, Italian, this entire nation is made up of people from different ethnic backgrounds. And it's a good thing that we're not all the same."

Tonie, with a look of solitude stated, "It meant that we were somehow different. Not to everybody, though. I didn't have it as hard as the ones who went before me; and, the ones who came after me didn't have it as hard as I did. Now, I say I'm Turkish. I've never been ashamed to tell anyone that I'm Turkish. I say it with pride and dignity. People think it's neat." Tonie helped me to understand that the meaning of the word has changed over time. The word "Turk," at one time, was used to distinguish Turkish people from others. Now the word conjures up feelings of pride regarding who we are.

Helen expressed her feelings on the matter by saying, "It just meant that you were being singled out. They made a point to let you know that you were different. Now, after I got older, I learned. People, if they try to live for the Lord, and if they are educated, they don't live like that. But it takes you a long time to get to the realization that they are just ignorant and just to let it go. But it takes a long time to get to that point."

I was curious to see how Jean perceived the word "Turk," so I asked, "If someone were to say the word 'Turk' around you when you were younger, how would that have made you feel?" She answered, "Awful bad, I'd just, I'd go into orbit, you know? Those were like fighting words because you didn't want to be called a 'Turk.' At that time, I think maybe it was just the way they treated us and we didn't want to be treated differently. It makes no difference now. It doesn't make any difference to me anymore."

These were very interesting conversations. My respondents had developed identities as Turkish people through many years of subcultural experiences and beliefs. Yet all four of them had difficulty expressing clearly their historical origins and ethnic identifications; and they often were ridiculed for calling themselves Turkish people.

After Browder completed his research, I recontacted these same respondents and shared with them the truth about their heritage and explained that we had discovered—through historical accounts, legal files, census data, genealogical reports, vital records, and DNA analysis—that Joseph Benenhaley was not only their forefather but he also had ancestral connections to the Mediterranean/Middle Eastern/North African area. What they had always believed was true—their patriarch and progenitor was Turkish.

I then asked them to tell me how they felt knowing that their traditional narrative has been validated. Boaz's response was positive and to the point, reflecting his lifelong conviction about who and what he is. He said, "It sounds great. I'm glad that you've been able to find some things that we haven't been able to find in the past. I will just be interested in reading about it because I think that's fascinating."

When I spoke with Helen, she was alternately intrigued, talkative, and indifferent. She seemed interested in knowing more about our progenitor, Joseph Benenhaley, especially regarding his parents. I told her that, unfortunately, we did not have any record of his ancestors. She asked,

> You reckon that's the one? Now wait a minute now. I used to hear people talking about "Old man Joseph Benenhaley." When Sumter came here, he brought a Benenhaley, a Lowrey, and a Hood man with him. I can't prove all of that. If that's an actual fact, I don't have any objections to what you are. You are what you are, right? These younger . . . especially if they have moved away, if they didn't grow up here and didn't go to school here, all of that stuff is Greek to them. My grandchildren, when I tell them about the school situation and how we were treated, they look at me and ask, "What? What are you talking about?" They absolutely don't believe it. It doesn't matter to me. So much has been written about that. If this is all factual, it's a good thing. Go forward. It doesn't matter to me what we are.

Jean and Tonie were not shocked that our research had led us to conclude that Joseph Benenhaley was Turkish. Jean said, "It's what we always thought. Well, I guess it's OK. It's a good thing to know that we are Turkish." Tonie added, "I always knew he was a Turk. Nobody's ever told me that. All the time I figured he was a Turk. Nothing surprises me anymore. I have no feelings about it. I don't feel any way. I never really thought about it. I took it for granted. Wasn't he a Benenhaley? All right, then. That's a Turk. Not surprised at all."

It was interesting that these four older respondents expressed mixed feelings about our resolution of long-stated doubts regarding the Turkish patriarch. For the most part, their responses reflected obvious joy as I went over these findings; and they asked a lot of questions. But, strangely, there also seemed to be an undertone of "this doesn't change anything" in their demeanor. It was as if they were happy to hear confirmation of what they had always believed but it did not undo all their suffering over the years. After what they had experienced, it was to be expected that such news might trigger a variety of emotions. Happily, Boaz, Helen, Jean, and Tonie finally learned the truth about their history and heritage.

~ Observations about the Community ~

Since I started working on this project, outsiders—including many of my friends—have expressed great curiosity about the lives of the Turkish people during their sustained, enclosed existence in rural South Carolina. They have asked me all kinds of things. Of course, many of their questions relate to the origins of the Turkish people and the early years of their settlement (which the we have already covered). But they also want to know about what daily life was like in the Turkish community during more recent times, during the 1900s.

I did not know much except what my mother and cousins had told me. But I learned a great deal in my research for this project. The general answer is that the Turkish people lived lives very similar to those of other common, working people in the rural South of the past century. Despite strange and exotic rumors befitting "golden-skinned creatures," the Dalzell settlement in many ways resembled other small communities in that part of the state. However, they rarely mixed or socialized with their Sumter County neighbors. Their ancestry and dark-complexions might explain why a few individuals or families experienced original and early seclusion; but it seems unlikely that such factors would dictate isolation, segregation, discrimination, and oppression of an entire community for so many generations.

What really marked the Turkish people as "different" and defined them as "other" in the 1900s was an engrained personality and lifestyle reflecting their long experience as an enclosed ethnic settlement. Over the course of their history, they had become a distinct subculture not only in terms of their Turkish ancestry but also in their outcast identity, exiled society, and strained relationship with the outside world. Furthermore, as with most isolated subcultures, they developed certain ways, attitudes, and practices that outsiders find intriguing and puzzling.

I decided to ask my four relatives, who lived there during much of the past century, to respond to the most common questions about their interesting community. The Turkish people are still sensitive about some of these topics. But they are important parts—or at least commonly perceived elements—of our story; and they need to be addressed in any "true history" of the Turkish community. So, here are the observations of my kinfolk, along with my commentary, about their lives and experiences in the 1900s.

Entrenched Separatism

Next to their curiosity about the original founding of the Turkish community, outsiders seem to be most interested in how white-Turkish separation became entrenched and ugly for so many generations. Was it the white people who drove this sustained, oppressive isolation of the Turkish people? Or did the Turkish people themselves choose to erect and maintain an iron curtain around the Dalzell settlement?

I approached Boaz about this question, since he has studied the Turkish community and is very knowledgeable about Turkish history. At first, he speculated that each ethnic group probably just felt more comfortable being with people like themselves. However, I probed Boaz further, and he acknowledged that it went beyond simple feelings of comfort for the white and Turkish people. He described the two-way separatism this way: "I don't want to have anything to do with you just as much as you don't want to have anything to do with me. It works both ways. If you can do without me, I can do without you."

Despite his explanation of mutual disdain, it was clear that Boaz viewed white discrimination as the main cause of the extended, lonely history of this community. He noted with sadness, for example, that "the Turkish boys and girls were not allowed on teams like the American Legion baseball teams and those types of things. The segregation was almost as bad as the segregation of the blacks. Not as bad, but bad enough. That's the reason that the community in that part of Sumter has lasted as long as it has as what some call a Turkish community."

Boaz also alluded to the chip-on-our-shoulder attitude among the Turkish people when he stated, "If you say something against one, you'd better be ready to back it up. You better not say anything against one of them. If you do, you're going to have all the family to deal with."

That last remark brought up another topic that seemed to stir up feelings among my Turkish relatives. They do not like the words "clan" and "clannish," so I asked questions regarding clannishness as tactfully as I could.

Clannishness

I told my respondents that just about everything I read said they were clannish, and I asked them to explain why they had a reputation for being closed-minded against outsiders.

All four tried to explain by going back to the previous discussion about both sides feeling comfortable among themselves; and, again, they kept bouncing back and forth about who started the estrangement. According to Boaz: "I think the Turkish people felt much more comfortable among themselves. Again, that was because it was being forced upon them. I think protection is a good word, but I think it was due to the fact that they knew how they had been classified because of their dark complexion and probably all kinds of questions asked—'What are you? Who are you?'—until one of the ways that they felt a protection of themselves was just to be clannish, stay to themselves. I don't think you could say it was a matter that they hated someone else of a different color. I think it was more of a protection of what the other people forced upon them. So the people stayed pretty much to themselves.

Helen stated that the clannishness of the Turkish people was due in part to their desire to live on their own, but that it could have been forced upon them, too. She explained that the Turkish people left the High Hills Baptist Church to begin a new church, Long Branch. Once they started a new church, they may have wanted their own schools, as well, but she was not sure about that. She and Boaz both told me that when they were allowed to attend the white schools, the Turkish students would sit together. She then explained further: "We all lived in the same area and everybody was the same. We made our biggest mistake when we settled into one area. Like your mama and daddy moved off and you and your brother didn't have to experience this. This is where our parents were born and raised. Your mother would have stayed here if she hadn't married your daddy. When we were growing up, we didn't go anywhere except to our cousins' houses. We didn't socialize with anybody else. But it could have been forced upon them."

Tonie repeated the notion that the clannishness of the Turkish people was due to their desire to live separately and to their not being accepted by other ethnic groups. We were discussing the isolation of the Turkish students when I asked her about the school she had attended. She responded, "We had one school bus for the whole school. It seems like there was a first bus load and then a second bus load. It seems like he would take one bus load of students home and then come back and get the rest of us. It was unique because there were only Turkish families going there." So I asked, "Was that by choice?" Tonie gave an emphatic "No!" But later she added, "Actually I think that most of them chose to stick to themselves."

Jean cut through this circuitous discussion with a shorter and candid statement of the situation. "I did all of my elementary school at Dalzell. Only Turkish people went there. They had no other place to go. You either went there or you stayed at home. They wouldn't let you in the white school." I decided it was time to move on to another topic, but it proved just as sensitive.

Intermarriage

From the beginning, the Turkish people married within their own group; and that practice continued into their second century as a community. They are still pretty sensitive whenever anyone brings up the intermarriage issue.

Boaz and I had a long and interesting discussion about intermarriage. I said, "I know that for a while the Turkish people weren't marrying outside of their ethnic group, for a very long time." Boaz had a look of wonderment in his eyes as if he was not sure as to where the conversation was leading. He then stated, "I think they just accepted it. In other words they got the idea, 'we are who we are, who they say we are. We're not going to try to force the issue. I'm as good as they are, but hey, if they don't want to date me, we'll marry within our own ethnic group.' I mean, I'm glad I married my wife. But I never thought about... of course, I got married when I was eighteen. I told my wife she didn't give me a chance."

I was curious as to what Boaz was going to say before he told me how old he was when he was married, so I asked, "Were you going to say that you never thought about marrying someone outside of the ethnic group?" He responded, "No," which meant that he had never thought about marrying someone outside of the ethnic group. I asked, "So that was just an understanding?" He responded, "I think so. It was just a matter of not being in a situation where you were with other people. I mean, you went to school with other Turkish people, so unless you were the kind of guy, back there then, that went to some of the bar rooms, or places like that, you did not intermarry with other ethnic groups."

I followed up by asking if it was acceptable among the Turkish people, when he was growing up, to marry outside of the Turkish ethnic group. He responded, "I don't think there would have been a problem. It was just a matter of... I had no dealing with anyone other than right there in the community because ten years of my life was at the Dalzell School. Sumter, which was only twelve to fourteen miles away, the only way we would have had to get there was to catch the bus or walk. No cars." I continued the conversation by asking, "Did it matter whether they married whites, versus blacks versus Native Americans versus Asians versus Hispanics? What was accepted?" He responded, "I don't know of any, really, that did. I know there were a number of Chinese airmen who visited, and they dated some of the girls, but there was no marriage. Probably if they had, it would have been accepted like anyone else."

When I asked Boaz if he believed that these other families who married into the Benenhaley family were also Turkish, he responded, "From the standpoint of if a Ray married a Benenhaley, the child that would come would certainly have some roots, yes. But I don't think it's fair for people in the community to take, say, Hood, for example, Hood is English, just as white as white can be, and to class him or her as a Turk is ridiculous. If my son married an Italian, that wouldn't make his ancestry Italian. Now if they had a child, it would mean that the child would have some connection, but not my son."

I then asked him what would have happened if someone would have married outside of the ethnic group or gone to church outside of the group. I was curious to know what would have happened within the group. He responded, "Nothing because there were some who did when they moved to other places. They married outside of the group. They would come back, and they were accepted."

When I asked Helen about marrying into other ethnic groups, she stated, "The opportunity they had was when people would marry people from Shaw Air Force Base." She concurred with Boaz that part of the reason that Turkish people did not marry outside of their ethnic group, at the time, was the lack of transportation.

She stated, "Turkish people used to marry Turkish people, but it is not like that anymore. I can't remember the last time a Turkish girl married a Turkish boy. It used to be if you were Turkish, you married a Turkish person. Now people are exposed to other people. When the older people were growing up, they were all together. They didn't get out because back then, older people didn't have cars or transportation to get out and mingle with others." I asked Helen the same question about the Turkish community's feelings about marrying outside of the Turkish community. She answered, "It was accepted to marry outside of the group, but the older ones never met anybody to marry. If they were classified as white, that was fine. I don't know about Native American. I know one person who brought a Korean wife back. I don't think the family objected to that."

Tonie mentioned that when she was growing up, they would go to Christmas parties on the base with white children and black children. "I dated white guys. The man I married is white. Most of the Turkish men and women, the older ones anyway, married other Turkish people. That doesn't exist anymore." Jean added, "If they would have married a person from another ethnic group, they were from out of state or something." In general, when Turkish people did marry outside of the ethnic group, it was to someone from somewhere else who was not familiar with the ethnic group isolation, and it was usually to white non-Turkish people. Very few Turkish people married black, Asian, or Hispanic partners.

Skin Tones

It seems that intermarriage is no longer a real issue. But another topic—skin tones—still creeps into today's discussions of the community. The Turkish people historically have been labeled as "dark-skinned" or "dark-complexioned" as an explanation for their peculiar status in this area. While that may have been true originally, it became less so in the past century as the community expanded and assimilated. Today, it is not uncommon for them to be light-skinned, blond-haired, and blue-eyed individuals.

The news media and journalists have always contributed to social stereotypes with references and inferred conclusions about the "looks" of the Turkish people. For example, newspaperman William D. Workman cited their distinctive appearance as a reason for their social isolation (Dec. 17, 1950); and F. Kinloch Bull later wrote that they "looked like Turks" with "straight black hair and copper colored complexion (*Random Recollections,* 1986, 106). *Ebony Magazine* even printed a picture of what they called a "Typical Turk" with "tawny complexion and coarse, black hair" ("South Carolina's Raceless People" 1957).

Such statements can still be heard today. Boaz told me about a comment he heard and his reaction: "I had a person say, 'All of you look the same.' That's ignorant. It's coming from somebody not knowing what to say. There are all kinds of shades of color."

I suspect that during the early part of the twentieth century, many Turkish people were dark-skinned; but, just as with black people and white people, some of them had different tones. Today, the Turkish people range from very dark to very light. In my own immediate family, we all look different. My mother has brown hair, green eyes, and dark skin. My brother has black hair, chestnut eyes, and dark skin. I have brown hair, dark brown eyes and lighter skin than he (unless I have been outside in the sun).

My coauthor and I also could see the diversity of appearance in the children of the people we interviewed for our chapter on today's Turkish community. One informant's daughter had beautiful olive-colored skin, dark eyes, and dark hair. I asked whether anybody ever asked her about her nationality, and she answered, "A lot of people think I'm Mexican." Another man's son was light-skinned and he had blue eyes. As I looked at him, I could not help but think that it is nearly impossible to look at someone today and identify him or her as being Turkish. But, if you listen closely to their conversations, you might be able to detect that someone grew up in the Dalzell community.

Speech Patterns

The isolated history of the Turkish people resulted in interesting and distinctive speech patterns. I can detect some of those distinctive patterns if I pay attention to word pronunciations among my relatives.

I asked each of the participants if the Turkish people had unique speech patterns, and they all said yes. Some of the participants were able to give some examples. When Tonie and I spoke, she stated, "Yes. Some don't pronounce their words correctly. Their accent, the way they talk is different. Not everybody is like that. Some have an accent that sounds almost Cajun, like the accent you hear in Louisiana." Helen agreed. She stated, "I've had people ask me, 'Are you from Louisiana?' Start observing people, Terri. We just don't talk like other people. Not everybody is like that. I haven't been asked very often what I am, but the few times that I've been asked, it was when I started talking. We talk differently. For instance, this sounds silly, but someone named Judy, we say, 'Juddy.' That's just an example. Someone named Connie, we say, 'Conie.' We grew up with our parents talking like that and not pronouncing things correctly. Sometimes we don't finish words or sentences. If someone asks a question, we don't say yes. We say, 'yay.'"

Boaz's thoughts on the matter were similar: "You can hear it anywhere where the people do not have the educational background, but a lot of times words are cut off, instead of saying it plainly. 'Gonna.' You know, and of course . . . I heard somewhere in a city in Georgia, somebody said, 'Yea, bo!' I said, 'He's from Sumter.' I said, 'I can guarantee you.' I've had people to ask me a lot of times if I'm from Charleston. I think that you would find that in the mountains or anywhere where a group of people are together, the way they use their words."

Jean mentioned that other people bring to her attention that she has a unique accent. She explained, "I get teased a little where I live with the different words I use. I'll say, 'Cut off the light' and they say, 'Shut off the light.' What do you do to the lights? Do you cut them off or shut them off?" I responded, "I turn them off." We both started laughing. She continued, "Turkish people just talk very flat. I don't want to say drawn out, because almost all of the southerners do have that anyway, but in their pronunciation of words, now this is the older people, I'm saying sixty [years old] and above."

~ Speculation about Our Eventual Demise ~

The Turkish people of Sumter County are not nearly as enclosed as in the past. Today, many Turkish people have moved to other areas either to start a family or to attend college and begin careers.

I asked each of the participants what they thought would eventually happen to the Turkish ethnic group. They all agreed that the Sumter County Turkish community might one day be extinct as Turkish people continue to marry outsiders and the traditional narrative fades into history. Boaz tried to remember the last time two Turkish people married each other. He stated, "It's been years and years since a Turk married a Turk." If they do not marry each other, they obviously cannot have Turkish children, which means that the ethnic group is slowly disappearing.

When I asked Helen if she thought that the ethnic group would not exist in the near future, she stated, "Not in my lifetime, but probably in your lifetime. It won't be long because if I sit here and started thinking about all the dark Turkish people who are left, they are up in their eighties. You'll be dead before it's completely gone. Soon there won't be any Turkish people left. The genuine Turks are dying out, the darker ones. The Turkish generation will soon be gone because Turkish people married Turkish people, but it is not that way anymore. I can't remember the last time a Turkish girl married a Turkish boy. It used to be if you were Turkish, you married a Turkish person, but it's not like that anymore. People are exposed to other people."

Jean stated, "Do I think that they will not exist? Oh, I think it's getting where there's remarrying out into other ethnic groups and so forth, just like I think . . . I don't know if it will ever be that it will totally not exist, but it won't be too much left there in another twenty years." Tonie concurred. She stated, "Most of the Turkish men and women, the older ones anyway, married other Turkish people. That doesn't exist anymore."

These were all interesting comments about Turkish ancestry and ethnicity; but Tonie's closing comment was a startling prediction. "Yes. I definitely think that they will be gone one day. Maybe in the next twenty-five to fifty years, no one will even know what a Turk was."

I hope these conversations give outsiders some idea about how Turkish lives reflected their outcast situation in Dalzell. The issues raised in these questions still bother some Turkish people; but for others, these matters are trivial or inconsequential. However, readers will not be surprised that another factor—race—has shaped the Turkish people's collective fate consistently and significantly, and it strongly impacts their sense of heritage.

~ Relations with White and Black People ~

Race has always been the most contentious and divisive element of southern society, and certainly this was true in Sumter County in the first half of the twentieth century. White, black, and Turkish people of this area at that time all attended segregated schools, lived in their own areas, went to their own churches, and often sat in separated places in theatres and buses.

It does not take a genius to figure out the strained arrangement among the three groups. The white people did not welcome the Turkish people; the Turkish crowd did not consort with black individuals; and the black community simply tried to survive in such an environment. Of course, this is an oversimplification. Many citizens of the three ethnic groups in Sumter County have always lived together and gotten along on friendly terms. However, there is no denying the adverse social environment for Turkish and black people during the past two centuries. This part of the conversation will address that situation and show how my Turkish respondents dealt with the two other ethnic groups in this adverse environment, especially during their integration of the white high schools of this county.

Rejection by White People

The Turkish people of Sumter County had sought to assimilate into the white culture for many years but they were denied access. Although the participants identified themselves as being white people, the community seldom accepted them as white. How white people isolated and segregated the Turkish people has been covered in a previous chapter, so those incidents and patterns do not need to be repeated here. However, below my four relatives share a few of their personal experiences about how they were rejected by white people.

To begin, the critical strategy whereby white people kept the Turkish people isolated was the same strategy that kept black individuals oppressed—the legal sham of "separate but equal." This was a tricky task, since the Turkish community had long enjoyed certain benefits of white privilege.

The white establishment managed this in great part through racial designations on official records—and this practice merits extended discussion. The Turkish people were usually labeled as "Turks" on birth certificates when my respondents were growing up—and this was a critical matter since that designation represented a formal declaration of inferior social status. These documents also were required in order for a child to enter school and participate in numerous other activities in the community. This arbitrary designation was left up to unspecified individuals, usually a nurse or doctor present at the birth of a child. Sometimes it was based, in the case of Turkish people, on the surname and sometimes on skin color. But, once "Turk" was inscribed on the birth certificate, that individual's future opportunities and relationship to whites in this area were set almost in stone; it was very difficult for anyone to undo this brand of second-class citizenship.

Jean experienced this practice with her own child. She said, "When my child was born, they had 'Turk' on my child's birth certificate, and I think we had it taken off. They saw me and classified my child as being Turkish. I couldn't believe they put that on the birth certificate. People were prejudiced back then." She also explained that at the local hospital, the Turkish people were not assigned to rooms where there were whites. She said, "They wouldn't put you in a room with a white if you had to be a patient in a hospital. I can remember that. They kind of put Turkish people in rooms to themselves."

Helen also mentioned the birth certificate issue and was appalled that the people who filled out her first child's birth certificate wrote "Turk" in the "race" section. When she had her second child, she was very vocal about how to fill out the "race" section. During the interview, she clenched her teeth together and pointed her finger at me as she explained, "At the time when I had my other child, they were still putting it on there and I had to tell the doctor to tell the nurse that she'd better not put 'Turk' on there, like she did the last time. He said, 'I'll tell her.' He stood right outside the door and she put 'white' on there because of him." It was obvious to me that Helen was very serious. After listening to some of her choice words, which have not been included in this book, I understood why the nurse did not put "Turk" as the child's race.

When I asked Tonie about this issue, she told me that her original birth certificate had "Turk" in the "race" section, too. She did not believe that this was a fair practice. She stated, "My first birth certificate, the original, had 'Turk' on it. They classified us as 'Turk' as if it were a race. That is not a justifiable term for the Turkish people. Absolutely not! The birth certificates should have said, 'white' or 'Caucasian' for race."

She also commented, though, that times have changed. People do not have the same type of mentality as they once did. She said, "I don't think any prejudice exists today like back then. They don't look at us as Turks anymore. They still know we're Turkish, but it's different. I don't have a problem going anywhere anymore. I am more confident, and times have changed."

I knew that the birth certificate problem was a big issue among the Turkish people; so I pursued the matter. I asked Boaz, "Why do you think they used to put 'Turk' where it says 'race' on birth certificates and even death certificates?" He stated, "I would like to say out of ignorance, but I think out of prejudice. They wanted to be sure that was set aside. The Turkish people knew they belonged to the white or Caucasian race and wanted to claim that. The whites did not want to give them that right."

Interestingly, however, being classified as Turk on birth certificates did not always prevent Turkish individuals from participating in community activities. Some were not always easy to identify based on their physical characteristics. Some had light complexions, whereas others had dark complexions. So they were able to move about and enjoyed the same freedom and opportunity of most other citizens in the county.

Helen told us about an interesting incident back in the 1950s. Her family had light complexions. One day a man approached Helen's dad about a new school that was opening. Helen explained, "A man came and told my daddy, 'Now we are opening a private school. If you want your children to go, go enroll them now because we are not letting Turks or blacks go.' So my daddy said, 'Well that excludes us, then, because my children are Turkish.'"

Helen also told me a story about one of her teenage friends. "This girl was dark, and she was a friend of mine. She said, 'I'd like to get my hair cut.' I said, 'There's a beauty shop up the street.' She said, 'Well, call and make me an appointment.' We walked up to the beauty shop, and we walked in. The lady said, 'I'm ready. Come in. You can sit in that chair.' I said, 'It's not for me. It's for her.' She said, 'Oh I can't cut her hair.' And she didn't. Some of the older white people still feel the same way about the Turks. They might put up a front, but some of them feel the same. Not the younger ones, but the older ones."

I asked Boaz to help me understand some of this discrimination and he volunteered that it was not always due to a calculated act of hatred; often it was a simple matter of respect—or disrespect. For example, he said that Turkish people were sometimes addressed by their first names, while they themselves addressed whites by their last names. Boaz began to tell me about a man he knew who experienced this very thing. He said, "Fred was a farmer. Two of the farmers that lived right close to him, when they would come, and again, this comes from politeness and the way you've been taught. But when they would talk to Fred, it would be 'Fred,' that's his first name. It wouldn't be Mr. It was Fred. But when Fred would refer to them, it would be Mr. So-and-so. A lot of it was the fault of the people not taking the stand for themselves that they ought to take."

Helen echoed his words. She said, "I have always taught my grandchildren to be respectful to elders and people in authority, but back then they would call all white people 'sir' and 'ma'am.' Say for instance Laura Bush and George Bush were to come here, we would say, 'Yes, ma'am' and 'Yes, sir.' That's how the Turks treated the white people. They treated them like they were royalty or something just because their skin was a lighter shade than theirs."

The problem obviously went beyond personal disrespect for the person sitting or standing or lying nearby. As already noted in the previous chapter, discrimination against the Turkish people was common and systemic. For example, Boaz once received a letter from the State Tax Commission in which the person who sent the letter addressed the letter to the "Turk Parsonage." Boaz was very upset that someone from the State Tax Commission would make an ethnic distinction in a letter to the church. Boaz decided to respond with a letter of his own, which he shared with me:

Dear Sir,

This letter is in reference to an application for tax exemption addressed to the "Turk Parsonage." Are all such applications sent to churches with the addresses stating to the English Baptist Church, Irish Catholic or Negro Church? I am appalled that people with such mentality are working for the State Tax Commission. It is tragic that some people still have Dark Age attitudes.

Also, that discrimination was sometimes scary. For example, when they tried integrating the white schools, the reaction was quick and fiery.

Jean told us this story: "One night, when the KKK was on the rampage, you wouldn't remember that, somebody burned a cross in my dad's yard. We got up the next morning and there was a cross burning in our yard and for about two weeks, a lot of people stood guard out there. That was when the KKK was in full swing. I was terribly upset and afraid because you know what the KKK was doing. It was just kind of dreadful. We were scared. We were afraid to go outside the house. It was a scary situation. And they used to . . . I know they used to meet right down the road from us, there. And they'd have their services. We could just kind of see from our house when they'd have the crosses burning and they'd have their meetings. It was not a good experience."

I then changed direction and asked Boaz about racial segregation of that time and whether Turkish people were in favor of segregation or whether they opposed it; and he explained that they just accepted it as a part of life and that they did not know any better. Being with one's own ethnic group was something that all ethnic groups in Sumter County were doing. They did not view it, necessarily, as something that needed to be rectified. The condition simply was. These conversations made me feel bad as I shifted my questions from Turkish-white to Turkish-black relations in Sumter County.

Separated from Black People

What I found here was more of the same, with uncomfortable realities for both Turkish and black people. These two groups have long lived their lives in an awkward social separation that reflected the overarching influence of perceived white supremacy.

I found it especially interesting that it was hard to get my relatives to talk about black people. They usually turned those conversations back to their own troubled relations with white people. For example, when I asked my respondents about their feelings toward black people, they would talk about how white people treated them compared to how white people treated black people. Apparently, the two minority populations had never experienced serious or sustained interaction; and their mutual resentment of the white establishment had served to minimize their grievances against each other.

But make no mistake about it—the chasm between the two groups was deep and wide. Befriending anyone of a different ethnic group was uncommon, and marrying someone of a different group was a rarity in this area. This was especially true of Turkish-black relationships. Since the Turkish people claimed to be white, they rarely associated with black people. For them to socialize with black people would have caused them to experience even more discrimination.

According to attorney Ira Kaye, this unfortunate situation had to be considered within the broader context of southern society ("The Turks"1963): "Over-emphasized in the position of the Turks has been their hatred of the Negro. Those who make this charge have been very superficial in their view of the problem. The fact that these poor people have insisted upon a White status for so long must be weighted in the light of history. In the pre-15th Amendment era of our history, even the free Negro was under severe legal handicaps. So were the Indians living in the South. Not to strive for recognition as White meant a loss of all hope of achieving anything for future generations" (15).

As mentioned above, Turkish people seemed reluctant to talk about their associations with black people. But I appealed to them to tell me about their experiences when they were teenagers, and they described a tangled web of racial perspectives and stratification. Boaz suggested that the relations among the three groups was a matter of coping in a rigid social hierarchy. "Just as much so as the white people of Dalzell would not want to associate with the Turkish people, the Turkish people did not want to associate with other groups. They were already prejudiced against, and they didn't want anything else adding to what they were already going through."

Helen told me that not being accepted by white people was one of the greatest challenges facing both the Turkish people and the black people. She said, "It was hard to be classified as being different." Helen claimed that "the Turkish people didn't discriminate against black people, but they didn't socialize with them either." She also said, "We were treated just as bad as the blacks, maybe worse. It was like we had leprosy or were outcasts or something."

Jean likewise claimed that she thought that the whites of Sumter County treated the Turkish people "worse than blacks." I asked her to elaborate about this comment; and she said: "The blacks weren't trying to get into schools or anything, at least in the earlier days, but the Turkish people were. I just think they thought we were pushing our way in, and that we shouldn't. I don't know how to explain this. . . . I mean we were just caught in between." Jean also said, "We weren't in favor of segregation, but we didn't have any choice. They just would not let us into the white school. . . . It was like they had a hatred for us and why, I don't know."

How did the black people feel about the Turkish people? The authors asked Roosevelt Miott, who grew up in Dalzell at the same time as the four respondents, about this situation. Miott, a career teacher and administrator in Sumter County, went to all-black Ebenezer School in the 1950s. He talked with us in a telephone interview on October 1, 2014, about those long-ago days. He said that the Turkish people were a small group that stayed to themselves. He also said: "We never considered the Turks a threat to us, because they were in the same fix that we were in. The whites didn't want us or the Turks to come to their school. Also, we got short-changed in funding just like them; and we all got our textbooks only when the white schools got rid of them. We knew it was wrong for them just as for us."

Miott did not concern himself during those times with where the Turkish community came from: "I just assumed they were from Turkey." He said he related to them because they did not have anything either; "like us, they were not in control in this part of the world." Miott also volunteered his opinion that time has changed a lot of things in Sumter County. "Things are different now, because people recognize that we're all human beings. Back then, it was taboo to mix, so we did not socialize together; but we had good relations as individuals." For example, he said, "One of the Turks, Hammond Ray, used to help my daddy bale hay and take our cows to market. He even loaned us the money to build our house."

These were difficult interviews. Obviously my respondents felt very uncomfortable talking about the differing roles and relationships among Turkish and black people in the white-dominated social arrangement of those times.

~ Oppressed by the System ~

After such depressing conversations, I asked each of my informants if they considered themselves to have been systematically oppressed by the white people of Sumter County.

Helen seemed shocked that I would even ask. She said, "Oh, yes. I mean, Terri, honey, you are so young you can't . . . there's no way that as much as I have talked to you, there's no way that you can imagine. Sure I did." Tonie explained that her feeling of oppression depended on where she was, "Yes. I didn't feel like that growing up, but going to school, yes, I felt oppressed. I felt like they were better than I at that time."

Jean was also emotional about oppression. "Yes, oh sure, you know. We just were all the time. I mean, you were just looked down on, you were just, they wanted you to think you were different. And we believed that we were, I guess. After so long, you just kind of think you are." Jean expressed these feelings even stronger in other conversations about their treatment; "The whites felt that we were just kind of trash under their feet."

Boaz answered in a way that seemed strange to me: "I had so much to do with playing and working until, I didn't think much of it. Sure, I knew how people felt." That statement sounded restrained and somewhat ambivalent; but it reflected Boaz's normal demeanor. He is a minister and he finds it hard to criticize people. However, I could tell by his comments in other discussions and his actions as an adult that he recognized the oppressive nature of the situation in Sumter County. For example, on several occasions, our conversations about discrimination led him to tears. I had watched, during one interview about Boaz's childhood, when his expression changed from glee to regret. He was talking about playing baseball during recess at the Dalzell School and he said: "But I've often wondered because of the tremendous ball players that they had how far they could have gone. I used to sit and listen at the American Legion teams from Sumter, and listen at them play, and I just wondered how it would have been to have been able to have had a good diamond and to have been able to play."

As I thought about my four relatives and their feelings of oppression during the Integration Movement, I noticed something very interesting. When I asked about fighting this oppression, all of the participants spoke of the action of the adults in the Turkish community; but the reality is that they themselves, as teenagers, were on the frontlines of the movement. For example, when I asked about the Turkish community's efforts to have Turkish children admitted to white schools, all four participants were able to tell me about the Turkish leaders who came together to bring their case to the Supreme Court. They were able to tell me the names of the men who led the movement as well as the years that they began to see a change. A few of the participants were even able to give me the names of the lawyers and community leaders who either helped or hindered their cause.

But the reality is that Boaz, Helen, Jean, and Tonie also were very involved as courageous young leaders in the fight against oppression. Of course, they were civil rights heroes by virtue of their pioneering role in integrating the white high schools—years before Little Rock. But their participation went beyond being symbols of change; they were activists everyday on the buses and in the classrooms. Take Helen, for example. In a discussion above, she is described as "feisty." Apparently, Helen regularly acted against discrimination that she encountered at Hillcrest. One day, a boy made a negative comment about her and she threatened him with a Coke bottle. She also confronted the bus driver when she discovered that he told the white students on the bus that they were not allowed to let Turkish students sit next to them. This confrontation caused her and another student to be taken off the bus that day. She also confronted people in authority when she perceived an injustice. The day of the boycott, for example, Helen asked the school official if he was finished "Turk talking" so that the Turkish students could come in.

Jean's most interesting battle—a physical confrontation—took place on the school bus. An adolescent boy was being abusive to Jean by pulling her hair. She decided to act. She turned around and clobbered him with her book bag. Once she stood up against this boy, he never bothered her again.

Tonie's individual fight was just as courageous but not as violent. She reminisced about going to the white high school on the first day of class and walking right past those who did not want her there. That may not sound like a big deal to some people but it took guts. Nobody had ever done that before. She felt victorious in her own individual act against oppression.

Boaz also defended himself in school when necessary, but his individual contribution to the fight against oppression occurred more during his adult life. He, being a community leader, often had to confront other community leaders who were prejudiced. One time he even spoke with the judge of probate about a mistake on a marriage license. The marriage license listed a Turkish person as being black and this made Boaz very angry. The judge of probate assured him that this document and any others that were brought to his attention would be corrected.

These conversations have painted an interesting but sad picture of what happens when ethnic groups separate themselves from other groups. I sometimes wondered as we conducted our investigation, whether it was racism or classism that led white people to segregate the Turkish students from their schools. Maybe it was both. Could it be that the Turkish people were distancing themselves from the black people to avoid further oppression? Perhaps. Did the black people view the Turkish people as belonging to the oppressive white group? I don't know. No one can really justify why the three groups isolated themselves from one another, but they did. Whatever the past and future of the Turkish people, I am glad that we are now telling our story, including both the good and the bad of that history; and I hope that this project will enlighten Turkish descendants about their traditional culture.

The conversations reported thus far, somewhat like family discussions around the dinner table, have revealed important issues and perceptions among the Turkish people. Apparently they had faith in their traditional narrative but they knew little in terms of real history regarding their ancestry and ethnicity. My older relatives had clear opinions about certain issues—particularly being derided as

"Turks" and whether or not they were Indians—and varying ideas about other aspects of life, like clannishness and intermarriage, in their community. Also, my respondents harbored serious feelings about race relations and stood up against discrimination and oppression when they were young people.

Tensions among the three ethnic groups escalated in the middle of the twentieth century as the Integration Movement threatened serious disruption of the established order in Sumter County. Suddenly, the thought of all these people being thrown together—and jeopardizing their traditional ways and cultural identities—caused great turmoil in the community. All of a sudden, the Turkish people had to rethink what they knew and how they felt about their ancestry, ethnicity, community, and relations with the other races in this area.

~ *Chapter Nine* ~
# Life at the Dalzell School for Turks and Integrating the White Schools

For most of their history, the Turkish people of Sumter County had their own schools, legally segregated from white and black students. They were forced by law to attend what was known by the community as the Dalzell School for Turks or simply the Turk School.

~ Dalzell School ~

The Turkish schoolhouse shifted location periodically. In 1913, it was located near Dalzell, with twenty-eight students and one teacher; and in 1928, there were about one hundred children and three teachers in two schools, one in Dalzell and the other in Stateburg. In the 1940s, there was a single school at Dalzell with eleven grades (Sumter County Genealogical Society 2005). We could not determine the total count of students or teachers at the school during that latter period; but it was clear that there were too few teachers to educate too many children in the too small building. As had always been the case, the school simply lacked the resources and certification for its assignment and it provided an inferior education to its students.

Class rolls for Dalzell School for Turks always reflected the familiar names of the Turkish people. For example, at one time during the mid-1940s, the student body consisted of eighteen Benenhaleys, twelve Rays, eight Oxendines, two Hoods, two Buckners, and one Amerson (Sumter County Genealogical Society 2005; there was no information available for grades one through three). Boaz, Jean, Helen, and Tonie attended that school, and their stories reveal nostalgic memories and the stark realities of those times.

~ Warm but Mixed Memories ~

For the most part, my respondents recalled their early school days as an enjoyable but meager experience. The Dalzell School of the 1940s was located in a three-room, one-story building. Each room contained several grades, so the three teachers had to divide their time for teaching multiple classes simultaneously.

When I asked Helen how many students were in her class she said, "Probably about twelve in my grade. I believe we had first, second, and third grades in a little room and then fourth, fifth, and sixth in another. The highest students were bunched in a third room. The school wasn't very big. We didn't have any running water inside. We had to use an outhouse. We didn't have any air conditioning. We had to collect wood to stay warm. The teachers kept order. One had a ruler, and she would hit you on the hand with it, but nothing serious."

Boaz explained an interesting phenomenon of how school officials from the Dalzell School handled the problem of overpopulation when there were too many third grade students for the amount of space that they had in the school. To rectify the situation, they decided to create a big third grade and a little third grade. This meant that some of the third grade students who were supposed to be promoted to the fourth grade would instead be promoted to what was called the big third grade; and rising second graders would be promoted to what was called the little third grade. In essence, some students had to repeat the third grade simply because there was no room for them in the fourth-grade classroom

All four of my informants spoke fondly of their memories of Dalzell School. They talked about many aspects of the school, including the building, their teachers, lunch, Bible study, and recess. However, they had strong negative feelings, because the school did not prepare them academically for the level of work expected of them at the integrated high schools.

Students who arrived early were expected to gather wood and start a fire inside until the teachers and other students arrived. Back then, the teachers trusted the students with such tasks. Everyone worked together to create an environment conducive to learning. When someone was off task, the teachers sometimes used corporal punishment to keep order. They were highly respected and, according to the participants, very strict. The students genuinely liked their teachers at the Dalzell School; and Boaz added that "they did the best they could."

At the Dalzell School, once everyone was warm and had studied a few subjects, it was time for lunch. The Dalzell School did have a cafeteria, and according to Tonie, they paid seven cents for lunch when she first attended the school, but the price rose to ten cents when she was older. She explained the lunchtime procedures this way: "The first grade would go first, then the older grades. The food was already prepared and placed on the table for the number of students that were there that day. They already knew how many students would be eating and they prepared the lunches ahead of time. When we entered the lunchroom, we just sat wherever we wanted. I usually sat where the biggest apple was." When I asked what was served at these lunches, Boaz responded, "Sometimes we would have soup, milk, peanut butter, crackers, maybe an apple," The lunches at the Dalzell School were a highlight of the day. The four participants also spoke very highly of recess and the Bible class they had once a week.

According to Anne King Gregorie, the Turkish people of Sumter County "embraced the Baptist faith" (*The History of Sumter County* 1954, 469). For this reason, the Dalzell School invited a Bible teacher to come once a week to teach Christian principles. All of the participants spoke very highly of this class. Jean stated, "Yes, they taught Bible, which I really appreciate because a lot of that stuck with you. We had to memorize scripture and as you get older your eyes go. Those things stick with you. That's one thing I'm grateful that I had. We had someone come teach Bible maybe once or twice a week."

Tonie was also grateful for the Bible teacher and class. She had a vivid memory of that time of the week. She recalled, "They used to have prayer and Bibles in the school. We would have this lady who would come and teach us Bible stories. We would sing and she would play the piano. She would take that flannel board and stick pictures of Jesus and Mary on it. She would tell us stories and illustrate the stories on that flannel board. I was infatuated with that. I think she came every Thursday. She stayed about an hour."

After a few hours of exercising their minds, the students needed to exercise their bodies. Recess at the Dalzell School was unsupervised. Students were allowed to go outside and play until the teacher called them back in. They were not given toys or athletic equipment, so they had to devise ways to entertain themselves. Boaz smiled, raised his eyebrows and reminisced, "Recess was one of the best times. At ball time, we would pick up and play ball. We'd usually have a rubber ball or a tennis ball, not a baseball. We'd get a piece off of a desk for a bat, didn't have any such thing as a baseball bat. Usually no gloves, if a person was lucky, he might have a glove, and he was thought of as the star player, having a glove. We had a good time during play time. Get out and play, talk about boxing with boxing gloves, we had naked fists. We'd get out there and say, 'Now you're not going to hit in the face.' Boy, before we'd get started somebody would pop somebody in the face."

Being unsupervised was freeing for the students, but it was also somewhat dangerous. Helen explained, "We would go in the woods and make play houses. In the woods there was an old car seat. A friend of mine would say, 'You get on the car seat. Be the patient. I'll be the doctor.' That day we were in the woods. The teacher would usually call the students in. That day the bus driver came to get us instead of the teacher. The bus driver came out there and we were playing doctor and patient. He said, 'If you don't get up real quick, you're going to be playing undertaker. Look at that snake!' Honey, that was the biggest rattlesnake I'd ever seen. It was wrapped around the springs of that car seat. We were lucky."

~ Limited Opportunities ~

Just as Helen and her friend were unaware of the potential danger of the snake under the car seat, they were also unaware of what attending the Dalzell School might mean for their academic futures. The Turkish students who received an eleventh-grade Dalzell certificate were not allowed to attend colleges because colleges required a twelfth-grade diploma.

So what were their options? Boaz answered, "Well if they wanted to go somewhere else to school, they would have to finish that twelfth grade. Most of them, sorry to say, just got a job in the community. Of course a number of the families took their children out of the area where their children could get the proper training for schooling."

I understood Boaz to say that the options basically were to try to go to another school or get a job. When I asked him, he responded, "Right." So I asked for clarification: "You couldn't just go into college from the Dalzell School graduation diploma, right?" To this, Boaz responded, "No."

Helen recognized that many Turkish students were not given the opportunities to succeed academically because their school only had eleven grades. She said to me, "If the other lawyers had any heart at all, they would have seen that these children didn't have a chance. What could you do with an eleventh-grade education that wouldn't even be recognized?" Jean seemed to answer her question. She explained, "Not too much of anything, farm work. I don't know if anybody worked as a secretary or anything. There's not much they could do. I don't even know if they could have worked as a clerk in a store. I don't remember any of them working in stores then."

Tonie was clearly upset when talking about not being granted an equal education and elaborated on how being unprepared affected her in her career. She looked at me from across the room and stated, "I never looked back on it until I got old enough to realize that I needed a job one day and had no qualifications and no education. Since the Dalzell School was so far behind a regular school, by the time I got into the ninth grade, I probably had a seventh grade education or a sixth grade education. I couldn't keep up with the kids because of that. By the time I got to the ninth grade, my peers were so far ahead of me that I failed that grade. But I do feel like I'm intelligent." She made a point that, though she had not received an equal education, it had no bearing on her intelligence today. It was clear that she did her best to overcome her childhood educational experiences in order not to be limited in her adult life or her self-esteem. Simply stated, the participants believed that attending a school with only eleven grades put them at an extreme disadvantage for future academic success.

I asked Helen why the school only had eleven grades. She thought for a while and then stated, "I don't know why there wasn't a twelfth grade. They didn't care. If it was up to them, there wouldn't be any grades, I suppose." The participants all agreed, though, that because they attended the Dalzell School, they were not prepared for future academic work or community work.

~ Demands for Change ~

During the early part of the twentieth century, my relatives were aware that they were living in a homogeneous Turkish community. Although they were aware of the segregation among the Turkish, black, and white people in Sumter County, they seemed unaware of the degree of overwhelming desire of many people to keep the groups separated. When they realized that their children were not receiving an equal education, they decided to seek equal educational opportunities from the court system. They came together to stand up for their rights.

Boaz explained the awakening of a desire to better themselves to me. He said, "What happened was that when the young men went off to World War II, of course, they fought as Caucasians. They were treated as such, and when they came back, they wanted to join the American Legion and things like that. At that time they were not allowed to because they were Turkish. So this is when they began to assert their rights and began to find out what could be done. And this is when it began."

I asked Boaz, "When people actually started fighting for your rights, do you remember who those people were?" Without hesitating, he remembered, "Yes, Mr. Henry Benenhaley was one, Woodrow Hood, especially, was one of the ones that really pushed this. Also Marion Hood, Hammond Ray, and Henry Ray were also involved." The other participants concurred that these men united; and Jean added one more person to the list, "Herbert Ray."

Boaz continued: "We owe so much to those people who had the courage to go through what they went through. In fact, Mr. Augustus L. Merrimon is the one who led them through getting into the high school. He was a lawyer from Sumter. Many of the lawyers were afraid to take the case because the people put pressures on them. In fact, one of the lawyers dropped the case because we feel that the people in Sumter put so much pressure on him that he dropped it. And then Mr. Ira Kaye came along, and he took the case and pursued it to a successful conclusion" Ira Kaye was the last lawyer who eventually defended the Turkish people in their fight for an equal education. He was very familiar with their situation and, once the Turkish people were proactive in acquiring him as counsel, he helped them to gain access into white high schools.

Unfortunately, the Turkish students experienced a high dropout rate at those schools. In fact, Jean was the only participant in this study to graduate from high school. I asked her if the Dalzell School was similar to other schools in the area.

She responded, "We were limited to a lot of things, and the facility was not like the others. It was a struggle going to high school. You had a lot of studying to catch up, because I felt that we didn't get everything that we should have gotten." Helen concurred. She said, "When you go to school for nine years and don't get the basics and get what you need, when you get to the ninth grade, you've pretty much lost it. They taught the three Rs ('Reading, Riting, and Rithmetic') but that's about the size of it."

Boaz claimed that the school system in Sumter County was responsible for the Turkish students' being unprepared. He stated, "I just don't think the school system put the effort there to provide and prepare the students. I refer to it now as Dalzell University, in jest. When I was in the ninth grade, I didn't know a noun from a verb. During my first year in college, I had never seen a microscope before, other than in a picture. Another thing, when I got to the third grade and was hoping I was going to the fourth grade, they didn't have room so they came up with what they called a big third grade and a little third grade. You had to go through the third grade again and not go to the fourth grade because they didn't have room."

The four participants were all forced to attend the "Turk School" in Dalzell. Though they had very pleasant memories of the school, the students, and teachers, they all agreed that it had not prepared them for the rigors of public high school or for their future careers. The school had only eleven grades, so going to college was not an option unless these students went to another school that had twelve grades. All of these factors caused the participants of this study to reflect on how things could have been if they would have been given the right to an equal education when they were younger.

The struggle to attend the white public schools of Sumter County would prove a long road for the Turkish people, and winning the legal battle did not end their troubles. Integration would subject the young students to personal difficulties due not only to resistance from white individuals but also to their own segregated backgrounds and academic deficiencies.

~ Integrating the White High Schools ~

Boaz, Jean, Helen, and Tonie had attended the Dalzell School for Turks during the 1940s, and they were among the first Turkish students to attend white public schools of that area in the 1950s. It was a heroic endeavor; but, as we shall see, they suffered severely for their heroism.

The participants were integrated into two different high schools. Boaz attended Edmunds High School in Sumter because he lived in the Edmunds High School district, and Jean, Helen and Tonie attended Hillcrest High School because they lived in the rural Hillcrest High School district. Their experiences were very different, depending on which high school they attended.

Edmunds was more accepting and Hillcrest was more resistant.

I asked Boaz why he thought there was a difference in the way that the Turkish students were accepted in these two schools and he stated, "This is my opinion, but I think that the majority of the Turkish people lived in the country and that's where Hillcrest was. That's where so much of the prejudice was. Hillcrest was pretty much in the center or close to the Dalzell area. That is why I would think the people in that particular area had more contact with the Turkish people, from the stand point, they just knew each other better. At that time there was hatred, prejudice, bigotry among the country people more so than those in the city. You had the country district and then you had the district in Sumter. Edmunds was in the city and Hillcrest was in the country. I just think it was because of the proximity and the dealings that they had with one another."

Edmunds High School was formally opened in 1939 and was named after a former educator and superintendent of schools in Sumter County, Samuel Henry Edmunds. Edmunds High School was very accepting of Boaz from the first day that he attended. He remembered, "The people at Edmunds were very kind, the teachers and the students. I didn't go but five weeks and quit because I was unprepared at the time going from Dalzell to Edmunds High in the tenth grade. But when I went to stop, to drop out, they begged me not to. As soon as I got there, the coach invited me for football. I was accepted as a peer. Any type of program they had was open to me."

When I asked him to describe a typical day at Edmunds High School he stated, "It was very structured, very different because the classes were divided. On a typical day, we would have algebra, then maybe typing, English class. I made the mistake of taking Latin. And I took it one day until the teacher asked me a question, and I couldn't answer, so I did not go back to that class." Boaz explained that the teachers, coaches, and students were all very supportive. He had very few problems with anyone at this school. He could only think of two incidents in which he was discouraged a little. He stated, "I had no problems with any of the students, except one boy in a class one day said something, and I just let him know what would happen and had no more problems with him."

The other incident was not at the school but rather at the bus stop. Boaz recalled with sadness, "When it came to my stop, there was a girl on the bus, and she would always make sure that she got way ahead so she didn't have to walk along with me in getting off of the bus." I asked, "Why didn't she want to walk with you?" Boaz seemed dejected and said, "She thought she was better than me. I was Turkish. She didn't want to be seen with me."

But for the most part, Boaz felt encouraged by everyone at Edmunds High School. In fact, he stated, "It's just five weeks, but coming from the background of Dalzell to Edmunds, just for those five weeks, I'll always be proud of those five weeks at Edmunds." He remembers one teacher, in particular, who tried to encourage him to stay in school. Not wanting to disappoint her, he dropped out without her knowing. He explained, "I went to the office to sign out, and my teacher found out about it and talked me out of it. But then when my teacher wasn't looking, I went back and signed out. Sneaky."

Like Boaz, who attended Edmunds High School, the Turkish students who attended Hillcrest High School felt unprepared for the challenges of a rigorous high school curriculum. They had great difficulty competing with their classmates. There were some teachers and students who tried to help them succeed, but because of the lack of preparation and because of the strong resistance of some toward Turkish students, many were not successful.

I asked Tonie to describe the classes that were taught at Hillcrest High School. She stated, "I took math, home economics, science, English, literature. We even went to agriculture classes with the boys once a week and watched farm films and gardening, which I enjoyed. I don't know why I liked it, but I'm still interested in gardening."

Regarding extracurricular activities, Tonie explained, "The only thing I remember about Hillcrest was football games, basketball games, the cheerleaders. Inside the gym we would watch basketball games." I asked, "Did you participate in any of these activities?" Tonie said with disappointment, "I didn't participate in any of it, but I went to watch basketball games in the gym, and I wasn't very fond of them."

Tonie, Helen, and Jean did not participate in any extracurricular activities including the prom. They explained that Turkish students were not allowed to participate in any of these activities. Tonie's explanation was, "We weren't allowed to participate in any sports, cheerleading, proms. . . . As a matter of fact, they kept the proms a secret—where they were going to be, what night they were going to be. That was hush, hush, so the Turkish people couldn't go. They just acted like we weren't there. They wouldn't give you a chance to try out for anything."

Jean echoed Tonie's thoughts about the prom. She stated, "I'll never forget the prom. They had it at a private place in Dalzell so we couldn't go. They had a private one so that my friend and I wouldn't be able to attend." I was not sure that I understood, so I asked, "Do you mean they kept it private just so two people wouldn't come?" She then spelled it out very clearly and said, "That is correct. That was terrible. Two people, I mean, just two of us."

Likewise, Helen stated, "When we went to Hillcrest we weren't allowed to participate in anything. When they were getting ready for their prom, they went to the Dalzell Community House. I guess they didn't tell us that we couldn't participate, but if they didn't want us to sit by them on the bus, they sure didn't want us at the prom."

In spite of the efforts of some to keep the Turkish students segregated, there were others who reached out to them. My respondents mentioned several teachers who were nice and helpful.

Tonie remembered one particular teacher with adoration and told me about one day in class when she was feeling defeated. She remembered, "I said, 'I don't know how to put a zipper in this skirt.' She said, 'I'm going to show you. I'm not going to do it for you.' So she encouraged me to do that. She always told me I did a good job. I was sewing. We had to wear what we made, and it was supposed to be a double collar. I said, 'I left the collar off of this blouse.' She said, 'It's fine. All you have to do is press the seams and press the collar. Then bring it back and let me look at it.' She said, 'Tomorrow everyone has to wear the outfits you made.' So I was embarrassed, but I wore it, and she said, 'Oh, it looks nice.'" The efforts of this teacher, and others like her, made the transition into the white high school more bearable for the Turkish students. The efforts of those who resisted integration, however, made the transition very difficult.

Upon reminiscing about her days at Hillcrest High School, Jean sighed. She began to tell me about several events that came into her mind. She explained, "My friend and I went through h-e-l-l together. We were put back in everything. It was hell on wheels. That's putting it mildly. We dreaded to go. They made it tough for us and treated us badly." As I listened, I understood more of why she had sighed before explaining her educational experiences to me. The difficulty for Jean began from the moment she boarded the bus until the moment she returned home in the afternoon. She told me, "When you get on the bus and people start picking at you and teasing you, that gets your day started off bad. In the classroom they would treat you badly. You never were treated nice, Terri. They looked at us as trash. They wouldn't be caught dead sitting on the seat beside you or anywhere close. And they'd call you names."

Jean then elaborated on how, as difficult as it was, she stood up for herself and did not allow others to stop her from attending Hillcrest. She said, "We stuck it out. It was hard. I don't remember literally fighting, except one day on the bus. That boy that I told you about pulled my hair and I clobbered him. We had book satchels back then and I clobbered him, and he didn't bother me anymore."

Tonie was the youngest participant in this study and attended Hillcrest High School seven years after Jean. Her experiences may not have been as drastic, but she still spoke of having to endure the resistance of some. She explained, "No one really wanted us there. I felt like they were better than I at that time. I don't anymore." I noticed that Tonie had a great amount of self-confidence during the interview. She was not ashamed to admit her struggles as a child, because these same struggles helped her to be sure of herself as an adult. When recalling the first day of integrated high school, she proudly claimed, "We went into the school to register and then we left. I think our parents took us up there, and we went into the school to register. It was like they didn't want us in the school, but we went anyway. We walked right passed them, signed our name." Tonie was making a statement that day. She might have known that there were some people who did not want the Turkish students to attend Hillcrest High School, but she knew she had just as much right to attend the school as anyone else. For this reason, she was fearless.

After attending the school, Tonie was faced with the resistance of some, but claimed, "The only ones who treated us badly were the ones who grew up here. The air force kids who didn't grow up here treated us well because they didn't know anything about Turks. Some of the teachers would try to turn some of the students against us. They'd get together, and some of them were the instigators. They would try to embarrass us in front of the class." Tonie's experiences may be difficult for some to comprehend. She stated, "Every time we tell someone, even from another county in South Carolina, they've never heard of it. They just think it's awful. They say, 'You are kidding. Oh my goodness!'"

Jean has also experienced disbelief by others who hear of her experiences. Younger Turkish people who have never experienced segregation, for example, find it very difficult to believe that their older relatives had to fight for the right to attend white schools. She stated, "When I tell my kids they don't want to believe it." Even in the church where Boaz was a pastor, some members of the congregation were very surprised to hear of his educational experiences during the Integration Movement. He explained their disbelief, "I've had church members who have read my little book say to me, 'I can't imagine that someone would act that way.' People in other areas are amazed that people would have been treated as such." Boaz was shaking his head when explaining this as if to assure me that it was true.

All of the participants agreed that not everyone at Hillcrest High School was resistant to integration. Some genuinely wanted the Turkish students to have a smooth transition and befriended them; others did not. Helen was the most vocal about some of the things that she endured. During one interview, she carried on a lengthy monologue in which she recalled the resistance. I listened intently without interrupting as she relived several difficult experiences at Hillcrest High School. She was visibly strained at the thought of having to retell these stories, and then she began. She stated,

> One day we were sitting on the grass and these apples and oranges came flying. And some of them hit me. There were some boys who would say mean things about us. I said, "If you repeat what you said again, I will hit you across the head with this Coke bottle." I stood up for myself.
>
> The lunchroom was still outside the main building. We would get ready to go in, and there were some students. The minute we would try to go in, they would elbow us and try to prevent us from entering.
>
> Then one day we were passing the cemetery and a boy made a comment, "One less Turk to deal with." One day I stepped on his foot and said, "Excuse me." He said, "You can't excuse a dog after he already bit."

The bus driver would start off driving, and then he would see how he could jerk the bus to make us fall down because all the Turkish students had to stand. One day I got on the bus. I said to a little girl, "Move your feet, honey, and let me sit down." She started crying and said, "The bus driver said no more Turks can sit by me." I said, "Let him tell me I can't sit down." He said, "Do you want me to slap your face?" That's when another Turkish student stood up and defiantly said, "Yes, slap her right now." The bus driver said, "I want both of you off of my bus right now." Some teachers would refer to us as "You people over there, you need to speak up." In class we would sit together. No one would ever sit with us.

I remember the first two Turkish girls to graduate from Hillcrest. One of the girls had on a beautiful white dress. There was one white girl who had on the identical dress. They called them the "Gold Dust twins." It was some type of detergent at the time. That girl called home and someone brought her another dress. She wouldn't wear the dress because one of the Turkish girls had on the same dress.

Math wasn't my cup of tea. When I got to the ninth grade, I wrote a letter to be taken out of math class, and the lady took me out. I wrote the letter, so I never would have graduated without math. I signed my parents name to it and she didn't even pursue it. She said, "If you want to drop out, drop out."

I hated to see the light of day come. A lot of mornings we would get to the point where we could see the road and we would let the bus pass right by because the bus driver would always jerk the bus. We'd tell my daddy and he would say, "Get in the car. I know you missed the bus on purpose." You see, he knew what we went through.

A friend of mine had a crutch. When she would get on the bus, she would usually hand the crutch to the bus driver and he would put it down for her. One day she handed him the crutch and he said, "Take care of your own self."

Some of the cafeteria women were so mean. They would push the choice pieces of chicken to the side and give us the backs.

We experienced the same thing in the classroom, where if the teacher called you to the board and you couldn't do something, everyone would laugh. "Ha! Ha! She can't do that." And it was devastating. They were right. We couldn't do that.

A lot of people around here just want to forget it happened. It's real. There's no need in denying it. Some people around here are in denial. They say, "Don't bring that up. It's in the past." Sometimes I think about what we could have been and what we could have done if we would have had an education.

~ Recollecting Segregation and Integration ~

I was particularly interested in how my four participants felt about the situation back then. So I asked each of them to tell me as much as they could remember about segregation and integration.

For Boaz, segregation was something that most people simply accepted. He stated, "I think they just accepted it as a fact. I don't think at the time, that they thought of it being anything other than . . . that they could have done anything else. I think they just accepted it. I did. I knew nothing better." Helen shrugged her shoulders and told me, "I didn't know any different. We were all there. I just thought, 'That's the way it is.' It had been like that for years and years. I knew I was separated from the other groups, but it didn't bother me." Tonie did not even realize she was segregated for many years. She stated, "I didn't even know I was a Turk until I went to Hillcrest. I never knew that I was any different from anybody else until I went to Hillcrest and found out."

Jean, on the other hand, admitted that she knew she was being segregated. She stated, "We realized it. We thought that maybe we were different and they didn't accept us, so you just planted it in your mind that you were different. So I guess we grew up thinking we were different." I inquired, "So was that OK with you?" She responded, "Oh, I'm sure it wasn't OK. No, but I just felt, what else can we do? It's either that or you don't go to school."

Since the ages of the participants ranged from sixty-five to seventy-five at the time of these interviews, some of them were very young during those years. But they were able to name many of the Turkish people who united to fight for an equal education, including Henry Benenhaley, Woodrow Hood, Marion Hood, Hammond Ray, Henry Ray, and Herbert Ray; and they said that about ten of the men in the community raised enough money to pay for the case. These individuals are considered to be heroes among the Turkish people and their efforts are commendable, because they were persistent in their fight for their children to have an equal education. In the end they were victorious.

The protests against integration undoubtedly made the transition into integrated high school a very difficult time. I asked the participants to recall their first day of integrated high school. Helen responded, "It was a bad experience, an experience I'll never forget." Jean added, "I was scared to death, scared to death. They didn't want us coming in, that's for sure. They would call us all kinds of names." Tonie recalled, "The first day I went to school there, all the kids came, and the Turkish kids went, too. The second day, the Turkish children were the only ones who showed up. All the white kids stayed at home. So that year I stayed out because we couldn't go back to the Dalzell School, and we couldn't go back to the other school because the white kids would stay home if we showed up. So some of us stayed out a year while the Turkish men fought the legal battle for equal rights. I fell behind. Staying out of school for one year as a child and then having to go back into the next grade, you forget a lot."

Helen also experienced the boycott. She explained it this way, "That particular day, we would usually go in when the bell would ring. There wasn't anybody there but us. Two white girls came but the teachers told them that they had to go back home. They told them to call their parents to come and get them."

Helen especially remembered a school official who came out to talk with the Turkish students one day during the boycott. "He said 'You all can come in now,' I said, 'Are you sure now? Are you finished Turk-talking so we can come in?' One girl punched me in the ribs. I said, 'Don't punch me now. I'm not afraid of these people up here.' It's a wonder someone didn't kill me when I was in school."

Helen also noted that "I can't explain this to my grandchildren. They can't comprehend any of this. People who aren't from this area, if you tell them this kind of stuff, it's like if I tell my grandchild about this, the response is, 'That's a bunch of junk.' My grandchild laughs, but I say that it's not a laughing matter. People from the outside can't believe it. It's hard to believe that people that lived here haven't heard about it."

~ Looking Back on the Movement ~

It has been more than a half century since those turbulent days of the Turkish Integration Movement. But all of my relatives remember those days vividly; they are proud of their role in changing the system, but they have strong, negative feelings about their experiences during that Movement.

Boaz tried to explain those unpleasant times by noting that so many people were bitterly and violently opposed to integration. Helen simply described it as a bad experience; but Jean said she was scared. Tonie remembered having to stay out of school for a year. "It was awful," she said. "You never knew what they were going to say to you or what they were going to do to you. Even the teachers were prejudiced. Traumatic. That's the word I think of, something I hope no one ever has to face again." I asked, "What made it so traumatic? Can you give me an example?" She said emphatically, "Yes. Kids calling you 'Turk,' the bus leaving me and I would have to go back home. I'd have to have an excuse the next day about why I wasn't in school, and I would put, 'The bus driver refused to pick me up.' They didn't care. If they were the only ones on a seat, they would put their books on the other side of the bus so that you couldn't sit there, and dare you to move them."

When probed further, Tonie explained that she had been sheltered and lived in a safe, homogeneous environment of mostly Turkish people, and her educational experiences during the Integration Movement caused her to constantly reflect on how her life had changed. An example of how her life had changed was through the roles that adults played in her life. Tonie commented that some of the teachers tried to embarrass the Turkish students and even tried to turn other students against them. Tonie's faith in adults no doubt dissipated. She understood that some people made her the object of oppression because of her ethnicity, but she did not comprehend why people judged others based on the color of their skin. She believed that she should fight oppression and in her own way, she did so. She stated that she knew that others did not want her to attend Hillcrest but that she walked right passed them and signed her name on the registration papers.

Jean also reflected on the past. I asked her if there was ever a day when she realized that she was Turkish and that that was something different. When she first began to reflect, she admitted that she had adopted the belief that she was different in her mind because that was what she had always heard. Society had caused her to believe that she did not deserve the opportunity to have an equal education. She had accepted this notion for a while, but the more she reflected, the more she wanted to devise a way to bring about change.

While Helen reflected on the past, she also made several comments about her thoughts on the Turkish community today and her thoughts about what could have been. She was perplexed that some Turkish people want to deny that they were mistreated during the Integration Movement. Helen is not one to overlook injustice. She believes that while the mistreatment happened in the past, people should still be aware of it today. Helen also spoke in wonderment of how things could have been different had the Turkish students been granted an equal education. She reflects on it frequently, even after all of these years. Like Helen, Boaz also commented on the wonder of what could have been. He reflected on the missed opportunities the athletes were denied because of the lack of facilities to play ball. According to Boaz, there were some talented athletes who might have been able to play professionally, but they did not have access to a good diamond on which to play baseball.

All four participants reflected on their state of being during the Integration Movement. Tonie and Jean discussed feeling different. Tonie stated that she was not aware that people looked at her as being different until someone pointed it out in high school. Jean declared that she had actually accepted her situation as being normal, because she had somehow been led to believe that she did not deserve an equal education. Helen and Boaz both reflected on the way things could have been if only segregation had never been a part of their lives. Boaz was even brought to tears as he spoke about this topic. The events that occurred in the personal lives of the participants over fifty years ago were still raw and close to their hearts. Over the course of their lives, my respondents had to overcome many obstacles in order to successfully liberate their minds—not just oppression but sometimes their own feelings of worthlessness. This lack of self-esteem was undoubtedly caused by other people pointing out their differences and prohibiting their participation in academic, community and social events.

Jean was one of the first two Turkish students to graduate from Hillcrest High School. They were faced with great opposition each day. She also had to overcome the obstacle of not letting others keep her down. She was determined to fight against those who wanted to hold her back. Tonie mentioned that once she became an adult, she realized that she did not have the qualifications to get a job. She also stated that when she was in high school, she felt like the other students were better than she was. She knows that she is intelligent, but she had to conquer her own self-doubt before she could move on. Helen, likewise, struggled against the odds. She overcame the hardships that she had endured while trying to graduate from high school. She did not allow her past to defeat her will to succeed. Boaz also had a strong determination to overcome adversity. He went to college on probation, because he never graduated from high school. In college, he was selected to be president of the senior class, and he received the President's Medal as the Student Most Likely to Succeed. He has walked across at least four different stages to get different types of degrees or diplomas and has never walked across a high school stage to get a high school diploma.

The following is a summary of the testimonials of my older relatives, not only about the Integration Movement but also about the lives of "Sumter Turks" in the past century. All four of them said that they were of "Turkish descent"; however, none of them could say exactly where they came from or describe clearly and precisely who they are. They believed that their people were forced to isolate long ago because of the way they were treated by outsiders; and they felt more comfortable living among themselves. They had very pleasant memories of the Dalzell School, but they agreed that they had not been prepared for the rigors of Edmunds or Hillcrest High Schools or for any future career. There was overwhelming feeling that integrating the white schools was a necessary and progressive step forward; but it was a negative experience for them personally. Only one of the four students graduated from high school; but they all have overcome the trauma of their younger years. They often think about what might have been if they had been given the opportunity that white people enjoyed back then and that young Turkish people now take for granted.

Boaz, Helen, Jean, and Tonie have now raised their voices and told their stories about the Turkish community's difficult history. I have been honored to be a part of this effort and hope that I have faithfully presented their lives and feelings in these pages. The following chapter includes a discussion on today's Turkish community and what is happening in Sumter County in the twenty-first century.

~ *Chapter Ten* ~

The Turkish Community Today

The Turkish community today is very different from when the informants of this study were students at the Dalzell School. Back then, the Turkish people were a very unique society with what many considered unusual cultural ways. They were close, not only in their relationships with one another, but also geographically. Most of them lived within a few miles of one another; and few left the comfort of family, home, and community.

Things have changed in the twenty-first century. The Turkish people now enjoy the blessings of American life just as do other citizens. Ironically, however, this assimilation into mainstream society jeopardizes their sense of cultural community and ethnic heritage.

~ A Different and Better World ~

Today, the Turkish people of Sumter County live in a very different and better world. The Turkish spirit endures and they are still intimate in their relationships, but they do not cluster together as an enclosed, isolated enclave. They are thoroughly mixed in the public, business, and social activities of this region. Almost all are marrying outsiders; and most are moving to other areas. They also have much more freedom and many more opportunities than were afforded those who grew up in earlier times. The global job market has provided many outlets for them to move to various parts of the world in order to chase a career dream, and they actually do live all over the world.

Additionally, the Turkish people are subject to less discrimination. Most important, today's Turkish young people have access to an equal education, thanks to their predecessors who fought for better schooling. This has granted them the freedom to dream big and follow their hearts to discover an entire world of opportunities waiting to be grasped.

Of course, it is impossible to determine fully and precisely how the Turkish community is evolving. The US Census provides no clear, consistent data; and no polling firms are tracking the attitudes and activities of Turkish people.

However, information drawn from miscellaneous government publications, genealogical sites, and knowledgeable local sources suggests a definite and consequential reality: their numbers are declining. The "Benenhaleys" grew from a single family of seven persons in 1810 to almost three hundred Turkish people in the settlement by the end of that century; and at midpoint of the twentieth century, the Turkish population peaked at about five hundred persons. Their numbers dipped to about four hundred in 1990, and extrapolation from the American Community Survey Data—a federal sampling project—suggests that the number of Sumter County citizens claiming Turkish ancestry has dropped to slightly over two hundred in the first decade of the current century. Curiously, this decline has occurred while the county population doubled over the past half century.

Church membership provides another clue to the changing environment in this community. In 1904, the Turkish people built their first church—Long Branch Baptist Church—near Peach Orchard Road in Dalzell. They then built a replacement church for their growing congregation on Raccoon Road in 1921; an even larger and current church on Peach Orchard Road has served them since 1960. According to reports of the South Carolina Baptist Convention, Long Branch began with forty-four members at its founding in 1904, grew to ninety-four in 1910, to 173 in 1930, to 230 in 1950, and topped at 391 in 1970. Then it dropped to 195 in 1990 and 150 in 2012. Of course, some members went to Springbank Baptist Church when that group was established on nearby Fish Road as an independent institution in 1971. Long Branch Pastor Jonathan Bradshaw told us during a 2015 interview that about sixty to eighty congregants attend church on most Sundays; and Springbank Pastor Steve Miller estimated in an interview that same year that Sunday attendance there usually exceeds a hundred persons.

Both churches still serve as a place of worship for many Turkish people in Sumter County, but neither considers itself a Turkish church today. In 2004, Long Branch pastor Carroll E. Waddell remarked to a reporter for *The Item* regarding the church's one-hundred-year anniversary (Baker, Oct. 30, 2004): "At one time, (the members) were somewhat suspicious of people who were not of Turkish descent because (the Turks) were treated badly when they came here. This was even as late as the '50s and '60s. It has taken a little bit of time for people to get used to each other, to accept each other as equal people." Current Pastor Jonathan Bradshaw, who had assumed his position at Long Branch just months prior to his interview with the authors, said: "We think of ourselves as a multicultural association;

and most of our new members really don't know much about the history of the Turkish community." Springbank also attracts worshipers of diverse backgrounds. Pastor Steve Miller of that church told us that he had never heard of the Turkish community prior to assuming leadership at Springbank eight years ago; and he similarly defined his church ministry broadly: "We consider our mission as ministering to anybody and everybody in the local community, to include Shaw Air Force Base."

It is clear that today's Turkish people are similar to most South Carolinians in terms of language (English), religion (Baptist), and interests (such as church, school, cooking, television, movies, football, basketball, baseball, hunting, and fishing)—about what would be expected of southerners long and far removed from their Old World origins. Many of them retain the dark looks that cause people to ask if they are Hispanic; however just as many are light-haired, light-skinned, blue-eyed individuals. Some have a slightly different way of talking or pronouncing certain words, which leads to questions about whether they are from Charleston or New Orleans.

In previous generations, questions or comments about such cultural matters would have triggered emotions among the Turkish people; however, nowadays most such observations are considered simply southern banter.

These demographic patterns and comments demonstrate that the Turkish people are changing in dramatic ways. The traditional community—defined as an ethnically and geographically concentrated population—is yielding to assimilation.

~ New Questions and Challenges ~

Their world has changed; and, as might be expected, important new questions now hang over the descendants of Joseph Benenhaley. For example, is there still a real "community" of Turkish people in Sumter County? What is life like for these people nowadays? And what does the future hold for them in the twenty-first century? I will try to answer these and other questions by visiting among and talking with the Turkish people now living in that area.

First, however, it is important to discuss a few new and different challenges facing the Turkish people. Interestingly, there are some downsides as they pursue the positive course of assimilation. The older members are dying and the younger members are marrying outside the traditional families and moving to other parts of the state and nation. In some ways, such developments serve to weaken the Turkish people's sense of community and cultural heritage.

Also, as has already been mentioned, some Turkish persons are rethinking their ethnic identities. Activists within the American Indian and Melungeon movements have posed alternative ideas about our origins and history; and those ideas seem to have resonated among some who traditionally considered themselves Turkish people. I was in Sumter in 2007 when an article came out in the local newspaper, *The Item,* about the Turkish people not actually being Turkish but rather Native American. This article stirred up a lot of angst among many members of the Turkish community who do not claim to be Native American.

As a researcher, I was intrigued. As a member of the Turkish community, I was perplexed. If there was proof that we are Native American, I would have accepted that as who we are. But I have found no such proof. Thus, while I am open to the truth about our origins, I have my own solid set of beliefs and attitudes regarding who we are; and this is based on my own personal research and the documentary research presented earlier in this book.

I relied at the outset on the earliest documents available regarding our origins, such as the written account of General Thomas Sumter's great-grandson, Thomas Sebastian Sumter, who claimed that Joseph Benenhaley was a "Caucasian of Arab descent" in a newspaper column for the *Watchman and Southron* (1917). Sumter also reported that his great-grandfather, General Thomas Sumter himself, defended the Turkish people's white status in court (1920, 243).

Also, the earliest birth certificates and death certificates with Benenhaley surnames listed "Turk" as the person's race. I did not find any that listed Benenhaleys as being Native American. Finally, I also researched census records for the purpose of tracing my family tree back to Joseph Benenhaley, which I was able to do.

Having said that, I realize that a family tree can go in many different directions. The reality is that our patriarch could have been Turkish; some members of the early family tree may have been Native American; and others may have married people from Native American tribes, which would make some members of my family partially Native American and some partially Turkish.

Actually, as was mentioned in the documentary section of this book, that mixed possibility has been suggested in DNA analyses among a few living Turkish people. These reports clearly indicate prominent Mediterranean/Middle Eastern/North African descent for the Benenhaley bloodline; but there are markers for different ethnic groups among some people of the other families. Since my interviews were about the historical experience of the participants, I did not pursue this issue as much as I would have if this had been a genealogical project. The findings of the documentary analysis are consistent with the traditional narrative; therefore, I am comfortable that we are what our ancestors before us claimed to be, that is, a community of Turkish descent.

The same is true about the Melungeons. A man from my church in Georgia, who identifies himself as being Melungeon, approached me about a Melungeon conference in Atlanta. The Melungeons, according to Brent Kennedy and Robyn Vaughan Kennedy, "are a diverse group reflecting a mixed ethnic, cultural, and religious heritage" (1997, 167). They mention their lineage from Turks marooned on the Carolina coast; and they cite the South Carolina Turkish people as likely relatives (153).

I went to the Melungeon conference. While there, I looked around and could not help but notice that the Melungeons in the audience appeared to be people of many different ethnic groups, yet they all claimed that they were from the same ethnic group. I saw people who appeared to be white, black, Latino, Native American, and Asian, but they all identified themselves as being Melungeon. At the conference I sat in awe for a while. Many social scientists claim that race is a social construct rather than a scientific or physical phenomenon; so I wondered to myself: Is this what it would be like to live in a truly raceless world? Were all these people Turkish cousins? Did they all share similar genes from the old Ottoman Empire? Recently, a DNA project (Yates and Hirschman 2010) supplied a mixed answer to my questions. The project tentatively suggested the Melungeons' genetic origins as "an amalgam of Mediterranean, Middle Eastern, North African, Sub-Saharan African, and Native American ethnic groups." The authors reported that this amalgam probably accounted for the darker coloring of Melungeon skins; they also said that this likely set them apart from northwestern European groups and targeted them for stigmatization. Eventually, my awe subsided. The Melungeons impressed me as educated people. But based on my personal research and our documentary study, I do not believe that the Turkish people are Melungeons.

Another growing challenge is the fact that younger members of the Turkish community in Sumter County seem to be drifting away from their roots. It is not surprising that their ethnic identity might fade as they assimilate into broader society; however, I am concerned that they probably lose something important if they forget their cultural heritage.

My friend, Eleazer Benenhaley, an elderly man of Turkish descent who was born and raised in Sumter County, has seen significant improvement for his people over the years. For example, whereas in the 1940s and 1950s he could only listen on the radio and dream about playing American Legion baseball, his son, Tim, was a star performer for the Dalzell-Shaw American Legion team in the 1970s; and numerous Turkish boys have played for Legion teams in the area since then. However, Eleazer Benenhaley believes that many are too young to understand what the older Turkish people experienced. He has written elsewhere about this situation (*An Analysis* 2008):

> While visiting one of the middle schools in Sumter County years ago, I came in contact with a history teacher and a group of boys who were of Turkish background kidding each other with ethnic slurs. The teacher said to me, "I hope you don't mind us having fun with each other." I replied, "You can do that with them, but you cannot with me." You see, those young boys knew nothing of the bigotry and prejudices that their parents and grandparents had faced. I doubt that the teacher knew.

> I will always be thankful for those who endured the indignities of those who tried to keep their children out of the White schools. Those brave people have gone on to their reward and those who opposed them have had to answer to the Great Judge of the Universe! (34).

I am hopeful that the current project will help these younger people understand and appreciate their Turkish heritage.

~ Conversations and Observations ~

Seeking answers to our questions about today's Turkish community, my coauthor and I traveled to South Carolina and met with several Turkish people during the past few years. We wanted to find out how the younger generations feel about their heritage and how the community has changed from the old days.

Seven different individuals, all of whom live in the Sumter area, agreed to talk with us. Unlike the structured interviews with Boaz, Helen, Jean, and Tonie, the sessions with younger Turkish citizens were free-ranging conversations and spontaneous observations. These interviews were just as interesting as the ones with the older respondents; however, the sessions with Greg, Chip, Brian, Adrienne, Richie, Harold, and Reilly about life today were less provocative than the revelations from the past century. The following report reveals what they told us about their lives and thoughts about their ethnic heritage.

Greg Thompson

I first spoke with Greg Thompson on the phone after Browder had already met with him to discuss our project. We had heard that Greg could be an integral contributor to this study, if he were willing. After the initial meeting with Browder, Greg decided that he would, in fact, help with this project; and it was anticipated that he would be a veritable gold mine. Friends had shared that Greg possessed valuable material and information, and he was committed to telling the story of the Turkish community in full and with respect for the Turkish people.

Also, we knew, from the beginning, that Greg knew more than we did about the Turkish people and their traditional narrative. For example, Greg was certain that Joseph Benenhaley was a "Caucasian of Arab descent" long before our research confirmed that claim. He revealed to us that he had run several genetic tests years ago; and he said, "I knew all along that he was an Ottoman; and I've been saying it for years. Blood does not lie. DNA does not lie. This backs up the traditional narrative. There's really nothing else to discuss in my opinion."

Although Greg is not Turkish by birth, he married into the Turkish community after moving to Sumter from Panama with his military family. He enrolled in Hillcrest High School during his junior year in 1980. A native of Iowa with a transient background, Thompson had been accustomed to meeting and living with all

Greg Thompson, a native Iowan who married into a Turkish family in the 1980s, provided critical information, documents, and photographs from his collection of Turkish material for this project. Thompson is writing his own manuscript about the early community. Courtesy of Greg Thompson.

kinds of people from different ethnic backgrounds. It had become a way of life for him, so when he moved to Sumter he did not see people in color. He also was unaware of the local culture and did not know that there was a community of Turkish people until he met the girl of his dreams. He met Kathy Peagler (whose mother was a Benenhaley) on the first day of school and noticed that her "jet black hair and olive skin stood out from the other girls." He was immediately attracted to her but was cautioned by his classmates to be careful with their relationship because she was a "Turk."

Ignoring their words of caution, Greg dated and eventually married Kathy in 1985, but it was not before he had a chance to ask her what their classmates were talking about when they said that she was a "Turk." She courageously told him that for a long time, the white people had treated her people as second-class citizens, questioning their history and showing them every kind of prejudice. She simply told him that he would have to decide for himself whether or not he would want to have anything to do with her.

Over time, Greg became close with Kathy and with her family as well. He noticed that the members of her family also shared her physical features and that they were all very close. He stated, "They looked out for each other and stood together against anyone who tried to cross them, not out of necessity, but more so out of the simple fact that they were family, and family sticks together." Greg also noticed that the older generation was more tight-lipped about their history than the younger generation seemed to be. His own mother-in-law did not share much with him about their history until Greg was an official member of the family. She then shared with him a great deal about the history of the Benenhaley family. She educated him on the fact that her parents were Benenhaleys, and that they descended from a man named Benenhaley who was brought to the area by General Thomas Sumter, himself, around the time of the American Revolution. She told him that her family located around the geographical area of Fish Road and Highway 441, which was land that the general had given to them during that time. She told him that, for the most part, they "called no other place home." This was also the area where they founded their own school and church.

Greg had been married for about four years when he spoke with his wife about the possibility of writing a book about her Benenhaley ancestors. He stated, "Of course she was all for the idea of finally getting her family's story and lineage on paper and in a manner that was truthful and accurate," since most written documentation of the Turkish community had been written by people who were not of Turkish descent nor part of the community through marriage. He began collecting information from family members whom Kathy suggested to him, gathering stories, courthouse information, census information, family Bibles dating to the 1870s, tintypes of the early Benenhaley generations that dated to the late 1800s, and old letters from those born in the 1840s.

He was very close to finalizing his research when, after sixteen years of marriage, his wife, Kathy, tragically died in an accident. Devastated by his loss, he put the research down and locked it into a trunk, because he "no longer had the desire to bring it to fruition." He had relied on her to help him connect with the older generation, which he never would have been able to do without her.

Six years after this terrible tragedy, Kathy's mother, Leah, approached Greg and told him that whether or not he ever did anything with the research was his decision to make. However she felt that all the hard work and time that was put into getting all the papers together was a waste if it just sat in a box somewhere. She, too, passed away a year after this discussion, and Greg still had not decided what to do with all of the information that he had gathered. Leah's brother, Isaac, or "Big Ike," had also helped Greg to recount numerous stories of places, dates and names, and he helped him locate the original home tract that General Thomas Sumter had given to the first Benenhaley man, Joseph Benenhaley. Sadly, Isaac also passed away in 2011.

Losing these three members of his family was agonizing, but Greg wanted to complete what they helped him start, so he agreed to share his information with us because of his great love for them. He told us that without them, it would not be possible to share his collection of "papers" because the papers simply would not exist. He is indebted to their memory for their willingness to share time and time again; and he wanted to honor his late wife, Kathy Marie Thompson, her mother, Leah Dorothy Benenhaley Peagler, and her uncle, James Isaac Benenhaley. In these pages, and in the hearts of their loved ones, their lives will always be remembered.

The authors traveled to South Carolina to meet with Greg and to see his massive collection of artifacts. I was impressed with everything that he had collected over the years, which he displayed for us from his living and dining rooms. He even had pictures of my distant relatives that I had never seen. Here was a man who clearly knew about the history of the Turkish people of Sumter, South Carolina.

We began with a brief discussion in his home before he took us on a tour of several sights in Sumter. He drove us to General Thomas Sumter's tomb, the Church of the Holy Cross, High Hills Baptist Church, Long Branch Baptist Church, and Springbank Baptist Church. He also took us to the area of land where it is believed that the first Benenahley, Joseph Benenhaley, was buried. While it was impossible to identify any graves due to construction, he assured us that this particular plot of land was indeed the burial site of Joseph Benenhaley. Then Greg drove us to the site of the old Dalzell School. While no remnants of the school building remained, the big tree that served as a landmark for the children who used to play beneath its branches during recess was standing strong. Its sad branches waved over us as a reminder of more difficult, heartbreaking times.

Greg told us on the way to the school, that when the Dalzell School had been given to the Turkish community, it was with the understanding that the community would provide its own driver for the bus. Therefore, the community came together and provided a Turkish bus driver for the school bus. The teachers, however, were white people and not Turkish.

After eating at a small Italian restaurant, we returned to Greg's home and were sitting around the dining room table when the question of the inevitable came up. Was Greg willing to open up the trunk that had been closed since the loss of Kathy? He told us that he never really felt the need to open that trunk because of the sad memories, and he added that he really did not know what was in the trunk anymore.

The authors assured him that he did not have to open it on our account, but it appeared that he truly wanted to honor his late wife, and by opening up the trunk, he would simultaneously face his fear of the unknown and also honor Kathy. We sat with him while he rummaged through many photos, papers, graduation speeches, articles, and other things. He shared anything that he thought would be of value. Afterward, he said that he was glad that he went through it, and that it had not been as hard as he had anticipated. In addition, by providing materials and information, he now had a sense of closure relative to the research he and Kathy started many years ago.

Meeting with Greg was inspiring. Here was a man who was not even Turkish by birth yet had the zeal and passion to tell the history of the Turkish people of Sumter, because he wanted the true story to be told by those who are part of the community. Marrying into the family made him a member of the community; he lived among the Turkish people, knew them intimately, and listened to their stories throughout the years. Because of his connection to the Turkish community, we asked him several questions.

We began by asking Greg if he believes that there is a Turkish community in Sumter today, and if so, how many people are part of the community and where do they live? Greg said there is a Turkish community in Sumter but that it is not definable. As he explained: "The general area centered around Long Branch Baptist Church, extending out in an arc for about a square mile or less. Since the arrival of Shaw Field in 1941, the Turks were gradually replaced as the dominant population. The past seventy years of demographic evolution has brought a large influx of new, non-Turkish residents to the area. Most people residing in that area today do not know that such a distinct community of people ever defined the area with their presence and history."

Greg also mentioned that many Turkish people have chosen to live outside of the original community's boundaries. This would include other states and even countries. When asked about the ethnic background of the Turkish people, Greg stated that he does not believe that the Turkish people are Native American. He does admit, however, that Native American Indians married into the community and, through intermarriage, some Turkish people, but not all, have some Native American blood:

> In my opinion, a very small percentage consider themselves Indian, and they are primarily of the younger generation (under fifty). Most of the older generation know their history. They know that the early Oxendines were Lumbee Indians from North Carolina and that Lumbee Oxendines married into the Benenhaleys—that is a fact. But their intermarriage only added another element of ethnic diversity to the community—just like the first intermarriages by the whites and others. The Oxendines today can identify themselves as Indian, because that is their origin prior to marrying into the community even though they have been diluted over time through intermarriage with the more numerous Benenhaleys, whites, and others. The original Turk, the first Benenhaley man, was married twice and both times to white women. The second generation of Benenhaleys was already half white by the time the Oxendine and other surnames were introduced to the genetic makeup.

Greg pointed out that any non-Turkish people who married into the Benenhaley bloodline brought with them a unique set of DNA that affected their children, not their forefather. "If the initial Benenhaley and Scott families did not start out as Indian, how can the community be Indian today?"

Although Greg is not Turkish, I asked him if he knew of any circumstances in which his family experienced discrimination of any sort. He told us that he did not know of any discrimination that his late wife might have experienced, unless she simply never told him. He said that most of the discrimination occurred in earlier times, sometimes in the writings of non-Turkish authors who referred to the Turkish people as "squatters, trespassers on Sumter's lands, etc." He also told us that early local census officials omitted surnames on census reports of the Turkish people. They simply wrote "Turk" as the last name or in some cases, skipped entire Turkish households. The same was true for some land plats recorded at the courthouse.

> Some older plats show adjoining properties as belonging to "Turks" instead of "Benenhaley." It is a well-known fact that the community was discriminated against in the school system. They were given an inferior school and sparse resources separate from the white county schools that they were forced to attend. Few of the younger generation even know that their grandparents had to sue in court in order to attend the white schools of the area. In addition, up until the mid-1950s, death certificates and birth certificates of Turkish community members had "Turk" as the race of the individual. The younger generation of today has no appreciation for and little knowledge of what the generations before them had to endure in order for today's community members to be able to have the choices and acceptance that they now have.

This comment led the authors to ask Greg if he believes that the younger generation should be informed of what their ancestors experienced. Of course, Greg said, it is important for younger people to know where they came from "or else they will not know where they can go." Greg seemed concerned that the Turkish community is slowly losing its identity through assimilation into the mainstream population. He attributed the disrespectful and untrue nature of past writings to outsiders writing about them in a demeaning fashion through the lens of a prejudiced society. He defended the Turkish people as a "good people with a proud heritage and an interesting history. They suffered through and overcame outright discrimination economically and socially to emerge as a vital component in the history of the geographic area of Sumter County."

Greg has two sons who are Turkish through the bloodline of their mother. For them and for others, he wants the story of the Turkish community to be accurate and honest. He told us that the older generation, which suffered the most, is dying off, and the younger generation has not been informed of the hardships that they suffered because it is not talked about. He believes that the younger generation deserves and needs to know their history.

Chip Chase

Chip is a Turkish man in his late forties who grew up in Sumter County after the Integration Movement of the 1950s. He is a professional public relations director for a telephone company; prior to that he had a long career in sportswriting and management with Sumter's daily newspaper, *The Item*.

When I asked Chip if he ever felt slighted or discriminated against because of his Turkish background, he responded, "Absolutely not. In our community, anyone of the Turkish lineage is thought of just like anybody else. Except for being maybe slightly dark-complected, nobody even knows anything. I get questions

Coauthor Terri Ognibene interviewing Turkish descendent Chip Chase, who can trace his lineage all the way back to the original patriarch. Chip said that he has experienced no significant discrimination as a Turkish person. Photograph provided by Glen Browder.

like, 'What's your ethnic background?' I just look like somebody with an olive complexion by most people's standards. A lot of them, like my mother, who was a Benenhaley, are much darker. I think in our community, the Turkish community is well thought of."

Unlike my informants who grew up during the Integration Movement of the 1950s, Chip's educational experiences were wonderful, in his opinion. In fact, he said that some of his best memories were from the time that he was a student at Ebenezer Junior High School.

Chip attended elementary and junior high school in the 1970s, and he attended high school in the 1980s. His educational experiences were exceptional. While he was the only Turkish student in almost all of his classes, he explained that he did not experience discrimination. I asked him how it felt being the only Turkish student in most of his classes and he answered,

> It didn't. I never thought of myself as the only Turkish person in the class. It was the same kids. We had been together since we were in middle school. White, black, it didn't matter, there was not differentiation between them and the Turks. I was well thought of, as were my cousins who were Turkish.
>
> It was definitely never a bad thing to be Turkish. I was class president when we did superlatives. I think I was the finalist for eleven of the twelve superlatives. I lost every one, though (laughter). So I finished second eleven times. You know what they say about second place. . . . It's the first loser.
>
> In the older group, it was a little different. You didn't mess with a Turk. They were generally considered a tough group. That was five years before me. And as we got older, it became less and less obvious who was who.

What a profound thought and testament to young people, who generally do not see in color. Chip's comment solidified the thought that prejudice is something that is taught.

When asked to elaborate on the word "Turk" in regard to it having either a negative or positive connotation, Chip explained, "I don't know that there's a connotation really with it. It doesn't have a perception in the community one way or the other, I don't think. I think it's a proud word. When I use it, I say it proudly. I think even the older generation of folks do. It's like somebody's white. Somebody's Turk. Somebody's black. It's what you are, but there's no stigma attached to any of it. I mean there's good people and bad people in any race and that's how we look at it."

Chip seemingly grew up when societal race perceptions were changing for the better. He is the product of the older generation's quest for a better life. He reaped the benefits of their fight, and now he passes this quest for a better life down to his own children. Regarding his own family he stated, "In my family, we don't talk about black and white. My kids don't have black friends or have white friends because they just have friends." While he did not experience discrimination himself and did not observe societal prejudice among the various ethnic groups when he was younger, his older brother did. He said, "I remember my brother telling stories of walking and somebody black coming up to him with a 2 x 4 and my brother got in a fight." I asked him, "Was there friction among the black people and the Turkish people?" He answered, "Yea, but see, my brother is lighter than I am, so it was just friction among all integration. To say that the Turks were singled out in this, they weren't. If my brother walked up here right now, you wouldn't think he was anything other than just a regular WASP."

As we were talking, Chip's youngest son joined our group. He said, "You've seen my son. You see how he looks. Can you think of a kid who looks more white than he does?" He had a point. Chip's son is light-skinned and has blue eyes. It is nearly impossible to look at someone today and identify him or her as being Turkish.

I asked Chip if he considered himself to be a white person. He responded, "I put on a thing that says 'race' I put white. I do think that Turkish descent is generally considered Caucasian." Browder asked, "Would you think of yourself as Turkish or Indian?" Chip did not hesitate but responded, "Turkish. I don't think it's going to be all or nothing. I don't think it's going to be everybody who is Turk is Indian or vice versa. I think that with the several different names that are attached to the Turkish community, they all don't have to be totally Turk or totally Indian or whatever. It's not an all or nothing situation."

Later in a phone conversation, I shared with Chip the information regarding Joseph Benenhaley's ties to the Mediterranean/Middle East/North Africa area and asked him his thoughts. He commented, "There are so many stories we've heard. I could easily see that being the case. I don't want to dismiss anything. It makes as much sense as anything else we've got. Am I worried about it? Not really. Our heritage can be traced back two hundred years. In this country, I think that's pretty neat."

When asked if he thought it is important for young people to understand their heritage, Chip stated, "I do think so. I think it's important for anybody to understand their heritage. How are you going to talk about where you came from if you don't know? If you start losing your heritage, there's no way that could be a good thing. If it's not something that's talked about, then it will be forgotten."

In the not-so-distant future, what will it mean to be Turkish? Browder asked Chip: "What about the future? What do you think the future is for the Turkish community in Sumter County?" Chip responded, "I think it's going to become watered down. Nobody's full anymore. My mother was a full Turk. Well, actually if you traced it way back, she probably isn't, but my sons are one fourth and their sons and daughters will be one eighth, and they will become a less and less prevalent name around the community. It's more so because as the older group who actually do look different, become less and less of them, the Turkish community, I could see, fade away. I think it's a bad thing." I echo his sentiments that it is a bad thing to anticipate that a community will fade away. It is my hope that this attempt to capture their voices will ensure that their lives and stories will last for many years to come.

Brian Benenhaley

The next interview was a very interesting and significant encounter—with an individual who is a lineal descendant of Joseph Benenhaley. Brian Benenhaley is an attorney in Columbia and served, at the time of this interview, as transitional pastor of Long Branch Baptist Church. Brian, a great-great-great-great-grandson of the patriarch, was direct and forthcoming about the changing world of the Turkish people in Sumter County: "Today, the older members of the community still remember their heritage; but I figure that in the next one, two generations the community will lose its distinctiveness. There are positive and negative aspects to this. I just hope they don't lose their heritage. It is important that they understand the positive aspects of their history." While he suspects the Turkish people eventually will assimilate into broader society, Brian estimated that the contemporary community—counting blood relatives and others who consider themselves part of that community—probably numbers five hundred to one thousand people. He also said the sense of community is still pretty strong, especially among older citizens.

The young pastor—forty years old at the time of the interview—was especially pleased to assert that the social lives of the Turkish people continue to revolve around Long Branch and Springbank Churches. "Besides our church worship services, we still have dinner-on-the-ground and special singing services. Everybody still likes 'The Old Rugged Cross,' 'How Great Thou Art,' and 'Victory in Jesus.' But at the same time, we are adapting and working to create a mindset among the people to understand that the mission of the church is to reach those who aren't here yet and make disciples rather than catering to the preferences of members."

Brian graduated from Hillcrest High School in 1992 and he never experienced discrimination that he can remember. He said that Shaw Air Force Base had had a big impact on the community by the time he came along and times had changed for the better. He said that there was not much problem either between the black and Turkish students. "We shared a curious bond, probably because of our histories of discrimination. There was a respect and a willingness to help one another in times of trouble."

But he knew that discrimination was a way of life for earlier generations of Turkish people. He recalled that, when he was seven or eight years old, his father explained the situation to him. They were at a baseball game involving their local team, made up of Turkish players. They were sitting with some of the other men, including his great uncle Leon "Dick" Ray, watching the game. Brian asked why his uncle Dick was black. His father replied that he was not black—he was simply a dark-skinned Turk. When Brian asked what that meant, his father told him about their people's history.

Brian's father also started telling him about his own experiences with discrimination as a teenager. "My father was one of the ones who integrated Hillcrest; and they had a tough time. One day, he had to take a brick on board the school bus and talked tough to some characters to show that he was not going to take any more harassment. High school back then was such a bad experience for him that he dropped out before graduating. He had gone out for baseball and was told that he wasn't welcome—that day he walked away from school and never went back."

According to Brian, that conversation was a turning point in his life. "I was bitter about what had happened to my daddy and other Turkish people in the past; and I determined that I would work hard to do the best that I could and prove that I was just as good as anybody else." Interestingly, he was a catcher for the Hillcrest High baseball team (where his father was "unwelcomed" in the 1950s) and for the Sumter P-15 squad (that Eleazer Benenhaley had aspired to play for back in the 1940s).

I asked Brian to tell how he felt about the word "Turk," and he said it depended on how someone said it. "If I think you're talking down to me or there's something negative in your tone, then I'll take offense about that." When asked to describe himself ethnically, he again said, "It depends." He explained that in the professional world, he's just another Caucasian. "But in my mind I feel that I'm a Turk and I'm proud of that heritage."

Brian seemed intensely concerned about the current situation where some of the traditional community have begun to identify as Native Americans.

> I can accept and respect that; but I don't like anyone turning his or her back on our history or insinuating anything negative about the Turkish heritage. I don't think they realize how deeply they have hurt many older members in the community who fought to set the label "Turk" on equal footing with anything else. Now that so much of that vision has been achieved, this Indian movement decides they don't want to be "Turk" any longer. The folks who waged the fight feel betrayed and it's understandable. They have taken the uniqueness of our story and traded it for a story that belongs to someone else. Fortunately, most Turkish people have remained strong and loyal to our culture.

Brian also was happy to hear that the mystery of Joseph Benenhaley and the history of the Turkish people had been solved. "I never was able to prove the Benenhaley story; but I love that it has now been documented." He also said "I'm glad that my children will know who they are and where they came from. Right now, all they know is that they are white kids who get a dark tan in the summer. It is important that they understand their unique history, the values of their culture, and that they stand on broad shoulders of brave ancestors."

Adrienne Love

Adrienne Love is a thirty-something school teacher whose blood runs warm and faithful for her Turkish ancestors. While she said she had never experienced discrimination, she expressed strong feelings about her heritage. "I was born a Benenhaley and didn't need to do any research about who I am. I had three great aunts and they told me all about our history. They taught me what it means to be a Turk; and I'm grateful to them for that. I also saw what my father went through; and that was enough to make me a strong Turkish person."

Schoolteacher Adrienne Love is a Benenhaley descendant. She told us that seeing what her father went through made her a strong Turkish person. Courtesy of Adrienne Love.

Adrienne seemed particularly influenced by her late father's experience. He faced discrimination as a teenager; and he never finished high school. She is convinced that those bad times handicaped him the rest of his life. "He suffered for being a Turk—and that had great impact on my proud identification as a Turk." She is also grateful to her mother, a white woman whose family came here with the military when she was in high school. "She told me about those days, when her father's coworkers at Shaw Field warned her not to get mixed up with the Turks, because 'they all carry knives and like to fight.' The truth is that the Turkish people had to stick together, and fight back at times because of mistreatment." But her mother told her that "our Turkish friends and neighbors were some of the best people I met in this area." And she eventually married a Benenhaley.

Adrienne said that, growing up, she never heard any insults or felt that she was treated badly. "It was kind of funny. My friends complimented me for my dark olive complexion and asked how I got so tanned—and I would laugh and explain that I was a Turk." She did hear tales about the old days, about a cross burning in her great-grandfather's yard, people throwing rocks at her kinfolks, and crowds threatening to beat them up. "Those stories bothered me," she said. She also was apprehensive about going to a new school, a private school in the area, because some of the kids' families had expressed hatred against Turks in earlier times. "But I experienced no unfairness there."

Adrienne said that her Turkish background never was a problem for her husband, a Sumter native, although he sometimes kids her for being so intense and agitated about the Turk-Indian debate. She also has been careful to pass along her heritage to their three children. "They are very aware of being Turks and they understand our history."

Adrienne expressed special excitement when told about our recent findings regarding Joseph Benenhaley and the Turkish narrative. "My feelings are happiness and relief. It is good to know that what my father and older relatives told me all my life was true." She feels strongly that all Turkish people should know that history. "Our history helped shape Sumter County and made us who we are today." And she is confident in the future of the Turkish people: "Being part of the younger generation and still living in the heart of the community, I see many others who are teaching our children about the pride that is known in being Turk. I believe that as long as there are people like myself we have no worries about the Turkish heritage being forgotten."

Richie Ray and Harold Benenhaley

On a cold, misty morning, the authors traveled to the home of Richie Ray to speak with him and his friend, Harold Benenhaley. Richie's eleven-year-old daughter, Reilly, was also present during the informal interviews and we were able to ask her some questions, too.

Richie and Reilly live on a farm that is located in Sumter County; this farm has been a part of their family for over seven decades. Richie's great-great-great-grandfather, James Ray, was a white European and his great-great-great-grandmother was Jensey Benenhaley, daughter of the patriarch. Richie said, "My father, grandfather, and great-grandfather all worked very hard on this farm and I began working alongside my father on the farm at age ten. I am thankful for the experience of growing up on this farm; I learned very quickly what responsibility and hard work was all about."

Richie identifies as Turkish and explained that the reason he believes that the Turkish people originated from Turkey is based on the information that was passed down to him by his great-grandparents, grandparents, and parents. He does not claim to be Native American based on the information given to him. He and Harold, both public employees, attended Hillcrest High School during the late 1980s and early 1990s. Before that, they attended Ebenezer.

Richie and Harold were asked about their educational experiences at Hillcrest High School in reference to their Turkish heritage, and specifically if they had had any problems. Richie explained that he did not have any issues at Hillcrest High School when he attended and explained two reasons: "Number one, some of the problems that my father and his father had . . . a lot of those issues had subsided by the time I was in school. Number two, Shaw Air Force Base. . . . Because of the military base, the children of the military personnel have traveled the world with their parents and for that reason, encountering Turkish people at school for those kids was not a big deal to them. Therefore, we all got along."

When asked his thoughts on discrimination he said, "I do not condone discrimination of any type for any reason. When I hear the word discrimination, I often think about the trials and tribulations that the Turkish community endured here in Sumter years ago. As a Christian I know that discrimination is wrong and that we are to love one another, we are all God's children."

When asked if he thought that the attitude of the Turkish people regarding other ethnic groups is the same or different now than the attitude of the Turkish people in the early part of the twentieth century, Richie stated, "I would imagine that it's different basically because the times are different now. An example would be that now our children can attend public school without fear of discrimination. Today, the Turkish people in my age group have not had to deal with the adversities that the Turkish community was faced with fifty years ago. Our Turkish ancestors in the early twentieth century were fighting for equality and just trying to survive, so I feel that there is a significant difference in the attitudes of the Turkish people now compared to then."

Harold, who traced his ancestry back to Joseph Benenhaley, said there were only about six to ten Turkish people at Hillcrest High School when they attended and stated that the Turkish people "hung together." Harold explained "I guess we just all grew up together and we were just comfortable together, and I guess there's just strength in numbers. So we never did really have any problems with anyone really messing with us because we were Turkish or, say, bullying or something like that. We never had any problem."

Harold and Richie concurred that sticking together was their choice and that most of the other groups did the same thing. According to their estimation, the school was probably made up of 50 percent white students and 50 percent black students, or possibly 40 percent white students and 60 percent black students. They both classified themselves as being white of Turkish descent. Richie agreed with Harold that the Turkish students never had any issues with the other ethnic groups while they were in school. He said, "We never had any issues, and we all got along just fine."

I asked them if they were ever discouraged from participating in extracurricular activities at their school. Harold said that he played baseball and explained,

"I never had any problem with that because it was a lot of people that came along ahead of us back in the '70s that played baseball, that played football, and I guess sort of paved the way for us, so to speak, because we never had any problems as far as sports or any extracurricular activities." He then began to name several Turkish boys who went on to play American Legion baseball. He quickly rattled their names off with pride. Among those names, Harold listed a Hood, an Oxendine, a Benenhaley, and a Buckner. It was obvious he was truly thankful to those men, and to many others before them, who endured certain hardships so that they and others would be able to play ball.

Richie and Harold both claim to be of Turkish descent. The authors were curious as to what the word "Turk" meant to them, and whether it had a positive, negative, or neutral connotation. Richie, who told us that he would consider himself "Turkish," explained it this way: "It depends on the context in which it is used. If someone were to ask you, 'Are you a Turkish person' or a 'Turk' I don't have an issue with that, and I'll be glad to sit down with them and explain to them what I know and how I know it. But I've heard that phrase used in a negative manner many times, and it doesn't set well with any of us."

Harold then expressed his feelings. He told us that it comes across as negative if someone says, "There goes one of those 'Turks' or something. . . . If you hear it in that context, it's a little offensive. It's kind of like a black person not wanting to hear the N-word, so to speak." Since neither Richie nor Harold experienced many issues growing up, I asked if they had heard their parents talk about growing up Turkish. Harold told us that his parents were certainly older than Richie's parents and that they did not have "any huge education." His dad had a sixth grade education and his mom had a second or third grade education. He said, "Back in those times, education wasn't a big thing for them. It was, you get on the farm, you work and that's it. Education was the furthest thing from their minds."

Harold said that his mom did not go into great detail with any stories, and that his dad would say a little bit more "only because he and his older brother had to get out, quit school and work." He said that the main experiences that he heard them talk about were stories about when they might walk up the street and someone would cross to the other side and sneer at them. Those were really the only stories that his parents ever shared with him, but he did share another story from someone else. He said, "One guy told me that when the schools were first integrated, he was on the side of the road waiting for the bus to take him to school and the person driving the bus just drove right on by him, almost ran him over, wouldn't even pick him up to go to school." He began to reflect on what he had just said, then added, "I'm so glad that we definitely didn't face that while we were in there."

Richie's mother is Caucasian, but not Turkish, so she had no issues. His father, on the other hand, was Turkish and attended the Dalzell School. He described his dad as a tough but quiet man, who did not talk a lot about his youth. Richie said, "There were a few conversations between my dad and me where he discussed some situations where he and some of his cousins were not treated fairly."

He also spoke about someone in the Turkish community who had lived through the Integration Movement and told him, "You don't know how good you have it now. It wasn't about education back then. We couldn't concentrate on that. There was always some type of conflict, and we often fought." Richie, like Harold, seemed extremely grateful to those who had gone before him to make life so much easier for him. He stated, "You know, we would hear these stories and they would be kind of hard to fathom because we didn't have any issues, but apparently they did."

While neither Richie nor Harold experienced any discrimination in school, they did feel that sometimes they experienced prejudice within the community. They each related their stories to dating. In particular, Richie explained that his experience was based on his younger days when he dated a non-Turkish white girl. His parents and grandparents did not attend the same schools that her parents and grandparents attended. He said that he dated this young lady for a number of years, but that there was a lot of tension in their relationship because of his Turkish background. Her family did not approve. If there was ever a family function, he was not invited. Her family put so much pressure on her not to date him that they eventually broke up. Twenty years later, their paths crossed again, and he received a sincere apology from her for the way that her family had treated him during that time, which he greatly appreciated. He said that he holds no animosity toward her or her family.

The Turkish community has changed significantly during the last fifty years regarding the number of people claiming to be of Turkish descent in Sumter. I asked Harold if he thought that there were still a lot of Turkish people in Sumter. Harold said that he believes that there are "still a good many around." He then explained, "Now, what you would call a full Turk or what not . . . there's not many full Turks left. A lot have been integrated and spread throughout the county. So, I would say there's a good many with Turkish blood in them."

Browder asked Richie if he thought the Turkish people were still a community. Richie responded, "Yes I feel that we are. Although there are fewer of us now and many have moved away from Sumter, we are still a community. Many within the Turkish community still worship, work, and socialize together just as any other community would. The history of the Turkish people of Sumter County is a tie that will forever bind us together." We were curious as to what the people do together as a community, generally speaking. Harold mentioned hunting, cooking and church. He said that hunting is a big thing and it is how the men get together and enjoy one another. He stated that cooking involved both the men and the women and that it was like having reunions. Of course church draws men, women, and children of all ages together to worship God and to fellowship together.

I asked them if being in close proximity with one another led to certain speech patterns that might be unique. They chuckled at first, then began to say that people sometimes ask them if they are from New Orleans after hearing some of their words. Specifically, Harold said, "A lot of the older Turkish people say, you know you say, 'Come here.' They say, 'C'myeer.' And 'Heyy'all." Richie tried to clarify by adding, "A lot of southern mixed in with it. I can remember being in school and we sat there and would be having a conversation, and we would be joking and laughing, and there would be somebody over there saying, 'You know something? I didn't understand the first thing you guys were saying.' Where are you guys from?'"

I can personally remember sitting around my grandfather's dinner table as he prayed. With my head bowed, I vary rarely understood what he was saying (he was not speaking to me anyway). I knew the prayer was over when he stopped speaking. I actually remember peeking around the table during the prayer sometimes and watching my aunts, uncles, and cousins stare at him so that they would know when the prayer was over. It was truly a unique speech pattern that was quick, quiet, and humble.

Richie further explained, "A lot of us growing up, we went to school together, to church together, hunted and fished together, we spent all of our time together, and it was just, and I imagine any group of guys spend enough time together they could have a conversation somebody else couldn't follow." So true. Harold likened it to what it might sound like to hear people of fundamentalist religion speak "in tongues."

Regarding physical appearance, Harold said that one time a man approached him and began speaking Spanish. Harold stopped the man and told him, "I am from here in Sumter, but my ancestor, from what I gather, is from Turkey. So he started speaking something else, and I'm like, 'Wait a minute. What are you saying?' He said, 'I'm speaking Turkish.' He had been in the air force and was stationed in Turkey, and I had to stop him again, and I said, 'I've never been to the motherland. Speak English to me.'"

When I explained to Harold and Richie that the data that we have collected actually shows that Joseph Benenhaley was tied to the Mediterranean/Middle Eastern/North African area, they did not seem very surprised. Harold stated, "It is everything that we were hearing before, that we were actually from that area. Nothing I've looked at or been told has basically shown where we had any type of Indian blood in us whatsoever. So, from what you've gathered and from everything I've seen, I believe he was from Turkey. That's what I think. All the information that you have gathered pretty much confirms it with me. Everything that I have heard and seen and been told is that we are from that area. It confirms what I believed anyway."

Richie added, "That coincides with everything that I've been told by my grandparents, parents, and other relatives in the community. So that does not come as a shock to me. We don't really have any concrete evidence to view, but by word of mouth that's been handed down through the years. So there's no reason for me to dispute that."

Reilly Ray

Reilly Ray is a sweet, demure eleven-year-old young lady. She came to the living room, with her father's permission, when we entered Richie's home. She sat quietly by his side, humble and curious. Reilly did not know much about her ancestors, and her father asked her to sit in on the interviews. I watched her during the interviews soaking in everything that Richie and Harold were saying. We could not help but ask Richie for permission to ask her a few questions. He gave her the option of answering for herself, showing full confidence in her and allowing her to speak her mind freely, if she chose to do so.

Reilly said that she did not mind answering a few questions, so I asked her if she had any issues or problems at school because of her Turkish background. She responded, "No, ma'am, because I go to a private school and nobody really knows what we are. I didn't even know until Dad told me last night. I knew what it was, but I didn't know all this happened. I just thought there were Turkish people."

Browder continued, "Does it seem strange to you to think about what they've told you?" Reilly said, "A little bit because I thought it was just like blacks and

Reilly Ray, daughter of Richie Ray, poses on a tractor at their farm. She and her father seemed happy to talk and learn about their Turkish heritage. Courtesy of Richard Ray.

whites that had that problem, but I didn't know it was them, too." He then asked Reilly, "Do you think of yourself as a Turkish person? Does it mean anything to you?" She politely responded, "Yes, sir, but I didn't go through what they went through, and what our granddads went through."

Reilly has olive-colored skin, dark eyes, and dark hair. I asked her if people ever ask her about her nationality. She said, "A lot of people think I'm Mexican, and they're like, 'Are you Mexican?' and I'm like, 'No, I'm not Mexican.' And then they'll ask, 'Well, what are you?' And I'll say, 'I don't know.'" She then told a very funny story about once when she was on a cruise. A man said "Hi!" to her, but Reilly did not hear him. He then said, "Hola?" She said, "No, no, no. Hi." Everyone laughed.

This conversation naturally led the authors to ask Richie if he believed that it is important for young people to know about their ancestral heritage. He responded, "You know, I do, and I'll be honest with you, I've never had this discussion with Reilly because I didn't want her to develop any negative thoughts about anybody . . . maybe having a problem with me or with her granddad or anybody for any reason because where she goes to school, there are no issues. Everybody gets along. That's the way I want it. But on the other hand, I now think it's important that she knows her heritage and where she came from and where her family came from, so I decided to let her be here today to hear this. I'm glad you guys asked her a question. She had the opportunity to speak." Indeed, our goal in writing this book is to allow the Turkish people's voices to be heard.

I then asked Reilly what she thought about what her dad had said to her the night before. She responded, "I thought it was kind of crazy because I didn't know that really happened." I could relate. I thought it sounded crazy when my mom would tell me stories, and I am a generation older than Reilly.

Browder asked Reilly if she thought she would read this book when it is finished. She very respectfully responded, "Yes, sir." He asked her why she would read it and she answered, "To learn more, I guess, to learn more about everybody else's experiences."

These conversations and observations reveal a great deal about the historic course of the Turkish people of Sumter County. They are no longer an isolated, enclosed community, and they now enjoy freedom and opportunities just as do other citizens in mainstream society. Both the original respondents from the previous century and those interviewed for this contemporary chapter acknowledge these changes; also, they express gratitude that Joseph Benenhaley's Turkish ancestry and their traditional narrative have finally been validated. However, there are significant new questions and challenges for this community. The older crowd is diminishing, the younger people are marrying outsiders and moving away, and some are reconsidering their ethnic identification. The following chapter summarizes my personal feelings about this project and our people's history.

~ *Chapter Eleven* ~

Our Story Has Now Been Told

This project has been a long and difficult assignment—ten full years of rigorous research and analysis. But it was worth it. I set the context for this investigation in the beginning, in my opening remarks regarding the troubled history of the Turkish people. I also asked several members of the Turkish community to share their stories of what it was like growing up during the middle part of the last century. This mission has succeeded. The reasons for taking on this task were laid out and those objectives have been achieved.

The first objective was to try to resolve the mystery of Joseph Benenhaley and his role in the early years of the Turkish community. The authors found that he was the Turkish patriarch, both founder and forefather of the Turkish people. The second objective was to help clarify the confusion regarding the Turkish people's cultural identity and to let them tell their own story about who they are and what life was like within their community. They have done so with courage and grace. A third objective was to present the Turkish account of their experience during segregation and integration in the middle of the past century. The participants of this study lived through their own civil rights struggle during those years; but, for all practical purposes, their voices had been unspoken and unheard. They have now spoken and they have been heard.

A final purpose of this project—reflecting the authors' responsibilities as teachers—was to inspire today's educators to embrace all students in the classroom. South Carolina, the South, and the United States of America have changed considerably over the past half century. The story and voice of these Turkish citizens should be very helpful as we welcome marginalized groups in contemporary society. My opening remarks and the personal interviews—combined with

Browder's documentary history—provide useful academic and historical context for the worthwhile contributions of this project.

Now, I would like to present my personal interpretations and feelings as an individual of Turkish descent. Summarizing these personal conclusions about the Turkish experience proved an emotional challenge. It was difficult selecting the proper points of emphasis, and the specific wording required careful balancing between my coauthor (a scholar who takes pride in his candor) and the Turkish people (some of whom still feel demeaning hurt from the old days). I also found it difficult to sort out my own reactions, because I am both an academic person with a unique perspective and a Turkish person still connected to Sumter. My hope is that I achieved the appropriate course in this assignment.

1. The Traditional Narrative. It was nice to learn that new evidence collected in this project validates the traditional narrative about the historical origin of the Turkish people in Sumter County, South Carolina. Our interviews in this project have revealed that most Turkish people believed the traditional narrative, but they had no real proof or clear answers when questioned about their history. Because of this, they must have endured many criticisms and embarrassments over the years. So it is good that we now know the true story. Joseph Benenhaley was an Ottoman subject who probably came from somewhere in North Africa; he was indeed the patriarch of our community; and his blood dominated the lineage for many generations.

2. Other Ethnic Groups. We also now know more about the ethnic groups that came together in our community during the formative generations. White Europeans, Native Americans, and perhaps others have joined our ranks; but, throughout many decades, the Turkish people of this area clung to their traditional identity.

3. Two Centuries of Adversity. Now it is known that the Turkish people endured and survived two centuries of adversity in the Carolina backcountry. The Turkish experience was similar, in some ways, to that of other stigmatized Americans—but there are important differences. For example, the Turkish people have yet to be recognized for their distinct culture and historical contributions to our county, state, and country.

4. Our Voice and Story. The "discovered voice" of the Turkish people—expressed here by Boaz, Helen, Jean, and Tonie—have told "our story," a story that varies from anything presented thus far in news media accounts and academic reports by non-Turkish individuals. My older relatives in this study have lived lives that were far different from my life, or the lives of other citizens in this part of the country.

5. Heroes of the Movement. The Turkish participants in this project were among many heroes of the Integration Movement of the 1950s. Several years before *Brown v. Board of Education* and the celebrated desegregation of Little Rock High School, these people achieved significant change in the relative obscurity of rural South Carolina.

6. Difficult Experience. However, these four participants reacted with pensive and sober uniformity in reflecting about their personal experience with segregation/integration back in the middle of the past century. They expressed feelings of resigned isolation and discrimination as young people; and, in retrospect, they characterized the integration process as "awful," "scary," and "traumatic."

7. Lingering Sensitivity. There seemed to be a lingering sensitivity among these respondents to any activity that focuses attention on them, their origins, and their community/culture. There was even concern about this investigation; and the interview questions sometimes made some of my informants uncomfortable.

8. Mixed Feelings. These participants considered themselves as Turkish people; but they reacted strongly to being called "Turks" by outsiders. This common reference, used by both white and black people, was especially painful in the past; the informants considered it reflective of an offensive attitude that viewed them as different, alien, and inferior. However, they seem to have mellowed over time; and some now take it as a source of pride.

9. Message for Today. The Turkish respondents in this study have a message for me and today's generation. While things are different and better nowadays, young Turkish people and outsiders need to remember and think about, with respect, what happened to our people in the past.

10. Better World. Today's Turkish people live in a very different and more tolerant world than did our ancestors. Conversations and observations among contemporary Turkish descendants demonstrate clearly that they are no longer an isolated, enclosed community; and they enjoy freedom and opportunities just as do other citizens in mainstream society.

11. Significant New Challenges. However, there are clear signs that the Turkish community is fading as a distinct ethnicity, and our people face significant new challenges in the twenty-first century. The older crowd is diminishing; the youngsters are marrying outsiders and moving away, and some are reconsidering their ethnic identification.

12. Importance of Ethnic Heritage. Thus, as the Turkish people of Sumter County experience the positive benefits of assimilation, it is critically important that we take action to understand, celebrate, and teach our children about our ethnic heritage.

The history and culture of the Turkish people of Sumter County, until now, have been virtually ignored, misrepresented, and even denied; and most of what we "knew" was written by people who were not of Turkish descent. This project has allowed these marginalized citizens to tell, in their own voices, who they are and what happened to them in a difficult environment. Now, finally, our story has been told, fully and accurately, and with dignity.

I hope readers will not object if this section closes with two notes of personal appreciation. The first note is addressed to one of my Turkish relatives who posted an online message a while back that picked me up whenever I grew tired and weary during this investigation. The writer was responding to an activist who claimed roundabout relationship and argued that the Turkish people are not really Turks. The following is her verbatim statement (with a few extraneous words omitted) on an Internet message board:

> I read your information on the turks. . . . Me I am not a turk descentant but I have been married into the family for 34 years. . . . Never once have I heard the stories as you have told them. . . . Many in my family have passed down stories of the origin and some of the story tellers are very old like 90 to 100. . . . Grant you the beginning came much earlier than that but this is a group of people that are proud of where they came from so they passed it down their generations. . . . I myself [am] tired of the benenhaley's being put down. . . . The Turks have had their fill of all trying to explain them. . . . They know who they are. . . . The turks are family loyal people that cause no problems in society and they would really like to be left alone. They know how they got here so why is it posted on the internet. . . . If their name was brown would there be all this attention? No I don't think so. . . . Any response to this would be appreciated. . . .
>
> A true Turk in every sense of the word.

I hope that the "true Turk" appreciates our response to her plea.

Finally, I want to to express thanks to my mother. Through the years, I have learned much about her struggles and her accomplishments. She has shared with me our history of adversity, but she has taught me not to be enslaved by it. She has given me a vision for a bright educational future, a future where there will be equal education for all students. Teachers will teach so that all of their students can be empowered, and students of every ethnicity will learn in order to be free. My mother gave me roots as well as wings. And this is what I hope to pass along to our readers.

Conclusion
What Have We Learned?

It has been well over two centuries since Joseph Benenhaley fought for America's freedom in the Carolina backwoods, and a full half century has passed since his descendants fought for equal educational opportunity in that same area of South Carolina. Now, for the first time, we know the full and accurate history of the Turkish people of Sumter County. This documentary analysis has solved the mystery of Benenhaley's ancestry and the origin of the Turkish community. Just as important, the Turkish people of Sumter County have discovered their voice; and their story has been told. So, what have we learned about the Turkish people of Sumter County from this project?

~ True Story of the Turkish People ~

The history of the Turkish people has long been ignored, obscured, and misrepresented by others. Now, the authors have authenticated—through historical accounts, legal files, census data, vital records, genetic analysis, and genealogical reports—their ancestry and history as conveyed in the traditional narrative. The authors also have heard from the inside what life was like in this unique community. Their collective oral histories and other interviews tell on a personal level about strong family relationships, living as second-class citizens, challenging segregation, and the mixed blessings of assimilation.

More general and significant, the authors have learned the true story of the Turkish people of Sumter County. They were not tri-racial isolates as that typology was professed by early scholars and journalists and activists; nor were they indistinct remnants of unknown origins as they so often have been trivialized; and they cannot be classified today as misdeemed Indians or the local branch of some larger group, like the Melungeons. It is clear that they were founded by an identified and documented

Turkish patriarch—Joseph Benenhaley, or Yusef ben Ali—late in the eighteenth century; and they organized and conducted themselves as a conscious, subcultural community throughout the nineteenth and twentieth centuries. Some white Europeans, Native Americans, and perhaps others joined them over time; but, as a group, they identified as the Turkish people. Furthermore, they never blended in with surrounding society nor dissipated among scattered fugitives. They were indeed the single historical case of an exotic ethnic leader and his followers pursuing their long, lonely course in backwoods South Carolina. Consequently, they lived lives of isolation, segregation, discrimination, and oppression; and only in the past few decades have they begun assimilating into America's mainstream.

In a strange way, the authors think that their findings may serve as delayed, deserved deliverance for Joseph Benenhaley and his descendants, particularly those Turkish people who lived through the old days. They silently endured as outsiders misdefined and often disparaged their community. Many of these citizens must have experienced prolonged, suppressed sadness over decades; and now, through this project, perhaps they have freed themselves from the quiet desperation of those times.

The younger Turkish people of the twenty-first century should be especially appreciative for this groundbreaking research and authoritative articulation. They have heard anecdotes about the old days; however, many of them apparently find such tales hard to believe or irrelevant in their contemporary lives. This project provides empirical information about their history and what their parents and other ancestors endured. Fortunately, both young and old Turkish people now understand who they were and are; and they can celebrate their heritage. Furthermore, they can pass that history and heritage along to their children and future generations.

The implications of this project also should be of great interest and value for today's professional educators. It is not enough for public schools to simply open their doors to previously marginalized groups; the leaders of these institutions must hear and respond to "other voices" and "other stories." Administrators and classroom teachers have special responsibilities and opportunities as they help these students journey from adversity to assimilation.

Perhaps the most immediate and practical impact of this project—an essential "to do" assignment for scholars, journalists, genealogists, and ancestral/ethnic/racial groups—is that serious analysts will need to go back and edit previous accounts of the Turkish people. There are many, many documents both in print and online that are absolutely inaccurate in their depiction of Turkish history; and they need to be corrected.

Clearly, too, this project—especially the genetic research—challenges how previous analysts have mischaracterized the Turkish people. Customary references have ranged from simplistic dismissal as randomly mixed remnants to harsh indictment as misguided racists. Now, analysts will have to acknowledge and reclassify the Turkish people as a distinct ethnic community with a Mediterranean/Middle Eastern/North African progenitor and a merging, over time, of other ancestral strains. Additionally, today's analysts can authenticate their accounts with personal testimony from real, live people in this community.

~ A Multicultural Narrative ~

Our primary conclusion from this project is that the Turkish people's history is a distinct ethnic narrative; however, the resolution of the Benenhaley mystery is not the singularly definitive aspect of our project. Readers should also note, for example, how intricately the Turkish narrative is interwoven with other cultures.

The history of the Turkish people must be seen and understood as a tale of progress that was shared with others—particularly white European, Native American, and African cultures—in this part of the world. We could have written different, worthwhile, and important narratives for those other cultural communities whose lives intervened and intertwined the Turkish people in this area and over this time period. For example, we could have chosen to focus on white Europeans of that environment who preceded the Turkish community in Sumter County but also married into that group and contributed significantly to their distinct existence and experience. So, too, did Native Americans. Our research clearly evidences an American Indian narrative that is a critical part of the unusual tale of the Turkish people. They also preceded the Turkish community, joined among its members, and shared much of its history of isolation, segregation, discrimination, and oppression. Finally, the authors could have spent some of their time investigating those of African origin in this region, who undoubtedly helped shape the Turkish experience. This research has not demonstrated any significant participation by the large black population of this area in the Turkish community. However, they also preceded Joseph Benenhaley here; and they contributed substantially to the cultural environment of Sumter County. The black-white divide in this region certainly impacted the lives and ways of the Turkish people as they struggled to survive as a miniculture during a difficult period of southern history.

The authors' point therefore is that the historical and current debate about whether the Turkish people really are/were Turkish or a distinct subculture or something else has led us for too long into unfortunate and sometimes contentious directions. The fact is that all these different people—Turkish people, white Europeans, Native Americans, African Americans—share different but entwined narratives; and they should celebrate their mutual heritages and legacies.

~ Diverse, Changing Regional History ~

In addition to correcting previous accounts, professional observers of various callings will need to incorporate this new evidence and true story into their conceptions of Sumter County, South Carolina, and the South. Clearly, the documentary analysis and oral history presented here add a new and interesting element to an expanding literature about regional society of the past and present. Let us revisit, for just a moment, an earlier discussion of southern culture (Ray, *Ethnicities,* 2007): "Southern culture, or the multiple southern cultures of the South's many subregions, is a complex amalgamation of disparate ethnicities and traditions from around the globe. After centuries of blending, the sum is undoubtedly greater than its parts but is hardly a finished product" (2).

The Turkish community of Sumter County actually fits very well into a regional narrative about historical adversity, enduring strength, and change. Their story is important—not only for particularized recognition and dignity of the Turkish community but also as a worthwhile addition to our understanding of southern culture. Our historic regional culture was much richer than we thought in earlier times; and this account of the Turkish people tells us something about important changes in southern society of more recent times.

~ Evolving, Inclusive American Experience ~

This project also speaks to our conception of the American experience. To paraphrase broadly from the above comment about southern culture, the United States likewise is an evolution that, over time, has produced a nation that is greater than its parts. And, most important, that inclusive evolution is far from finished. In this particular case, we are witnessing the problematic but promising dynamic—e pluribus unum—of the American experience. As was recognized a few years ago in an assemblage of South-watchers far, far away, a healthy relationship between the "people" and the "peoples" requires the elimination of notions about "other" and "alien" ethnicities (Theodosiadou 2008; Yates 2008).

Developments here in South Carolina, essentially, tell how a unique subculture, after two centuries of isolation and segregation, is assimilating into the broader culture. The various groups of people in this area—in our case the Turkish people, white Europeans, Native Americans, and African Americans—have shared a curious but intertwined history. Now, the Turkish people are struggling to hold onto their traditional heritage while embracing the ways and values of broader society. In this situation, the discovery of their voice and telling of their story will make that difficult struggle to be part of America more successful and a healthy relationship more likely.

~ Counsel of the Elders ~

The authors consider it fitting, in this closing discussion, that the central characters of our investigation—Revolutionary War hero Thomas Sumter and Turkish patriarch Joseph Benenhaley—express themselves, at least through their direct, living descendants, about the Turkish people and their traditional narrative. Here then are the reflections of Thomas Sumter Tisdale Jr. (great-great-great-great-grandson of the "Fighting Gamecock") and Eleazer Benenhaley (great-great-great-great-grandson of the Turkish patriarch).

Both Thomas Sumter Tisdale Jr. and Eleazer Benenhaley are well qualified to articulate this counsel of the elders. Tisdale, a Charleston attorney and past-president of the South Carolina Historical Society, has lectured frequently about his famous ancestor; and he is the author of an impressive book about life on the Sumter plantation (*A Lady of High Hills* 2001). Eleazer Benenhaley, who was born, grew up, and pastored in the community, is likely the most respected Turkish person living today, and he has authored a fascinating biography about his life among the Turkish people (*Moulded Clay* 1983). Both men provided their remarks in several telephone interviews and e-mail exchanges during January and February of 2014.

Tisdale appropriately references the friendship forged long ago, at the birth of our nation, between General Thomas Sumter and Joseph Benenhaley: "The relationship between my family, the Sumter family of Stateburg, and the Turkish people of Stateburg has been honored and appreciated in every generation since they came together during the American Revolution, and it is honored still in our time." Tisdale cautions that we have to learn from the past so that we can shape our lives for the future; and the key to learning from the past is to honor those who have done so much for us. "By honoring those who have gone before us, we can attempt to repay them the debt we owe to them for all we have, although it is a debt that can never really be repaid."

He accordingly pays special tribute to the Turkish people, specifically recalling the words of another ancestor: "My great grandfather, Thomas Sebastian Sumter, wrote in the early 20th century about the steadfast loyalty the Turkish people exhibited in the great American Civil War when they took up arms to protect our common homeland. After describing the particular personal contributions to the war effort of Warren, Dick, and John Benenhaley, he wrote, 'I am writing this now so they (the Turkish people) can have it to keep, and the young men who go to the War (World War I) may have a copy to show where they came from, who they are, and what they deserve.'"

Finally, he counsels today's generation to incorporate the Turkish people into American history. "Throughout American history, the Turkish people of Stateburg in Sumter County, South Carolina, have made invaluable contributions that have benefitted their own and the wider community. The public recognition of their contributions is long overdue. The history of their families deserves to be woven into the history of this country, as the Turkish people of Stateburg have been an important integral part of it for over 200 years."

Eleazer Benenhaley agrees that the world needs to hear the real story of this community. "Most writings about the Turkish people in Sumter County have been based on hearsay, speculation, or a prejudicial position. It is time for the truth of the struggles and victories of the Turkish people to be told!" He is especially proud that the Turkish people themselves finally get to talk about their history. "This is an accurate and exciting account of the Turkish people. But what distinguishes this project from all others is that they got much of their information from talking with Turkish people who attended the schools during the shameful and hurtful days of the past century." He thinks this story carries a strong civic message; and he hopes it will help ease the pain of the past for many in his community. "Hopefully, this history will be a reminder that no person should be treated as a second-class citizen because of his or her name or background. For the older people of Turkish descent, this history will help them to look away from the period when they were looked down on; and they can hold their heads proudly high today. The young people of Turkish descent also need to know of the hard-won victories of their parents, their grandparents, and others for them to have the privileges they have today."

Eleazer Benenhaley's closing counsel befits his hope and faith. "Even with all her faults, I am proud to be an American. The good experiences of being born in Sumter County outweigh the bad. Let's use the pains of the past as stepping stones to the future. As citizens and past citizens of Sumter, let's join hands and hearts together to make Sumter a better place where everyone, no matter the background, can live with dignity and respect."

After such moving counsel from the lineal descendants of Thomas Sumter and Joseph Benenhaley, perhaps we all should thank the Turkish people of Sumter County, South Carolina, not only for sharing their voice and story but also for helping us better understand the historical South and evolving America.

Bibliography

Abd-Allah, Umar Faruq. "Turks, Moors, and Moriscos in Early America: Sir Francis Drake's Liberated Galley Slaves and the Lost Colony of Roanoke." 2010. Accessed Feb. 11, 2014. http://www.nawawi.org/wpcontent/uploads/2013/01/roots_of_islam_p1.pdf.
"ACLU Helps 'Turks' in School Bias Case." *Civil Liberties*, Number 186, February 1961.
Adams, Robert, and Charles Adams, eds. *The Narrative of Robert Adams, a Barbary Captive: A Critical Edition*. New York: Cambridge University Press, 2005.
al-Ahart El, Muhammed. "Early American Settlers 1500–1850." Accessed Aug. 8, 2015. https://moorishorthodox.wordpress.com/muslim-settlers.
Allen, James Paul, and Eugene J. Turner. *We the People: Atlas of American Ethnic Diversity*. New York: MacMillan Publishing Company, 1988.
"Anne King Gregorie Papers." South Carolina Historical Society. Charleston, SC.
Austin, Alan D. *African Muslims in Antebellum America: Transatlantic Stories and Spiritual Struggles*. New York: Routledge, 1997.
Baepler, Paul. *White Slaves, African Masters: An Anthology of American Barbary Captivity Narratives*. Chicago: University of Chicago Press, 1999.
Baker, Robert. "Long Branch Marks 100 Years." *Sumter Item*, Oct. 30, 2004.
———. "Tribe Seeks Recognition." *Sumter Item*, Dec. 28, 2006.
Barringer, Paul B. *The Natural Bent: The Memoirs of Dr. Paul B. Barringer*. Chapel Hill: University of North Carolina Press, 1949.
Bass, Robert. *Gamecock: The Life and Campaigns of General Thomas Sumter*. New York: Holt, Rinehart and Winston of Canada, 1961.
Beale, Calvin L. "American Tri-Racial Isolates: Their Status and Pertinence to Genetic Research." *Eugenics Quarterly* 4, no. 4 (Dec. 1957): 187–96.
———. "An Overview of the Phenomenon of Tri-Racial Isolates in the United States." *American Anthropologist* 74 (1972): 704–10.
Benenhaley, Eleazer. *Moulded Clay*. Orlando, FL: Daniels Printing Co., 1983.
———. *An Analysis of Neophytes and Would Be Historians*. Belvedere, SC: Quality Printing, 2008.
Berry, Brewton. "The Mestizos of South Carolina." *American Journal of Sociology* 51, no. 1 (1945): 34–41.
———. *Almost White*. New York: The Macmillan Company, 1963.
Beyond Borders. "Moroccans in Britain and America." Accessed July 2, 2015. http://beyond-borders.webs.com.
Bird, Stephanie Rose. *Light, Bright, and Damned Near White: Biracial and Triracial Culture in America*. Westport, CT: Praeger, 2009.
Black, Jeremy. *The Atlantic Slave Trade in World History*. New York: Routledge, 2015.
Buchanan, John. *The Road to Guilford Courthouse: The American Revolution in the Carolinas*. New York: John Wiley and Sons, 1997.

Bibliography

Bull, F. Kinloch. *Random Recollections of a Long Life, 1896–1986.* Unknown Binding, estimated 1986; located at South Caroliniana Library.

Bullard, Mary Ricketson. *Robert Stafford of Cumberland Island: Growth of a Planter.* Athens: University of Georgia Press, 1995.

Cisneros, Sandra. *The House on Mango Street.* New York: Arte Público Press, 1984.

City of Sumter, SC. "NewcomerInfo." Accessed Nov. 7, 2005. http://www.sumter-sc.com/NewcomerInfo/Default.aspx.

Considine, Craig. "George Washington Was a Friend of Muslims." *Huffington Post*, February 18, 2013. Also, see "Honoring Muslim Americans on Memorial Day." *Huffington Post*, May 26, 2013; and "Saluting Muslim American Patriots." *Huffington Post*, Apr. 10, 2015.

Crain, Janet. "Melungeon Myth of Drake Dropping off Passengers on Roanoke." May 12, 2012. http://historicalmelungeons.blogspot.com/2012/05/melungeon-myth-of-drake-dropping-off.html.

Cramer, Clayton E. *Black Demographic Data, 1790–1860.* Westport, CT: Greenwood Press, 1997.

Curtis, Edward E., IV. *Muslims in America: A Short History.* New York: Oxford University Press, 2009.

Dangerfield, David W. "Hard Rows to Hoe: Free Black Farmers in Antebellum South Carolina." PhD diss., University of South Carolina, 2014.

Davis, Robert C. *Christian Slaves, Muslim Masters: White Slavery in the Mediterranean, the Barbary Coast and Italy, 1500–1800.* New York: Palgrave MacMillan, 2004.

———. *Holy War and Human Bondage: Tales of Christian-Muslim Slavery in the Early-Modern Mediterranean.* Westport, CT: Praeger, 2009.

DeMarce, Virginia. "Review Essay: The Melungeons." *National Genealogical Quarterly* 84, no. 2 (June 1996): 134–49.

DesChamps, Margaret Burr. "The Free Agricultural Population in Sumter District, South Carolina, 1850–1860." *North Carolina Historical Review* 32, no. 1 (January 1955): 81–91.

Diouf, Sylviane A. *Servants of Allah: African Muslims Enslaved in the Americas.* New York: New York University Press, 1998.

Dirks, Jerald F. *Muslims in American History: A Forgotten Legacy.* Beltsville, MD: Amana Publications, 2006.

Dolan, Mary. "Sumter Cheraw Indians Seek State Recognition." *Sumter Item*, December 1, 2007.

Draper Manuscript Collection. Wisconsin Historical Society.

Dunbar, J. C. "Benenhaley School Closes." *Watchman and Southron*, May 20, 1916.

Edgar, Walter. *South Carolina: A History.* Columbia: University of South Carolina Press, 1998.

———. *The South Carolina Encyclopedia.* Columbia: University of South Carolina Press, 2006.

Elliott, Carl. "Adventures in the Gene Pool." *Wilson Quarterly* 27, no. 1 (Winter 2003): 12–21.

"Ellison Family Papers." South Caroliniana Library. University of South Carolina.

Embassy of the Kingdom of Morocco, "US-Morocco Diplomatic Relationships." Accessed Nov. 15, 2013. http://www.embassyofmorocco.us/USMoroccorelationship.htm.

Emiralioglu, Pinar. *Geographical Knowledge and Imperial Culture in the Early Modern Ottoman Empire.* Surrey, England: Ashgate Publishing, 2014.

Ertan, Sevgi Zubeyde. "A History of Turks in America." 2002. Accessed Feb. 11, 2014. http://kucukcoban.8m.com/YAZILAR/turks_america.html.

Estes, Roberta J., Jack H. Goins, Penny Ferguson, and Janet Lewis Crain. "Melungeons, A Multi-Ethnic Population." *Journal of Genetic Genealogy* (April 2012). Accessed Feb. 11, 2014. http://yellowhammernews.com/nationalpolitics/ny-times-bashes-kochs-praises-billionaire-enviro-counterpart/.

Failinger, Marie A. "Islam in the Mind of American Courts: 1800 to 1960." *Boston College Journal of Law and Social Justice* 32, no. 1/1 (January 2012). Accessed Nov. 1, 2015. http://lawdigitalcommons.bc.edu/jlsj/vol32/iss1/2.

Faroqhi, Suraiya. *The Ottoman Empire and the World around It.* London: I. B. Tauris, 2006.

Bibliography

Federal Writers' Project. "Pockets in America: The Turks in Sumter County, South Carolina." Ca. late 1930s; Southern Historical Collection, The Wilson Library, University of North Carolina at Chapel Hill.

———. *South Carolina: A Guide to the Palmetto State.* New York: Oxford University Press, 1941.

Flood, Charles Bracelen. *Rise, and Fight Again.* New York: Dodd, Mead, 1976.

Furman, Kate. "General Sumter and His Neighbors." *Southern History Association, Publications* 6, no. 5 (Sep. 1902): 382–88.

"Furman Papers." Documents of Charles James McDonald Furman, at South Caroliniana Library. University of South Carolina.

Gainey, Claudia Benenhaley. "Sumter CherawIndians.com" Accessed Dec. 1, 2013. http://www.sumtercherawindians.com.

Games, Alison. *The Web of Empire: English Cosmopolitans in an age of expansion, 1560–1660.* New York: Oxford University Press, 2009.

GhaneaBassiri, Kambiz. *A History of Islam in America: From the New World to the New World Order.* New York: Cambridge University Press, 2010.

Gilbert, William Harlen, Jr. "Memorandum Concerning the Characteristics of the Larger Mixed-Blood Racial Islands of the Eastern United States." *Social Forces* 21, no. 4 (May 1946): 438–77.

———. "Surviving Indian Groups of the Eastern United States," in *Smithsonian Report* for 1948. Government Printing Office, 1949: 407–38.

Golden, Harry. *Mr. Kennedy and the Negroes.* Cleveland, OH: World Publishing Company, 1964.

Gomez, Michael A. *Exchanging Our Country Marks: The Transformation of African Identities in the Colonial and Antebellum South.* Chapel Hill: University of North Carolina Press, 1998.

———. *Black Crescent: The Experience and Legacy of African Muslims in the Americas.* Cambridge, MA: Cambridge University Press, 2005.

Goodrich, Thomas D. *The Ottoman Turks and the New World: A Study of Tarih-i Hind-i Garbi and Sixteenth-Century Ottoman Americana.* Wiesbaden: O. Harrassowitz, 1990.

Gregorie, Anne King. *Thomas Sumter.* Columbia, SC: R. L. Bryan Company, 1931.

———. *History of Sumter County, South Carolina.* Sumter, SC: Library Board of Sumter County, 1954.

Griessman, B. Eugene. "The American Isolates." *American Anthropologist* 74 (1972): 693–734.

Griswold, Rufus Wilmot, William Gilmore Simms, and Edward Duncan Ingraham. *Washington and the Generals of the American Revolution.* 2 vols. Philadelphia: Cary and Hart, 1847.

Gross, Ariela J. *What Blood Won't Tell: A History of Race on Trial in America.* Cambridge: Harvard University Press, 2008.

Hagy, James W. "Muslim Slaves, Abducted Moors, African Jews, Misnamed Turks, and an Asiatic Greek Lady: Some Examples of Non-European Religious & Ethnic Diversity in South Carolina Prior to 1861." *Carologue* 9 (Spring 1993): 12–27.

Handler, Jerome S., and John T. Pohlmann. "Slave Manumissions and Freedmen in Seventeenth-Century Barbados." *William and Mary Quarterly* 41, no. 3 (July 1984): 390–408.

———. "Escaping Slavery in a Caribbean Plantation Society: Marronage in Barbados, 1650–1830s." *New West Indian Guide* 71, no. 3 (1997): 183–225.

Hartley, Cecil B. *Life of Major General Henry Lee, Commander of Lee's Legion in the Revolutionary War and Subsequently Governor of Virginia; To Which Is Added the Life of General Thomas Sumter of South Carolina.* Philadelphia: G. G. Evans, 1859.

Heinegg, Paul. *Free African Americans of North Carolina, Virginia, and South Carolina: From the Colonial Period to About 1820.* Vol. 1. Baltimore, MD: Genealogical Publishing Co., 2001.

Heitzler, Michael James. *Goose Creek, a Definitive History: Rebellion, Reconstruction and Beyond.* Charleston, SC: History Press, 2006.

Hicks, Theresa M., and Wes Taukchiray. *South Carolina Indians, Indian Traders, and Other Ethnic Connections, Beginning in 1670.* Spartanburg, SC: Reprint Company, 1998.

Bibliography

"High Hills AME Church." Accessed Nov. 1, 2013. http://highhillsamechurch.org/mod/entity-information.

"High Hills Baptist Church." Accessed Feb. 19, 2014. http://www.rootsweb.ancestry.com/~scsumter/cemeteries/highhillsbaptist/highhills.html.

High Hills Baptist Church Annual Report, 1887 (Thompson Collection and Interviews).

"High Hills of Santee Baptist Church." Accessed Jan. 13, 2016. http://www.sciway.net/sc-photos/sumter-county/high-hills-baptist-church.html.

Hill, S. Pony. *Strangers in Their Own Land: South Carolina's State Indian Tribes*. Palm Coast, FL: Backintyme, 2010.

Hilton, Johnny. "These People Don't Know Who I Am." Accessed May 29, 2014. http://johnbhiltonjr.blogspot.com.

Hirschman, Elizabeth. *Melungeons: The Last Lost Tribe in America*. Macon, GA: Mercer University Press, 2005.

Hobson, Geary, Janet McAdams, and Kathryn Walkiewicz. *The People Who Stayed: Southeastern Indian Writing after Removal*. Norman, OK: University of Oklahoma Press, 2010.

Hodge, Frederick Webb, ed. *Handbook of American Indians North of Mexico. Smithsonian Institution, Bureau of American Ethnology, Bulletin 30*. Washington, DC: US Government Printing Office (fourth impression, Sep, 1912).

"Hood v. Board of Trustees of Sumter County School District No. 2, Sumter County, South Carolina." Civil Action No. 3880. 1953.

"Hood v. Board of Trustees of Sumter County School District No. 2, Sumter County, South Carolina." 232 F.2d 626. Case No. 7163. 1956.

"Hood v. Board of Trustees of Sumter County School District No. 2, Sumter County, South Carolina." 286 F.2d 236. Case No. 8221, 1961.

"Hood v. Board of Trustees of Sumter County School District No. 2, Sumter County, South Carolina." 295 F.2d 390. Case No. 8383. 1961.

Hooks, Bell. *Teaching To Transgress: Education as the Practice of Freedom*. New York: Routledge, 1994.

"Hopewell Baptist Church." Accessed Oct. 1, 2014. http://www.angelfire.com/sc2/grantm.

Howe, Daniel Walker. *What God Hath Wrought: The Transformation of America, 1815–1848*. New York: Oxford University Press, 2009.

Huggins, J. D. Letter to the Editor, *Manning Times*, Mar. 31, 1909

Irving, Washington. *A History of the Life and Voyages of Christopher Columbus, Vol. 1*. New York: G. and C. Carvill, 1828.

Jewish Heritage Collection. "Oral History Interview with Ira Kaye and Ruth Barnett Kaye." June 15, 1996. Accessed Jan. 14, 2014. http://lowcountrydigital.library.cofc.edu/cdm4/item_viewer.php?CISOROOT=/JOH&CISOPTR=631&CISOBOX=1&REC=16.

Johnson, Michael P., and James L. Roark. *Black Masters: A Free Family of Color in the Old South*. New York: W. W. Norton, 1984.

Johnson, Michael P., and James L. Roark. *No Chariot Let Down: Charleston's Free People of Color on the Eve of the Civil War*. Chapel Hill: University of North Carolina Press, 2001.

Journals of the House of Representatives, 1789–90. Jan. 20, 1790: 363–64, 373–74.

Kaye, Ira. "The Turks: Alice in Sumterland." *New South* (June 1963): 9–15.

Kennedy, Brent. "The Melungeons: An Untold Story of Ethnic Cleansing in America." May 15, 2003. Accessed Aug. 10, 2015. http://www.mediamonitors.net/brentkennedy1.html.

Kennedy, Brent, and Robyn Vaughan Kennedy. *The Melungeons: The Resurrection of a Proud People*. Macon, GA: Mercer University Press, 1997.

King, Martin Luther, Jr. "I Have a Dream." Aug. 28, 1963. Accessed Feb. 21, 2014. http://www.archives.gov/press/exhibits/dream-speech.pdf.

Bibliography

Klein, Herbert S. *African Slavery in Latin America and the Caribbean*. New York: Oxford University Press, 1986.

———. *The Atlantic Slave Trade*. New Approaches to the Americas. New York: Cambridge University Press, 2010.

Kupperman, Karen Ordahl. *The Jamestown Project*. Cambridge, MA: Belknap Press, 2007.

Lockley, Timothy J. *Maroon Communities in South Carolina: A Documentary Record*. Columbia: University of South Carolina Press, 2009.

"Long Branch Baptist Church." Accessed Nov. 11, 2013. http://www.longbranch-baptist.org.

Lowcountry History Initiative. "European Christianity and Slavery." Accessed May 27, 2015. http://ldhi.library.cofc.edu/exhibits/show/africanpassageslowcountryadapt/introductionatlanticworld/europnea_christianity_and_slav.

Lowery, Malinda Maynor. *Lumbee Indians in the Jim Crow South: Race, Identity, and the Making of a Nation*. Chapel Hill: University of North Carolina Press, 2010.

Lowery, Woodbury. *The Spanish Settlements within the Present Limits of the United States, 1513–1561*. New York: Russell & Russell, 1959.

Macron, Mary Haddad. "Arab Americans and Their Communities of Cleveland" (1979). *Cleveland Memory*. Book 22. Accessed Jan. 14, 2016. http://engagedscholarship.csuohio.edu/clevmembks/22/?utm_source=engagedscholarship.csuohio.edu%2Fclevmembks%2F22&utm_medium=PDF&utm_campaign=PDFCoverPages.

Markham, Clements R., ed. *The Journal of Christopher Columbus (During His First Voyage, 1492–93) and Documents Relating to the Voyages of John Cabot and Gaspar Corte Real*. London: Printed for the Hakluyt Society by Chas J. Clark, 4, Lincoln's Inns Fields, W. C., 1893.

Matar, Nabil. *Turks, Moors, and Englishmen in the Age of Discovery*. New York: Columbia University Press, 1999.

McCrady, Edward. *The History of South Carolina in the Revolution, 1780–1783*. London: MacMillan, 1902.

McElveen, W. A. "Bubba." "Our Town: Tuomey Changes Alter Downtown through the Years." *Sumter Item*, July 4, 1996.

McIntosh, Gregory C. *The Piri Reis Map of 1513*. Athens: University of Georgia Press, 2000.

McPherson, O. M. "Report on Condition and Tribal Rights of the Indians of Robeson and Adjoining Counties of North Carolina," in *Indians of North Carolina: Letter from the Secretary of the Interior, Transmitting in Response to a Senate Resolution of June 30, 1914, a Report on the Condition and Tribal Rights of the Indians of Robeson and Adjoining Counties of North Carolina*. Washington, DC: US Government Printing Office, 1915.

Migliazzo, Arlin. *To Make This Land Our Own: Community, Identity, and Social Adaptation in Purrysburg Township, South Carolina, 1732–1865*. Columbia: University of South Carolina Press, 2007.

Milling, Chapman J. *Red Carolinians*. Chapel Hill: University of North Carolina Press, 1940.

Mills, Gary. "Tracing Free People of Color in the Antebellum South: Methods, Sources, and Perspectives." *National Genealogical Society Quarterly* 78, no. 4 (Dec. 1990): 262–78.

Mitchell, J.H. "Long Branch Church in the Santee." *Baptist Courier*. Apr. 1, 1943.

"Morocco's Contribution to America's Independence." Accessed Nov. 14, 2013. http://www.ufppc.org/us-a-world-news-mainmenu-35/3026-history-moroccos-contribution-to-american-independence.html.

Muhammad, Amir Nashid Ali. *Muslims in America: Seven Centuries of History (1312–2000)*. Beltsville, MD: Amani Publications, 2001.

Myers, Portia. "Our 'Turk' Community Is One of a Kind." *Sumter Item*, Aug. 5, 1989.

Nagai, Tyrone. "Multiracial Identity and the US Census: 1790–1890," ProQuest. 2010. Accessed Oct. 6, 2014. http://www.csa.com/discoveryguides/census/review.php.

Bibliography

Nassau, Mike. "Melungeons and Other Mestee Groups." 1994. Accessed Nov. 11, 2013. http://www.melungeonmestee.webs.com.

National Archives at Atlanta. "The Evolution of a Government: A Study of the United States Constitution." Accessed Nov. 24, 2013. http://www.archives.gov/atlanta/education/chronological-topics/images/constitution-guide.pdf.

New, Sue. "Joseph Being Called Yusef Ben Ali Was First recorded by Thomas Sumter's Grandson." 2005. Accessed July 17, 2005. http://sciway3.net/clark/freemoors/JosephBenenhaley.html.

———. "Benenhaley, or a Story of the 'Turks' of Sumter County." 2002–2010. Accessed Nov. 15, 2013. http://sciway3.net/clark/freemoors/benenhaley.html (dated 2002–2010 and accessed).

———. "Census Data for the 'Turks' of Sumter County." 2002–2005. Accessed Feb. 21, 2014. http://sciway3.net/clark/freemoors/scturkcensus.html.

Nicholes, Cassie. "County's 'Turk' Community Unique." *Sumter News*, Mar. 26, 1970.

———. *Historical Sketches of Sumter County: Its Birth and Growth*. Sumter, SC: Sumter County Historical Commission, 1975.

Ognibene, Terri Ann. "Discovering the Voices of the Segregated: An Oral History of the Educational Experiences of the Turkish People of Sumter County, South Carolina." PhD diss., Georgia State University, 2008.

O'Malley, Gregory E. "Beyond the Middle Passage: Slave Migration from the Caribbean to North America, 1619–1807." *William and Mary Quarterly*, 3d Series, 66, no. 1 (Jan. 2009). 125–72.

———. *Final Passages: The Intercolonial Slave Trade of British America, 1619–1807*. Chapel Hill: University of North Carolina Press, 2014.

Oxendine, Charles L. *Oxendine Census Records, 1790–1920*. Madison, FL: Jimbob Printing, 1997.

Paredes, J. Anthony. *Indians of the Southeastern United States in the 20th Century*. Tuscaloosa: University of Alabama Press, 1992.

Pollitzer, William S. "The Physical Anthropology and Genetics of Marginal People of the Southeastern United States." *American Anthropologist* 74, no. 3 (June 1972): 719–34.

Price, Edward T. "A Geographic Analysis of White-Negro-Indian Racial Mixtures in Eastern United States." *Annals of the Association of American Geographers* 43 (June 1953): 138–55.

Quinn, David Beers. "Turks, Moors, Blacks, and Others in Drake's West Indian Voyages." *Terrae Incognitae*, 14 (1982): 97–104.

———. *The Roanoke Voyages, 1584–1590: Vols. 1–2*. New York: Dover Publications, 1990 and 1991.

Ray, Celeste. "Ethnicity." In *The Greenwood Encyclopedia of American Regional Cultures*, edited by Rebecca Mark and Rob Vaughan. Westport, CT: Greenwood Publishing Group, 2004.

———. *The New Encyclopedia of Southern Culture: Ethnicity*. Chapel Hill: University of North Carolina Press, 2007.

"Redbone Nation." Accessed Nov. 15, 2014. http://www.redbonenation.com.

Reed, John Shelton. "Mixing in the Mountains." *Southern Cultures* 3, no. 4 (Winter 1997): 25.

Rice, Benjamin H. "A History of Selim, the Algerine Convert." In William Meade, *Old Churches, Ministers and Families of Virginia*. Vol. I. Philadelphia: J. B. Lippincott, 1857: 341–48.

Roberts, Peter A. *From Oral to Literate Culture: Colonial Experience in the English West Indies*. Kingston, Jamaica: University of the West Indies Press, 2000.

Salzmann, Ariel. "Migrants in Chains: On the Enslavement of Muslims in Renaissance and Enlightenment Europe." *Religions* 4 (2013): 391–411.

Sass, Herbert Ravenel. *The Story of the South Carolina Lowcountry*. Vol. 1. West Columbia, SC: J. F. Hyer Publishing Co., 1956.

Sider, Gerald. *Living Indian Histories: Lumbee and Tuscarora People in North Carolina*. Chapel Hill: University of North Carolina Press, 2003.

Sidhwa, Bapsi. *Cracking India*. Minneapolis, MN: Milkweed Editions, 1991.

Bibliography

Simour, Lhoussain. *Recollections of History beyond Borders: Captives, Acrobats, Dancers and the Moroccan-American Narrative of Encounters*. Newcastle upon Tyne, UK: Cambridge Scholars Publishing, 2014.
South Carolina Commission for Minority Affairs. "Request for State Recognition: Native American Indian Tribe." Filed by Sumter Band of Cheraw Indians, 2013.
South Carolina Legislative Times: Being the Debates and Proceedings of the South Carolina Legislature, Session Commencing November 1855. Columbia, SC: E. H. Britton, 1956.
South Carolina Royal Council Journal. March 3, 1753; 198–99.
South Carolina Radio Network. "South Carolina to Recognize New Indian Tribe". Nov. 22, 2013.
"South Carolina's Raceless People." *Ebony Magazine*, Jan. 1, 1957: 53–56.
Southern Campaigns of the American Revolution. "Thomas Sumter Symposium and Battlefield Tours." Apr. 2005. Accessed Nov. 11, 2014. http://southerncampaign.org/newsletter/v2n4.pdf (dated Apr. 2005 and accessed November 11, 2014).
Spivey, Michael. *Native Americans in the Carolina Borderlands: A Critical Ethnography*. Southern Pines, NC: Carolina Press, 2000.
"Springbank Baptist Church." Accessed Nov. 11, 2013. http://www.springbank.org.
Steen, Carl. "An Archaeology of the Settlement Indians of the South Carolina Lowcountry." *South Carolina Antiquities* 44 (2012): 19–34.
Stockbridge, Kay M. Presentation on the "Turks" of Sumter County, at the Sumter County Museum, Sumter, SC. 1995.
Sumter, Thomas Sebastian. "An Interesting People: Origin of the Bennanhaly and Scott Families." *Watchman and Southron*, Sep. 15, 1917.
———. *Stateburg and Its People*. N.p.; probably published ca. 1920 in Stateburg or Sumter, SC.
Sumter County, SC. "Population." Accessed Feb. 25, 2008. http://www.city-data.com/city/Sumter-South-Carolina.html.
"Sumter County Colony Locally Called Turks." Columbia *State*, Mar. 18, 1928.
Sumter County Genealogical Society. *Sumter Black River Watchman*, Jan. 2005, 17.
Taukchiray, Wesley DuRant, and Alice Bee Kasakoff. "Contemporary Native Americans in South Carolina." In *Indians of the Southeastern United States in the Late 20th Century*, edited by Paredes, 72–99. Tuscaloosa: University of Alabama Press, 1992.
Tayac, Gabrielle. *IndiVisible: African-Native American Lives in the Americas*. Washington, DC: Smithsonian Books, 2009.
Taylor, Rosser H. *Ante-Bellum South Carolina: A Social and Cultural History*. Chapel Hill: University of North Carolina Press, 1942.
Theodosiadou, Youli, ed. *Southern Ethnicities*. Thessaloniki, Greece: Kornelia Sfakianaki, 2008.
"Thomas Sumter Papers, 2VV87." Draper Manuscripts Collection. Accessed at Houston Cole Library, Jacksonville State University.
Thompson Collection and Interviews. Extensive material (documents, photographs, conversations) shared by Greg Thompson with the authors during the writing of this book.
Thompson, Greg. "Turks Can Be Traced Back to Thomas Sumter." *Sumter Item, Progress 2000*, Apr. 2000.
Thomson, George Malcolm. *Sir Francis Drake*. New York: William Morrow, 1970.
"Timmerman Refuses Sumter Turk Appeal." *Sumter Daily Item*, Dec. 2, 1955.
Tindall, George Brown. *Natives and Newcomers: Ethic Southerners and Southern Ethnics*. Athens: University of Georgia Press, 1995.
Tisdale, Thomas Sumter, Jr. *A Lady of the High Hills: Natalie Delage Sumter*. Columbia, SC. University of South Carolina Press, 2001.
Trillin, Calvin. "Sumter County, SC. Turks." *New Yorker*, Mar. 8, 1969, 104–10.
"'Turk' Case Is Closed." *Sumter Daily Item*, Feb. 15, 1961.

Bibliography

"Turks Lose Ground on Grammar School." *Sumter Daily Item*, May 29, 1956.

US Air Force, Air Combat Command. "Archaeological Resources Overview of Shaw Air Force Base and Poinsett Electronic Combat Range." Apr. 2006. Accessed Nov. 15, 2013. http://www.dtic.mil/dtic/tr/fulltext/u2/a453315.pdf.

US Department of State, Historian. "Barbary Wars, 1801–1805 and 1815–1816." Accessed Nov. 28, 2014. https://history.state.gov/milestones/1801-1829/barbary-wars.

VisaJourney. "Your US Immigration Community." Accessed Nov. 18, 2013. http://webcache.googleusercontent.com/search?q=cache:lR9OltEGIZoJ:http://www.visajourney.com/forums/topic/307576moroccans/%2Bmorocco+white+caucasian&hl=en&gbv=2&ct=clnk.

"Wayman Chapel AME Church." Oct. 1, 2014. http:www.waymanchapelame.com/history.html.

Weiss, Gillian. *Captives and Corsairs: France and Slavery in the Early Modern Mediterranean.* Stanford, CA: Stanford University Press, 2013.

"Wes Taukchiray Collection." Special Collections/Archives. University of North Carolina Pembroke.

"Wes Taukchiray Papers." South Caroliniana Library. University of South Carolina.

Weslager, C. A. *Delaware's Forgotten Folk: The Story of the Moors and Nanticokes.* Philadelphia: University of Pennsylvania Press, 1943.

"Wesley D. White Papers." South Carolina Historical Society. Charleston, SC.

Wheat, David. "Mediterranean Slavery, New World Transformations: Galley Slaves in the Spanish Caribbean, 1578–1635." *Slavery and Abolition: A Journal of Slave and Post Slave Studies* 31, no. 3 (2010): 327–44.

White, Wesley, Jr. *A History of the Turks Who Live in Sumter County, South Carolina, from 1805 to 1972.* Unpublished manuscript, 1975, Smithsonian Institution in Washington, DC. This report is a collection of diverse data and analysis, with unnumbered pages; and White apparently has updated certain findings, with handwritten notes on various versions over the years.

Wikramanayake, Marina. *A World in the Shadow: The Free Black in Antebellum South Carolina.* Columbia: University of South Carolina Press, 1973.

Woody, Howard, and Allen D. Thigpen, A. *South Carolina Postcards, Volume 10, Sumter County.* Charleston, SC: Arcadia Publishing, 2005.

Workman, William D., Jr. "Sumter County 'Turks' Are Old Inhabitants," *News and Courier,* Dec. 16, 1950.

———. "'Turks' Seeking Educational Opportunities for Children," *News and Courier,* Dec. 17 1950.

———. "Old Legislative Petition May be Clue to Identity of Sumter County 'Turks,'" *News and Courier,* Feb. 12, 1951.

———. "Sumter 'Turks' Descendants of Men Who Served in American Revolution," *News and Courier,* Sep. 10, 1953.

———. "Sumter 'Turks' Stem from Early Soldiers," *News and Courier,* Sep. 10, 1953.

Works Progress Administration. Survey of State and Local Historical Records: 1936. Digital Collection housed at the South Caroliniana Library of the University of South Carolina. Accessed Jan. 13, 2016. http://digital.tcl.sc.edu/cdm/compoundobject/collection/hrs/id/3270/rec/1.

Yates, Donald N., and Elizabeth C. Hirschman. "Toward a Genetic Profile of Melungeons in Southern Appalachia." *Appalachian Journal* 38, no. 1 (Fall 2010): 92–111.

Yates, Donald N., and Richard Mack Bettis. *Old World Roots of the Cherokee: How DNA, Ancient Alphabets and Religion Explain the Origins of America's Largest Indian Nation.* Jefferson, NC: McFarland, 2012.

Yates, Gayle Graham. "The North Carolina Lumbee People as Seen Through a Visit with Linda Oxendine." 113–30, in Youli Theodosiadou, ed., *Southern Ethnicities.* Thessaloniki, Greece: Kornelia Sfakianaki, 2008.

"Yesteryear." *Sumter Item,* July 5, 2009.

Index

Abd-Allah, Umar Faruq, 49, 54, 58, 59
Adams, Charles, 53
Adams, Robert, 53
al-Ahart El, Muhammed, 43, 45, 49
al-Azemmouri, Mostafa (Estevanico the Moor), 49
Allen, James Paul, 22
American Civil Liberties Union, 143
American Legion Baseball, 28, 154, 166, 172, 188, 203
American Revolution and Revolutionary War, 26, 27, 33, 34, 35, 39, 44, 45, 49, 52, 66, 75, 76, 78, 99, 104, 109, 123, 132, 146, 215, 216; as it relates to the Turkish people, 3–6, 30–31, 41–42
Amersons, interred in Long Branch and/or Springbank cemeteries, 92
analytic model used in this project, xii–xv
ancestry, ethnicity, and race; explanation of terms as used in this project, 17–21
Arab, Moor, Muslim, Turk; discussed as historical terms used in this analysis, 12
assimilation, 20, 104, 127, 138, 144, 184, 185–86, 194, 210, 212, 213
Austin, Alan D., 50
awkward questions, 16–21, 154

Baepler, Paul, 53
Baker, Robert, 30, 71, 185
Baptist Courier, 46
Barbouchi, Limame, 47
Barringer, Paul B., 55–56, 57
Bass, Robert, 30, 32, 33–34, 52, 72–73, 82, 146
Beale, Calvin E., 9, 18, 38
ben Ali, Yusef. *See* Joseph Benenhaley

Benenhaley, Eleazer (author), 28–29, 35–36, 71, 103, 139–40, 143, 188–89, 215–17
Benenhaley, Joseph (Yusef ben Ali and the Turkish patriarch), 7, 12, 19, 20, 22, 31, 33–34, 35, 36, 39, 46, 47, 51–52, 56, 59, 60, 61, 62, 63, 64, 65, 66, 67, 101–4, 132, 138, 46, 148, 152, 186, 189, 192, 193, 194, 197, 201, 202, 205, 208–9, 212–14, 215–16; as depicted in the Turkish traditional narrative, 3–6, 30–31, 41–42; assumptions, uncertainties, and inconsistencies, 43–45; "Caucasian of Arab descent," 32; "first family," 94–95; founding and forefathering the community, 81–83; genealogical record, 80–85; genetic profile, 95–99; Matilda Ellison Benenhaley's letters, 75–80; Thomas Sumter's deed and survey, 72–73; proclaiming the patriarch, 99–100; unknown burial site, 89–90; 145
Benenhaley School, 139
Benenhaleys, as "First Family" of the Turkish community, 5, 94–95; demonstrated in cemetery records, 85–93; death notices, 93–94, and master list, 83–85; founding and forefathering, 81–83; genealogical record, 80–89; genetic profile, 95–99
Benenhaleys, individuals as cited in this book (listed by first name): Aaron Benenhaley, 87; Adrienne Benenhaley Love, 200–201; Alberta Benenhaley, 86; Alice Benenhaley, 84; Annie Benenhaley, 87; Blanche Benenhaley Buckner, 84; Brian Benenhaley, 198–99; Catherine or Katie Benenhaley, 82, 84; Cathreen Oxendine Benenhaley, 87; Claudia Benenhaley Gainey, 71;

Index

Benenhaleys (*continued*): Connie Carolyn Benenhaley Buckner, 141; Dick Benenhaley, 216; Dolly Benenhaley, 87; Edward Benenhaley, 87; Eleazer Benenhaley, 28–29, 35–36, 71, 103, 139–40, 143, 188–89, 199, 215–17; Eliphare Oxendine Benenhaley, 84, 92; Elizabeth Miller Benenhaley, 76, 81, 82; Ernest Benenhaley, 133; Etta Benenhaley, 86 ; Ferdinand Benenhaley, 82, 84; Florence Benenhaley, 86; Francis Benenhaley, 45, 82, 84 ; Harold Benenhaley, 201–6; Henry Benenhaley, 128. 131, 132, 133, 173, 180; Heyward Nathaniel Benenhaley, 141; Isaac Benenhaley ("Big Ike"), 75, 76, 79, 80, 81, 86, 87, 88, 89, 132, 191, 192; Isabella Benenhaley, 82, 84; Jensey or Jency Benenhaley, 74, 76, 78, 82, 84, 201; Jesse Noah Benenhaley (Noah Jr.), 86, 88; John Benenhaley, 87, 216; Joseph Benenhaley (*see* Joseph Benenhaley); Joseph H. Benenhaley II (Joseph H. Benenhaley Jr.), 82, 86; Julius Benenhaley, 133; Katie Benenhaley, 87; Lawrence Benenhaley ("Curly"), 75–79; Leah Benenhaley Peagler, 88, 101, 140, 191–92; Leo Cadeo or Cadia Benenhaley Taylor, 82; Lillie Benenhaley, 88; Lyrander or Lysander Benenhaley, 82, 84; Martha Benenhaley, 87; Martha Ann Benenhaley Hood, 84, 86; Martha Jane Oxendine Benenhaley, 86; Mary Magdalene Benenhaley, 87; Matilda Ellison Benenhaley, 75–80, 81, 82, 89, 102 ; Maybelle Benenhaley, 78, 86, 88; Mertis Ray Benenhaley, 130, 131; Moses Benenhaley, 87; Myrtle Benenhaley, 141; Nell Benenhaley, 141; Nellie Benenhaley Ray, 130, 131; Noah Benenhaley, 26, 77–80, 86, 89, 131, 132; Nora Benenhaley, 87; Peggy Ann Benenhaley Hood, 141; Raymond Benenhaley Sr., 141; Rosa (Rose) Benenhaley, 77–80, 86, 88; Soloman Benenhaley, 87; Sophronia or Sophonia Benenhaley, 82; Stella Miller Hood Benenhaley, 141; Thomas Hampton Benenhaley Sr., 131; Tim Benenhaley, 188; Virginia Benenhaley, 84; Wallace Levore Benenhaley Jr., 133; Wallace Levore Benenhaley Sr., 141; Warren Benenhaley, 216; William Benenhaley Jr., 86, 87; William Joseph Benenhaley, 87, 131, 132

Benenhaleys and Oxendines, historical relationship, 69–70

Berry, Brewton, 24, 25, 30, 36, 37, 39

Bethesda Baptist Church, 69, 93

"Beyond Borders" (website), 51

Bindon, James, 17, 46, 98–99

Bird, Stephanie Rose, 37

birth and death certificates, 138, 160–62, 187, 194

Black, Jeremy, 54

blacks/black people (Africans, African Americans): defined as a cultural group in this book, 10–12; 116; Turkish relations with black people, 163–65

Blanding, Jas. D., 32

Boliver, Mike, 6

Bolsers, interred in Long Branch and/or Springbank cemeteries, 92

Bradshaw, Jonathan, 185–86

Brown v. Board of Education, 143, 210

Browns, interred in Long Branch and/or Springbank cemeteries, 92

Buchanan, John, 32

Buckners, as a core family of the Turkish community. *See* core families

Buckners, individuals as cited in the text of this book: Blanche Benenhaley Buckner, 84; Charles Wilson Buckner, 84; Connie Carolyn Benenhaley Buckner, 141; Irma Buckner Ray, 141; Ray Buckner, 133; Samuel Lewis Buckner Jr., 141; Samuel Lewis Buckner Sr., 84; Sarah Oxendine Buckner, 76; Vernon Buckner ("Chic"), 133; Vickie Buckner Underwood, 137

Bull, F. Kinloch, 28, 30, 33, 43, 46, 66, 103, 157

Bullard, Mary Ricketson, 30, 39

Burgess, Doyle, 133

Cain, W. O., 128

Caribbean area, and intercolonial slave trade, 54–60

Index

Carpenters, interred in Long Branch and/or Springbank cemeteries, 92
Carters, interred in Long Branch and/or Springbank cemeteries, 92
cemetery records, 89–93, 102
Charleston, S.C., 31–34, 49–50, 56, 57, 59, 75, 77, 82, 158, 216
Charlotte Observer (Charlotte, N.C.), 143, 144
Chase, Chip, 195–98
Chavis/Chavises, 67, 68, 69
Church of the Holy Cross, 93, 192
Cisneros, Sandra, 115
Civil War, as it relates to the Turkish people, 2. 23, 24, 40, 109, 130, 132, 216
clannishness, 25, 129, 142, 127–29, 154–55
Cobb, Charles R., 46
Columbus, Christopher, 47, 48, 49, 50
Confederacy, as it relates to the Turkish people, 109
conjoined lineages, 66–69
Considine, Craig, 30, 43, 45, 49
core families of the Turkish community (Benenhaleys, Buckners, Hoods, Lowreys, Oxendines, Rays), 20, 95, 103, 116; as demonstrated in cemetery records, 85–93; death notices, 93–94; genealogical record, 80–89; genetic profile, 95–99; master list, 83–85
counsel of the elders, 215–16
Crain, Janet Lewis, 59
cultural groups and preferred self-descriptors, 10–12, 116

Dalzell, Stateburg, Sumter, and Sumter County, S.C., discussed as setting for this project, 123–126
Dalzell School (Dalzell School for Turks), 35, 74, 117, 122, 147, 148, 156, 166, 183, 192, 203; buildings and locations, 74, 128, 134, 136–37, 139, 179–80; education and activities, 28–29, 134–38, 141, 143, 169–72, 192; graduation speech incident, 140; limited opportunities, 172–73; second-class citizens, 139–44; standing up and demanding change, 173–74; warm but mixed memories, 169–72
Dangerfield, David W., 24, 30
Daubrig, Henry, 50

Davis, Robert C., 53
dealing with the issue of Indian-Turkish origins, 65–72, 104; conjoined lineages, 66–69; enduring, distinct Turkish community, 70–72; Turkish responses to the question of Indian-Turkish origins, 71, 147–48, 186–87, 193, 197, 199
Deas/Deases, 69, 83, 92
death notices (death certificates and obituaries), 93–94
decade of trial and triumph, 141–44
DeMarce, Virginia, 59
depiction by academic, media, and other observers, 23–29
DesChamps, Margaret Burr, 24, 30
Diouf, Sylviane, 39, 50, 56
diverse, dynamic regional history, 214–15
Dirks, Jerald, 48
Dolan, Mary, 30
Don Quixote (Cervantes), 46
Drake, Francis, 54, 58–59
Draper, Lyman, 72; and "Draper Manuscripts Collection," 64, 72–73
Dunbar, J. C., 27, 30, 139

Ebenezer School/Ebenezer Junior High School, 165, 196, 201
Ebony Magazine, 15, 25, 46, 119, 144, 157
Edgar, Walter, 2
Edgeworths, interred in Long Branch and/or Springbank cemeteries, 92
Edmunds High School (Sumter, S.C.), and integration of Turkish students, 174–76, 183
Elliott, Carl, 2, 96
Ellison, Matilda (Matilda Ellison Benenhaley), 75–80, 81, 82, 89, 99, 102; and Matilda's letters, 75–80
Ellison, William, 24, 75–76; and "Ellison Family Papers," 64
"Embassy of the Kingdom of Morocco" (website), 49
Emiralioglu, Pinar, 47
enduring, distinct Turkish community, 70–72
entrenched separatism, 5, 35, 153–54
Erbs, interred in Long Branch and/or Springbank cemeteries, 92
Ertan, Sevgi Zubeyde, 59

Index

Estes, Roberta J., 59
Evergreen Cemetery, 93
everyday life in Turkish community, 19, 26–29, 186
evolving, inclusive American experience, 215

Failinger, Marie A., 30
Fair, Randy, 113
Faroqhi, Suraiya, 47
Federal Works Progress Administration, 35
Federal Writers' Project, 7–8, 27, 30, 34–35, 43, 66
Flood, Charles Bracelen, 32, 52. 82
founding and forefathering, 81–83
Free Moors, 51
Frierson, John N., 73
Furman, Charles James McDonald, 67, 69; and "Furman Papers," 47, 64, 67, 69
Furman, Richard, 130

Games, Alison, 53
genealogical record, 80–95
genetic profile, 95–99, 102
Georgia, 22, 32, 113, 115, 149, 158, 187
Georgia State University, 113, 114
GhaneaBassiri, Kambiz, 50
Gibbes/Gibbeses, 67, 68, 69
Gilbert, William Harlen Jr., 9, 18, 37, 38
Goins, W. W., 69
Goins/Goinses, 66, 67, 68, 69
Golden, Harry, 26, 30
Gomez, Michael, 22, 30, 44, 50, 61
Goodrich, Thomas D., 47
Goose Creek, S.C., 31, 32
Gregorie, Anne King, 23, 30, 32, 33, 42, 43, 66, 130, 139, 171; and "Anne King Gregorie Papers," 42, 64
Griessman, B. Eugene, 30
Griffins, interred in Long Branch and/or Springbank cemeteries, 92
Griswold, Rufus et al, 32
Gross, Ariela J., 68

Hagy, James W., 2, 30, 36, 43, 49, 50
Hamed and Guylance (Moroccan petitioners), 50
Handler, Jerome S., 59
Heinegg, Paul, 38
Heitzler, Michael James, 32

heroes of the Integration Movement, 141, 166, 173, 180, 210
Hicks, Theresa M., 99
High Hills AME Church, 93, 130
High Hills Baptist Church (black congregation), 93, 130
High Hills Baptist Church (white congregation, also High Hills of the Santee Baptist Church), 26, 90, 92, 93, 129, 130, 155
Hill, Steven Pony, 9, 40, 46
Hillcrest High School (Dalzell, S.C.), and integration of Turkish students, 112, 121, 128, 140, 141, 142, 144, 167, 174–83, 189, 198, 199, 201, 202
Hilton, Johnny, 30
Hirschman, Elizabeth C., 59, 188
Hobson, Geary et al, 37
Hodge, Frederick Webb, 66, 67
Hood v. Board of Trustees, 83, 141–44
Hoods, as a core family of the Turkish community. *See* core families
Hoods, individuals as cited in the text of this book: Marion Hood, 133, 173, 180; Martha Ann Benenhaley Hood, 84, 86; Peggy Ann Benenhaley Hood, 141; Reese Hood Sr., 84; Stella Miller Hood Benenhaley, 141; Viola Hood Ray, 141; Woodrow Wilson Hood Jr., 141, 173, 180
hooks, bell, 113
Hopewell Baptist Church, 93, 131
Horns, interred in Long Branch and/or Springbank cemeteries, 92
Howe, Daniel Walker, 37
Huggins, J. D., 26, 30
Hurst, Sarah, 84
Hursts, 83

Indians/Native Americans/Native American Indians, indigenous peoples: defined as a cultural group in this book, 10–12, 116; entwined, conjoined lineages among Indians and Turkish people, 66–69
Indian Removal Act of 1830, 36, 37, 68, 70
Integration Movement of the 1950s, 110, 114, 117, 119, 123, 133, 136, 197, 200; decade of trial and triumph, 141–44; Edmunds High School, 174–76, 183; Hillcrest High School, 112, 121, 128, 140, 141,

Index

142, 144, 167, 173–83, 189, 198, 199, 201, 202; *Hood v. Board of Trustees*, 141; integrating the white schools, 35, 173–83; Ku Klux Klan, 163; looking back on the Movement, 181; Movement heroes, 141, 166, 180, 210; national civil rights movement, 138–39, 144; recollecting segregation and integration, 179–81
intermarriage, 7, 10, 20–22, 35, 155–57, 193
Internet, as source of information in this project, 64–65
Irving, Washington, 48, 49
Item (*Sumter [S.C]. Item*, and *Sumter Daily Item*, 21, 71, 128, 138, 143, 144, 185, 187, 195

Jacksons, interred in Long Branch and/or Springbank cemeteries, 92
Jefferson, Thomas, and Sally Hemings descendants, 96
Jernigan, Sara, 140
Jewish Heritage Collection, 142, 143
Johnson, Michael P., 24, 75
Journals of the House of Representatives (South Carolina), 50
journey from isolation to assimilation, 5, 10, 19–20, 21, 22, 28–29, 104, 115, 120, 122, 141, 142, 144, 153, 154, 155, 157, 160–68, 173, 178, 180, 182, 210, 213, 214, 215; isolation and segregation, 128–32; discrimination and oppression, 132–38; assimilation, 144

Kasakoff, Alice Bee, 68, 99
Kaye, Ira, 22, 30, 141, 142, 143, 164, 173
Kennedy, Brent, 9, 47, 49, 58, 59, 187
Kennedy, Robyn Vaughan, 9, 47, 49, 58, 59, 187
King, Martin Luther Jr., 114
Klein, Herbert, 54, 60
Ku Klux Klan (KKK), 163
Kupperman, Karen Ordahl, 47

LaRoche, Daniel, 50
legend of Turkish origins, 41–62, 146–47, 148–51; Joseph Benenhaley / Yusef ben Ali, 42–45; meandering saga of the patriarch, 45–47; possible trail from Ottoman Empire to Dalzell, S.C., 47–52; speculative slave-trade connection,

53–61; tendentious but plausible explanation for Joseph Benenhaley's presence in South Carolina, 61
Lockley, Timothy J., 59
looking back on the Integration Movement, 181–83
Long Branch Baptist Church, 45, 46, 71, 79, 90, 91, 102, 133, 134, 140, 192, 193, 198; founding, 35, 130, 131–32, 135, 155, 185; locations, 74, 185; mission 135, 185–86
Lowcountry Digital History Initiative, 53
Lowery, Malinda Maynor, 21
Lowery, Woodbury, 43, 49
Lowreys, as a core family of the Turkish community. *See* core families
Lowreys, individuals as cited in the text of this book: Henry W. Lowrey, 141; Robert Columbus Lowrey, 84; Ruth Annette Ray Lowrey, 141
Lubbock Evening Journal, 142, 144
Lumbee Indians, 21, 71, 193

Macron, Mary Haddad, 30, 34
Manning Times, 26
Markham, Clements R., 48, 49
Marsh, Charles, 3
master list of Turkish people living in the 1800s, 83–85, 102
Matar, Nabil, 54
McCrady, Edward, 32
McElveen, W. A., Jr. ("Mayor Bubba"), 30, 125, 138
McIntosh, Gregory C., 47
McPherson, O. M., 66, 67
Mediterranean/Middle Eastern/North African area, 12, 59, 96, 97, 152, 187, 188, 197, 205, 214; and transatlantic slave trade, 53–55, 99, 102
Melungeons, and possible linkage with Turkish people, 9, 58–59, 127, 187–88, 212
Merrimon, Augustus M., 141, 173
Middle East/Middle Easterners, 17, 19, 44, 148, 188. *See also* Mediterranean/Middle East/North Africa area
Migliazzo, Arlin, 3
Miller, Steve, 185, 186
Milling, Chapman J., 36
Miott, Roosevelt, 165

231

Index

Mitchell, Joseph H., 30, 46, 131, 132
Mohammed III (Sultan of Morocco), 49
Moody, Mr. (testimony in "Draper Manuscripts Collection"), 72–73
Moroccan Cultural Studies Centre, 51
Moroccan-American Treaty of Friendship (1786), 49
Moors of Delaware, 16, 39
Morocco/Moroccans, 39, 41, 43, 44, 48, 49, 50, 51, 52, 54, 55, 61, 125
"Morocco's Contribution to America's Independence" (website), 49
Muhammad, Amir Nashid Ali, 48
multicultural narrative, 214
"My Story," 112–17
Myers, Portia, 30

Nassau, Mike, 39
national civil rights movement, 138–39, 144
New, Sue, 43, 148
New Orleans, La., 55, 186, 205
New York Times, 144
New Yorker, 22, 26
News and Courier (Charleston, S.C.), 25, 128, 141, 144
Nicholes, Cassie, 23, 30, 33, 43, 66
Nino, Pedro Alonso, 48
North Africa/North Africans, 12, 17, 19, 22, 34, 35, 43, 44, 45, 50, 51, 52, 54, 55, 56, 61, 82, 96, 97, 99, 102, 104, 152, 187, 188, 197, 209, 214. *See also* Mediterranean/Middle Eastern/North African area
North Carolina, 2, 21, 32, 49, 56, 59, 66, 67, 68, 69, 70, 71, 72, 100, 193
North Carolina Supreme Court, 69

"odd enclaves" and "little races" of the American Southeast, 2
Ognibene, Daniel, 112
O'Malley, Gregory E., 57–60
Ottoman (Arab, Moor, Muslim, Turk), 12
Ottoman Empire, 44
Oxendine, Charles L. (author), 67
Oxendines, as a core family of the Turkish community. *See* core families
Oxendines, individuals as cited in the text of this book: Cathreen Oxendine Benenhaley, 87; Charles W. Oxendine, 84; Eliphare Oxendine Benenhaley, 84, 92; Jacob Oxendine Jr., 133; Jacob Oxendine Sr., 133; Jessey Oxendine, 69; Mandy Oxendine Chapman, 71; Martha Jane Oxendine Benenhaley, 86; Ralph Justice Oxendine, 70–71; Sarah Oxendine Buckner, 76; Thomas Oxendine, 84; Washington Oxendine, 84

Peagler, David, 75, 76, 79, 80, 81, 86, 87, 88, 132
Peale, Rembrandt, 3
Pinkhams, interred in Long Branch and/or Springbank cemeteries, 92
Pinzon, Martin Alonzo, 48
Pinzon, Vicente Yanez, 48
Piri Reis, and Piri Reis map, 47
Pittsburgh Courier (Pittsburgh, Pa.), 144
Platt, Lucy G., 8
"Pockets in America," 7, 8, 27
Pohlmann, John T., 59
Pollitzer, William S., 38
Price, Edward T., 9, 38
Privateer township, Sumter County, S.C., 66, 67, 68, 69, 70, 93
proclaiming the patriarch, 99–100
Providence, S.C., 7

Quinn, David Beers, 49, 59

Ray, Celeste, 1, 17, 215
Ray, individuals as cited in this book: Eugene Ray, 141; Hammond Ray, 133, 165, 173, 180; Henry Ray, 173, 180; Herbert Ray, 133, 173, 180; Herbert Ray Sr., 132, 180; Irma Buckner Ray, 141; James Ray (1878–1929), 130; James Ray (1795-unknown), 201; James Ray Sr., 84; Jensey Ray, 74; Katie Ray, 139; Leon Ray ("Dick"), 198; Lever A. Ray, 141; Mertis Ray Benenhaley, 130, 131; Nellie Benenhaley Ray, 130, 131; Pearl Ray Corcoran, 112; Reilly Ray, 206–7; Richie Ray, 201–5, 206; Ruth Annette Ray Lowrey, 141; Viola Hood Ray, 141
Rays, as a core family of the Turkish community. *See* core families
recollecting segregation and integration, 179–81

Index

"Red Bones" of Sumter County, 24, 35, 37, 66, 67, 69, 126
"Redbone Nation" (website), 67
Red Sea Men, 15
Reed, John Shelton, 2
relations with white and black people, 5, 10, 15, 16, 83, 160–65; rejection by white people, 160–163; separated from black people, 164–65
Rice, Benjamin H., 55–56
Roark, James E., 24, 42, 75
Roberts, Peter A., 60
Robeson County, N.C., 67, 69

Sackets, interred in Long Branch and/or Springbank cemeteries, 92
Santa Elena Island, S.C., 49
Sass, Herbert Ravenel, 15, 30
Savannah, Ga., 32
Schwartz, Ramon, 141
Schwartz, Ramon Jr., 141
Scott, "a man who gave his name as Scott" (John Scott): first reported by Thomas Sebastian
Scott, Catherine, 84; Elizabeth, 84; Sarah, 84
Scotts, 7, 67, 69, 82–83, 84, 92
self-identification as "Turks," "Turkish people," or "Caucasians of Arab descent": claimed statement of Joseph Benenhaley first reported by Thomas Sebastian Sumter in 1917, 32; declared self-description by Turkish litigants in federal court case during the 1950s, 148; reported self-identity of the Turkish people by Wesley D. White in Smithsonian research during the 1970s, 68; self-ascribed designation reported in analysis of the 1980 census by James Paul Allen and Eugene J. Turner, 22; stated identity by Eleazer Benenhaley in his 1983 autobiography, 29; and as Turkish people have self-defined themselves in interviews with the authors over the past decade, 103, 149, 162, 194, 197, 199, 200, 203
Selim, 55, 56
Shaw Air Force Base (Shaw Field), 35, 89, 112, 124, 138, 145, 156, 186, 193, 198, 200, 202

Sider, Gerald, 66, 67, 68, 69
Sidhwa, Bapsi, 114
Simour, Lhoussain, 53–54
Simses, interred in Long Branch and/or Springbank cemeteries, 92
Sinkler, Anna L., 35
skin tones, 6, 10, 11, 19–20, 23, 27, 32, 34, 35, 42, 46, 52, 67, 82, 99, 103, 104, 109, 110, 116, 126, 128, 132, 140, 142, 153, 157–58, 159, 163, 182, 186, 190, 195, 197, 198, 200, 207
Smiling/Smilings, 66, 67, 68, 69
Smiling (Smilings) Indians, 66
Smithsonian Institution, 52, 67, 100
South Carolina Baptist Convention, 185
South Carolina Commission for Minority Affairs, 65–66, 95
South Carolina Department of Archives and History, 50, 52, 136
South Carolina Gazette (Charles Town, S.C.), 59
South Carolina General Assembly, 51
South Carolina Historical Magazine, 42
South Carolina Historical Society, 42, 99, 216
South Carolina Radio Network, 71
South Carolina Royal Council, 50
South Carolina Royal Council Journal, 50
"Southern Campaigns of the American Revolution" (website), 32
Southern Studies Forum (European Association for American Studies), 1–2
speech patterns, 158–59, 205
Springbank Baptist Church, 90–94, 102, 192, 198; founding, 131, 135; location, 74, 185; mission, 135, 185–86
S'Quash, 55–57
State (Columbia, S.C., newspaper), 7, 8, 25, 27, 70, 134, 139, 144
Steen, Carl, 37, 68
Sub-Sahara Africa/Africans, 11, 18, 19, 53, 55, 59, 96, 97, 99
Sultan Suleiman the Magnificent, 47
Sumter, 7, 22, 31, 32–33, 34, 52, 73, 77, 78, 79, 81, 92, 194; in Turkish genealogy 82–83
Sumter, Sebastian D'Amblimont, 43
Sumter, Thomas (the "General" and the "Fighting Gamecock"), 25, 26, 31–40,

233

Index

Sumter, Thomas (*continued*): 45, 61, 82, 99, 102, 104, 125, 126, 130, 132, 145, 146, 152, 187, 191, 215–16; depicted as a central character in Turkish traditional narrative, 3–6, 31, 41–42; new evidence regarding relationship between Thomas Sumter and Joseph Benenhaley, 72–80, 102
Sumter, Thomas Sebastian, 7, 8, 31, 32, 33, 43, 67, 82, 103, 146, 149, 187, 216
Sumter Cemetery, 93
Sumter County Genealogical Society, 169
Sumter County Office of Mesne Conveyances, 73, 74
Sumter County Probate Court, 73
Sumter Tribe of Cheraw Indians, 40, 65–72, 95, 116, 148
systemic oppression, 165–68

Tarih-i Hind-i Garbi ("A History of the India of the West"), 48
Taukchiray, Wesley DuRant. *See* Wesley White, Jr.
Taylor, Rosser H., 39
Taylor/Taylors, 83
Team, Helen, 93, 148
Theodosiadou, Youli, 2, 215
Thigpen, Allen D., 30, 134
Thompson, Greg, 21, 64, 73, 79, 80, 88, 89, 133, 140, 145, 189–95; and "Thompson Collection and Interviews," 64, 75, 76, 79, 80, 81, 86, 87, 88, 130, 131, 132, 133, 136, 137, 190
Thompson, Kathy Marie Peagler, 190–93
Tisdale, Thomas Sumter Jr., 215–16
traditional narrative of the Turkish people, 3–6, 30–31, 41–42, 146–47, 148–51; basic account of the narrative, 3–6; important assumptions, uncertainties, and inconsistencies, 42–45; supporters, skeptics, and naysayers, 36–40; traditional narrative confirmed, 100, 101–5, 152–53, 209–10, 212–13
transatlantic and intercolonial slave-trade, as possible explanation for Turkish origins, 53–61
tri-racial isolates, and early designation of the Turkish people as a tri-racial community, 18, 36–40

Trillin, Calvin, 22, 26, 30
true story of the Turkish people, 40, 101–5, 208–11, 212–14
"Turk," "Turks," "Turkish people"; definition and use of terms in this project, 10–12, 116
Turkey, 10, 16, 19, 39, 44, 46, 52, 67, 68, 125, 146, 148, 151, 201, 205
Turkish community today: different and better world, 184–86; new questions and challenges, 186–89; observations and experiences of contemporary citizens, 189–207
Turkish heritage and the challenges of assimilation, changing identities, declining population, fading ethnicy, and possible demise, 8–9, 65, 104, 159–60, 185–86, 210–11
Turkish people/community, as theoretically and operationally defined in this project, xii–xv
Turkish reflections on: their ancestry, 146–48; ethnicity, 148–52; entrenched separatism, 128–30, 153–54; eventual demise, 159–60; clannishness, 142, 127–29, 153–55; intermarriage, 157, 193, 155–57; relations with white and black people, 160–65; skin tones, 157–58; speech patterns, 158–59; and systemic oppression, 165–67
Turner, Eugene J., 22

unique cultural situation, 21–23
U.S. Air Force, 35, 113
U.S. Census, used and cited as source of information about Turkish people, 2, 9, 18, 20, 22, 43, 45, 65, 66, 67, 68, 69, 74, 81, 82, 83, 84, 85, 89, 94, 95, 96, 99, 102, 111, 123, 152, 185, 187, 191, 212
U.S. Department of State, historian, 49
U.S. Senate, 66

Vanovers, interred in Long Branch and/or Springbank cemeteries, 92
Vaughn, Julie, 73

Waddell, Carol E., 185
Washington, George, as friend of Muslims, 43, 49

Index

Watchman and Southron (Sumter, S.C.), 27, 31, 187
Wayman Chapel AME Church, 93, 130, 187
Weiss, Gillian, 53
Weslager, C. A., 16
Wheat, David, 43, 54–55, 60
White, Wesley Jr. (Wesley DuRant Taukchiray), 22, 30, 43, 52, 66, 67–68, 69–70, 99–100, 131; and "Wesley D. White Papers," "Wes Taukchiray Collection," and "Wes Taukchiray Papers," 64, 99
whites/white people (non-Turkish whites, white Europeans, Europeans): defined as a cultural group in this book, 10–12, 116; Turkish relations with white people, 160–63. *See also* Integration Movement of the 1950s
Wikramanyake, Marina, 15, 30
"Wisdom and Woe at the Dinner Table," 110–12
Woody, Howard, 30, 134
Workman, William D., 25, 30, 128–29, 141, 157
World War I and Turkish people, 109, 132, 216
World War II and Turkish people, 79, 81, 109, 132, 173

Yates, Donald N., 44, 59, 99, 188
Yates, Gayle Graham, 215
"Yesteryear," 30, 128